An Introduction to
Classical Korean
Literature

An Introduction to
Classical Korean Literature

From *Hyangga* to *P'ansori*

Kichung Kim

An East Gate Book

M.E. Sharpe
Armonk, New York
London, England

An East Gate Book

Library of Congress Cataloging-in-Publication Data

An introduction to classical Korean literature : from
hyangga to p'ansori / Kichung kim
p.   cm.
"An East gate book."
ISBN 1-56324-785-2 (hardcover : alk. paper). —
ISBN 1-56324-786-0 (pbk. : alk. paper)
1. Korean literature—History and criticism.
I. Kim, Kichung, 1934–
PL956.K48   1996
895.7'09—dc20   96-11505
CIP
Printed in the United States of America

The paper used in this publication meets the minimum requirements of
American National Standard for Information Sciences—
Permanence of Paper for Printed Library Materials,
ANSI Z 39.48-1984.

∞

BM (c)   10   9   8   7   6   5   4   3   2   1
BM (p)   10   9   8   7   6   5   4   3   2

For Kumja, Kenneth, Karen, and Colin

Contents

Preface

My study of classical Korean literature has been part of an effort to discover the sources of my own being. Not knowing classical Korean literature, I felt excluded from the soil in which I ought to have rooted my intellectual, emotional, moral, and spiritual being. Whatever other literatures I studied, I felt that I would better understand them once I understood my own cultural roots. And so began an exploration of classical Korean literature that has lasted for nearly ten years, a step-by-step journey on which one discovery has led to another and yet another.

Thus my encounter with the enigmatic, enchanting *hyangga,* the earliest surviving vernacular Korean poetry, led me to the incomparable lyric songs of the *Koryŏ kayo,* the earliest poetry recorded in the Korean script. Similarly, when I set about writing on the works of Chosŏn women writers, I had planned one brief essay, mainly about *Hanjung nok,* the memoirs of Lady Hong, and the shijo written by kisaeng poets. But as I discovered the poetry of Hŏ Nansŏrhŏn and the *kyubang kasa,* the unpublished poetry of yangban women, one essay grew into two and then three. And as I completed the third essay I came to see I had only scratched the surface of my subject; there was so much more literature by Chosŏn women writers to be studied and discussed. I believe the same is true of every subject I have explored in this volume.

From the beginning, therefore, this study has been a personal undertaking. More than anything else, it is a report on my reading of those works of classical Korean literature I came to love. Naturally I wanted to share with others what I had come to appreciate and love, especially those who, like myself, wished to become acquainted with classical Korean literature. Ruskin has said that all our work should be in praise of what we love. It is in this spirit that I have undertaken this study.

This volume is intended for the nonspecialist reader, and I have tried to write it as plainly as possible, avoiding jargon. At the same time, wishing to make my discussion up-to-date, I have consulted as much of the available scholarship, in Korean and English, as I could. I believe scholarship and general accessibility are not mutually exclusive.

This is only a first report. In my further explorations I hope to expand my coverage to include the *kasa* of literati men and more on oral and *hanmun* literature.

My thanks go to the many scholars and translators without whose published works this exploration into classical Korean literature would not have been possible. Foremost among them are Cho Tong-il, whose five-volume *Hanguk munhak t'ongsa* (A Comprehensive History of Korean Literature) has taught me a great deal, Peter H. Lee, and Richard Rutt. I owe special thanks to my two mentors, Suh Doo Soo, my first and most influential guide, who initiated me into classical Korean literature, and Kim Yong-suk, who for many years has been generous with her time and encouragement. In addition, I have incurred many debts during the years this study has taken shape. I wish to thank the Korean Culture and Arts Foundation for providing a generous publication grant; the Korea Foundation, for a summer fellowship and gifts of books; California State University at San Jose, for sabbaticals, research grants, and other assistance too varied to detail, and especially the staff of the university interlibrary loan service, for locating all the obscure titles I needed; Robert Buswell of UCLA and *Korean Culture,* who encouraged me by publishing several of my essays on classical Korean literature in *Korean Culture* and gave permission to reprint that material; and Bruce Fulton, my editor, friend, and colleague whose help has been indispensable in completing this book. Poems from *Anthology of*

Korean Literature, compiled and edited by Peter H. Lee, *The Bamboo Grove* by Richard Rutt, *Form and Freedom in Korean Poetry* by David R. McCann, and *Anthology of Japanese Literature,* compiled and edited by Donald Keene, are quoted by permission of the translators and publishers. Unattributed translations are my own.

An Introduction to
Classical Korean
Literature

1

What Is Korean Literature?

Why begin with such an obvious question? Isn't Korean literature simply all the literature produced in Korean by Koreans? But it's not quite as simple as that. This question, in fact, is central in determining both the boundaries and the character of classical Korean literature—that literature written in Korea from the earliest times to the end of the nineteenth century.

What makes the question a central one is the historical fact that *hanmun*—literally "letters of Han," that is, Chinese characters—was the written language of practically all literate Koreans from about the beginning of Korea's recorded history to the end of the nineteenth century.[1] For this reason most of the written literature in Korea from the earliest times through the nineteenth century was written in hanmun even though *hangŭl,* the Korean alphabet, had been available since the mid-1400s. How did such a situation come about? The answer to this question lies in the history of written language in Korea.

Until 1446, when King Sejong promulgated the *hunmin chŏngŭm*—the twenty-eight-letter phonetic alphabet uniformly referred to today as hangŭl—the Korean people had lacked an indigenous writing system that represented their spoken language. There had thus developed two entirely different language systems in Korea—native Korean for speech and Sino-Korean hanmun for writing. Because Korean and Chinese are linguistically unrelated and Chinese characters are more ideographic than phonetic, it was nearly impossible for Koreans to use Chinese characters to represent their spoken language. And yet to express themselves in writing they had to first translate their

thoughts and speech into classical Chinese. Understandably, therefore, they made repeated efforts to adapt Chinese characters to the
Korean language. Two examples are the hybrid writing systems
hyangch'al and *idu*—both little more than modest efforts to add a
phonetic dimension to what was basically an ideographic writing
system. Neither was effective in representing Korean. The gross
inadequacy of such writing systems was perhaps best summed up
by King Sejong in the royal rescript of 1446 by which he promulgated the hunmin chŏngŭm:

> While there is a great difference between the Korean language and
> Chinese, there are no proper letters that the Korean people can use in
> writing their language and expressing their thoughts. From the time
> of the Silla Dynasty a system of writing known as Idu has been used
> in the daily life of ordinary people as well as in government busi-
> ness. But it is too complicated, imperfect, and inconvenient a system
> for the Koreans to use freely in expressing their own ideas and
> thinking, because too many Chinese characters are involved in it.
> Koreans are in great need of their own letters with which they can
> write the Korean language.[2]

The invention of hangŭl should have marked a turning point in
the history of written language in Korea. For hangŭl was a writing
system so simple, convenient, and accurate that almost any Korean
could master it in a matter of weeks—instead of years, as in the
case of hanmun. Hangŭl made it possible, for the first time, to
banish the alien writing system used in Korea for more than a
thousand years. As it happened, however, the history of hangŭl
from the time of its creation until the very eve of the twentieth
century was one of missed opportunities.

Even during the time of King Sejong the use of hanmun among
the lettered classes was too deeply entrenched to be easily displaced. The lettered classes had invested a great deal of time and
energy in learning hanmun. Their literacy in that system was among
the accomplishments that distinguished them from the lower
classes, and it gave them cause to continue using hanmun exclusively and to oppose the dissemination of Sejong's new phonetic

alphabet. Their opposition, buttressed by the forces of tradition, could not be overcome. Even the most zealous promotion of hangŭl by the king himself could not bring about widespread acceptance and use of the new alphabet.[3] Dubbed ŏnmun ("vulgar letters") whereas hanmun was called chinsŏ ("true writing"), hangŭl was soon relegated to an inferior status. It was considered suitable for use only by women and common people and was to be shunned by the literati and others highly placed. And in fact hangŭl was used mostly by women and people of the lower classes, and for this reason it was also called amgŭl ("female letters"). This debilitating split between the spoken and written languages persisted in Korea until the eve of the twentieth century. Hanmun continued to be the principal vehicle of reading and writing for practically all literate Koreans, especially men of letters.

We can now return to the original question, "What is Korean literature?" That most of the written literature in Korea from the earliest times through the nineteenth century was composed in hanmun goes to the very heart of this question. Should these hanmun works be considered Korean literature? It is a problem utterly unlike that posed by the tiny fraction of English literature that was composed in Latin, such as John Milton's Latin verses and Thomas More's *Utopia*.

Let us consider a few examples that illustrate the scope of the problem. If we assume that the recorded history of Korea goes back about two thousand years, then the period before the invention of the Korean alphabet—that is, from the earliest times to 1446—amounts to about 1,500 years. From this first 1,500 years of recorded Korean history only about four dozen works written in vernacular Korean survive: twenty-five Shilla poems called *hyangga* and another two dozen or so Koryŏ poems called *Koryŏ kayo*. In contrast, the same period has yielded thousands of works in hanmun, both prose and poetry. One individual alone, Yi Kyu-bo (1168–1241), a scholar-statesman of the Koryŏ period, left an estimated 1,500 hanmun poems, not to mention many hanmun prose works.[4] More hangŭl works survive from the period between 1446 and the late nineteenth century—that is, the end of the premodern period—but still the ratio of hangŭl and hanmun works is heavily in favor of the latter. The reason, as I have mentioned, has to do with the historical fact that even after the invention of the Korean alphabet, practically all literate men kept on writing in hanmun because it continued to be the only proper writing system for men of education and importance.

Given an opportunity to write in Korean, however, some men and many women did so, composing both poetry and prose. The most important of these hangŭl works were *shijo*. The single most important Korean poetic form, the shijo probably originated in the fourteenth century during the late Koryŏ period, before the invention of the Korean alphabet. Sung and declaimed, and at first transmitted orally, it was written down after hangŭl became available. The *kasa,* a longer and open-ended hangŭl poetic form, probably originated in the mid-fifteenth century. By the sixteenth century it was established among both men and women. Much of the popular prose fiction was also composed in hangŭl, since it was written mostly for a female readership. The most significant work of epistolary literature, *Hanjungnok,* by Lady Hong, for instance, was composed in hangŭl, possibly because it was originally a series of letters to her family. And toward the end of the premodern period popular works of oral literature such as *p'ansori* tales were written down in hangŭl as their literary status increased.

But the most gifted and best educated men of the Chosŏn period (1392–1910), such as Kim Shi-sŭp, Chŏng Yag-yong, and Pak Chi-wŏn, had all written exclusively in hanmun. So for the most part had Hŏ Kyun (1569–1618), an important poet-scholar-statesman, and his sister Hŏ Nansŏrhŏn. Although much of Hŏ Kyun's literary legacy was lost or destroyed after his execution for treason, over 1,500 hanmun poems[5] and numerous hanmun prose works have survived, compared with the single hangŭl prose tale, *Hong Kiltong chŏn,* attributed to him. Most of the important histories, travel journals, and diaries written by men were likewise composed in hanmun.

Should this enormous body of literature written in hanmun be considered Korean literature? The answer to this question determines not only the age but also the volume and character of classical Korean literature. For example, if we were to define Korean literature as literature that has survived in vernacular Korean, either orally or in writing, we would be limiting Korean literature before 1446—the year hangŭl was promulgated—to only the handful of vernacular poems surviving from the Shilla and Koryŏ periods, along with an oral literature of indeterminate age. We would in effect be excluding practically all of the literature written in Korea before 1446, and also much of the literature written between that year and the end of the nineteenth century. More important, we would be excluding not only the works of many gifted Chosŏn writers but also such central works of early Korean history, myth, and legend as the *Samguk sagi* and *Samguk yusa.* We would also have to exclude the oldest recorded version of the Tangun myth—the foundation myth of the Korean people—as well as the foundation myths of the Three Kingdoms and the Kaya state.

During the terrible years from 1910 to 1945 when Japan occupied Korea, Koreans felt a strong need to recover and reassert their own national and cultural roots and identity as a way of resisting the Japanese effort to destroy everything culturally Korean. An important part of this movement was a systematic, reinvigorated study during the 1920s of the Korean language and Korean literature.[6] A number of Korean scholars and writers dedicated themselves to this task despite harsh persecution by the Japanese authorities. These scholars and writers aimed to recover or rediscover what they believed was unmistakably Korean both in language and literature; in the process they hoped to remove what they considered foreign, as impurities are removed from precious metal. They tried, therefore, to separate what they believed was Korean literature from what they believed was not. They asked, for instance, "How could anything not written in the language of the Korean people be considered Korean literature?" Hence, Korean literature had to consist only of those works written (or orally transmitted) in the Korean language. They concluded, therefore, that literature written in hanmun could not be included. In 1929, for example, Yi Kwang-su, one of the most important literary figures of that period, argued that "Korean literature is that literature written in the Korean language" only, and that nothing else could be called Korean literature.[7] Many others felt the same way.

Most Korean scholars and writers today regard such a definition of Korean literature as too limited. At the time, however, it was a perfectly legitimate and understandable response to the attempt by a colonial power to obliterate all that was Korean. But such a narrow definition of Korean literature ignores two essential historical facts: first, hanmun was the most widely used writing system in Korea until the end of the nineteenth century; second, Koreans who read and wrote in hanmun included not only the literati but most literate Koreans, men as well as women. Excluding hanmun works would therefore mean excluding the literature written by most of the literate segment of premodern Korean society. Therefore, a way had to be found to include these works in the body of Korean literature. Such considerations prompted a modified definition of Korean literature: hanmun works would constitute a secondary body of Korean literature, while those works written or transmitted in vernacular Korean would compose the primary body of Korean literature.

Still another approach was proposed by Chang Tŏk-sun of Seoul National University. He argued that we should accept unconditionally all literature written in Korea before 1446 as part of Korean literature, whether it was composed in hanmun or in a hybrid writing system such as *hyangch'al*. As for hanmun works written after 1446, Professor Chang proposed to include them only if they possessed "the spirit of Korean thoughts and sentiments."[8] Obviously, the difficulty with such an approach is the impossibility of defining to everyone's satisfaction "the spirit of Korean thoughts and sentiments." Compounding the difficulty is the historical fact that the promulgation of the Korean alphabet in 1446 did not appreciably lessen the use of hanmun by the literati and the ruling classes.

Hanmun, though devised by the Chinese, was adopted by Koreans, Japanese, and Vietnamese as their literary language, just as it had been the literary language of the Chinese. It could therefore be argued that hanmun developed into a common literary and written language of the East Asian peoples. Furthermore, in appropriating Chinese characters, each of these peoples adapted them to the needs of their own language. Thus, for example, though Chinese characters are identical whether written by Chinese, Koreans, or Japanese, each people pronounced them in their own way and read them with grammatical markers from their own language. And in the case of Koreans, while many wrote in impeccable classical Chinese style, others such as Iryŏn and Pak Chi-wŏn introduced Korean words, phrases, and syntax into their hanmun prose. Thus, hanmun could be considered the earliest of the Korean literary styles, rather than a strictly alien writing system.[9]

Since the mid-1960s the scholarly consensus in Korea has shifted toward accepting all hanmun works as part of Korean literature; in other words, accepting hanmun simply as one of the writing systems used to record Korean literature. This emerging consensus sees classical Korean literature recorded in three writing systems—hangŭl, hanmun, and the hybrid idu and hyangch'al—all equally Korean and reflecting the changing needs and conditions of Korean society over the centuries. Additionally, in recent years the task of translating hanmun works into hangŭl has flourished and the study of hanmun itself has been revitalized, especially among younger scholars.

Another part of Korean literature that has increasingly become the focus of scholarly interest has been oral literature. In Korea too, before there was written literature there was oral literature, that is, the literature of spoken Korean. And out of this oral literature came the first written Korean literature, composed in hanmun or one of the hybrid writing systems. In recent years Korean oral literature has been vigorously researched, and today it is studied not only as the literature of ordinary people but also as the most important source of all premodern Korean literary forms, whether hyangga, Koryŏ kayo, shijo, or kasa. Indeed, classical Korean literature has been called an offspring of oral and hanmun literature.[10] Thus, oral literature—the study of which had been neglected in the past—has now taken its rightful place in the canon of classical Korean literature.

Notes

1. Although the first use of Chinese characters in Korea cannot be dated precisely, it is generally agreed that their use was fairly widespread by the fourth or fifth century A.D.

2. Lee Sang-Beck, *The Origin of Han'gŭl*, trans. Dugald Malcolm (Seoul: Tongmunkwan, 1957), 2.

3. There was considerable opposition within the court itself to the new alphabet. Several highly placed court officials had to be reprimanded, and at least one minister dismissed, for their vehement opposition. See Chang Tŏk-sun, *Hanguk munhak sa* (A History of Korean Literature) (Seoul: Tonghwa munhwa sa, 1987), 159.

4. Peter H. Lee, comp. and ed., *Anthology of Korean Literature*, rev. ed. (Honolulu: University of Hawaii Press, 1992), 37.

5. Yi Yi-hwa, *Hŏ Kyun ŭi saenggak* (Hŏ Kyun's Thoughts) (Seoul: Yŏgang ch'ulp'ansa, 1991) 210.

6. A renewed interest in hangŭl, spearheaded by Chu Shi-kyŏng and others, had been apparent since the 1880s.

7. Quoted by Kim Hŭng-gyu in *Hanguk munhak yŏngu immun* (An Introduction to the Study of Korean Literature), ed. Hwang P'ae-gang and Cho Tong-il (Seoul: Chishik sanŏp sa, 1982), 11.

8. Quoted in a news story about a speech given by Professor Chang upon his retirement from Seoul National University. See also *Hanguk munhak yŏngu immun*, ed. Hwang and Cho, 12.

9. Cho Tong-il, *Hanguk munhak t'ongsa* (A Comprehensive History of Korean Literature), 2nd ed. (Seoul: Chishik sanŏp sa, 1989), 1:18.

10. Kim Hŭng-gyu, cited in *Hanguk munhak yŏngu immun*, ed. Hwang P'ae-gang and Cho Tong-il, 16.

2

The Mystery and Loveliness
of the Hyangga

Although poetry must have flourished along with other art forms in the early Korean kingdoms of Koguryŏ, Paekche, and Shilla, very little vernacular poetry survives from the first thousand years of Korea's recorded history. We have reason to believe, however, that there was a considerable body of vernacular Korean poetry composed during this period, since early chronicles, both Chinese and Korean, tell us that Koreans were a people fond of singing and dancing, especially on certain festival days observed annually in celebration of their harvests and in propitiation of spirits. On these occasions both young and old are said to have sung and danced day and night for days on end. Furthermore, we know from historical records that an anthology of vernacular Korean poetry called *Samdaemok* (Collection from the Three Kingdoms) was compiled in Shilla in 888 A.D. It included hundreds of poems, not only from Shilla but from Paekche and Koguryŏ as well. But of *Samdaemok* only the title has survived. Thus, even though there had been a considerable body of vernacular poetry by 888 A.D., only the twenty-five songs of Shilla called hyangga have survived, along with a few poems in hanmun and the titles of several Korean poems.[1]

Each of the two dozen hyangga that has survived is a gem to be valued and carefully scrutinized, for these verses are all that remain of a much larger body of vernacular Korean poetry from the earliest period. The word *hyangga* literally means "native songs," that is, Korean songs as opposed to Chinese songs. Since Koreans had no writing system of their own during the first 1,500 years of their recorded history, how were the words of the hyangga recorded and preserved in writing? They were transcribed in hyangch'al, a system in which certain Chinese characters were used for meaning and others only for sound. Because the system was very complex and unorthodox, the hyangga poems were not deciphered until the first half of the twentieth century. In fact, many of them have yet to be fully deciphered to everyone's satisfaction.

Strange as it might seem, however, it is the very difficulty of deciphering the hyangga that accounts in part for their mystery, resonance, and loveliness. For they can best be appreciated if one can participate, even vicariously, in the long and difficult process of deciphering, transcription, and translation of them into modern Korean. I myself can never read any of the hyangga without recapitulating in my mind the process by which these ancient Korean poems, transmitted to us in the enigmatic hyangch'al, were deciphered. Each letter, each word, each phrase, and each line of the hyangga have literally been decoded, much as individual stones of an ancient ruin must be excavated and individually restored. Just as each stone or burnt remnant of an ancient structure is unearthed, washed, labeled, and restored, so too are each letter and each word of these ancient poems reconstructed through painstaking scholarship. And through these ancient poems we are given glimpses of ancient Korea across the gulf of many centuries, just as we are given glimpses of a vanished world through a handful of artifacts recovered from an ancient ruin.

Another key element in our appreciation of the hyangga is the prose account that accompanies them; most of the hyangga are integrally related to these prose narratives. In fact, with some hyangga it is impossible to say which is the kernel and which the shell, because a hyangga is often no more than one part of an extensive description of an event chronicled in the *Samguk yusa* (Memorabilia of the Three Kingdoms). Also, since the prose account is written in standard classical Chinese, it is perfectly intelligible to anyone who can read that language. For these reasons the prose account constitutes the indispensable first step to an understanding of the hyangga.

With the information provided by the prose account, the scholar can begin puzzling out the hyangga letter by letter, word by word, and phrase by phrase. The initial breakthrough in this work was made in 1929 by a Japanese scholar, Ogura Shimpei. This stimulated Yang Chu-dong to do the thirteen years of research that resulted in his landmark study of the hyangga, which was published in 1942.[2] This study has provided the basis for all subsequent readings of the hyangga, including Peter H. Lee's first English translation of the poems in his *Studies in the Saenaennorae: Old Korean Poetry,* published in 1959.

Of the twenty-five surviving hyangga, fourteen are found in the *Samguk yusa* and eleven in *Kyunyŏ chŏn* (Life of the Great Master Kyunyŏ). The hyangga are of three lengths: one four-line stanza; two four-line stanzas; and two four-line stanzas with a two-line concluding stanza. The varying lengths of these verses probably reflect the development of the hyangga from a simple folk song to a carefully designed poetic composition. Altogether they date from approximately the sixth to the tenth centuries A.D., during the Three Kingdoms and United Shilla periods.

One of the briefest but loveliest and most mysterious of the hyangga is a four-line verse called "Hŏnhwa ka" (Flower Dedication Song), a Shilla poem dating back more than a thousand years. Because the setting of the poem is essential to a proper appreciation of it, let us first consider the prose account accompanying the poem in the *Samguk yusa.*

The east and west coasts of Korea differ considerably in terrain. While the west coast slopes gently into the Yellow Sea—the muddy shallows at places stretching for miles when the tide is out—on the east coast low hills and rocky cliffs abut the clear waters of the East Sea, leaving only enough room for a narrow ribbon of coastal road in between. On this narrow coastal road a new provincial governor and his party are traveling to his new post. They have probably left Kyŏngju, the Shilla capital, the day before or very early that morning and are now making a leisurely progress to the north. They stop for lunch at the foot of a cliff. The governor is on horseback, his beautiful young wife, Lady Suro, perhaps rides in a carriage, and just before they alight they pause to admire the splendid scenery. For Lady Suro it might be her first journey out of Kyŏngju. She is struck by the scenery before her, the sparkling East Sea and the rocky cliffs. And what is that she sees high up on the cliff, near the very top? A beautiful flower in full bloom ... a red azalea perhaps? It almost takes her breath away. "Oh, I wish I could have that flower! I would give anything, if someone would only get it for me!" she says out loud. The attendants, in the meantime, mutter among themselves loudly enough for Lady Suro to hear: "That cliff is nearly a thousand feet high, and there are neither trails nor animal tracks leading to where the flower is. It is impossible for anybody to get it."

It is precisely at this point that the event celebrated in our poem occurs. An old man appears, leading a cow. Overhearing the governor's beautiful young wife, he approaches and offers to clamber up the rocky cliff and pick the flower for her:

> If you would let me leave
> The cattle tethered to the brown rocks,
> And feel no shame for me,
> I would pluck and dedicate the flower![3]

Why does he say he would climb to pluck the flower only if she should "feel no shame for [him]"? Is it because he feels self-conscious about his age, his weathered skin cracked and scaled with dirt, and his face blackened and wrinkled from too much exposure to the sun?

These four lines are all we have across the silence of a thousand years, and yet what a living, breathing picture! This brief ancient poem seems to me even more precious and wondrous than any of the gleaming Shilla gold crowns dug up, polished, and displayed before us. For through the words of this painstakingly restored poem we listen in on the living voices of a man and woman, the voices of the beautiful Lady Suro and an unnamed man who though old in years is still young at heart. There is almost a mythic quality to the homage he pays her, a kind of exemplary homage that has always been paid to the beautiful, young, and female by the ordinary, aged, and male.

Although there are no significant textual problems with this poem, there are puzzling questions as regards its content. For instance, who is the old man? Is he more than what he appears to be? The prose account accompanying the poem gives no clue; it simply says that no one knew who he was. And what about Lady Suro, the beautiful young wife of a new governor, who makes the old man completely forget his age?

About Lady Suro the *Samguk yusa* does have more to say, for it describes what happens as the governor's party travels farther north toward its destination. When the party stops for a seaside lunch two days later, a sea dragon suddenly appears and abducts Lady Suro, taking her into the sea. Once again an old man appears to aid the governor's party. He says that in order to recover Lady Suro the governor must assemble the people of the area and have them compose a song and chant it while beating the cliff face with sticks. The song the assembled people chant, given in hanmun in the *Samguk yusa,* goes as follows:

> Tortoise, tortoise, return the Lady Suro.
> Do you know the gravity of your sin?
> If you behave against our will,
> We will catch you in a net and roast you.[4]

When the song is chanted the sea dragon duly returns Lady Suro to her husband. The *Samguk yusa* account adds that because of Lady Suro's unparalleled beauty she had been abducted several times in the past, whenever she traveled through deep mountains and along lakes. Now what are we to make of all this? What exactly is the relationship between the two accounts of this beautiful young woman whose loveliness makes both men and dragons alike behave so extraordinarily? Do the additional details help us better understand the Lady Suro of "Flower Dedication Song"? And what about the old man in the second incident? Is he in any way related to the old man in the first incident?

There is still another intriguing detail. The hanmun tortoise

song compelling the dragon to return Lady Suro is clearly an expanded version of an earlier hanmun song given in the *Samguk yusa*
account of the miraculous advent of King Suro to Karak, a kingdom
later annexed to Shilla. That earlier song goes as follows:

> O tortoise, tortoise!
> Show your head.
> If you do not,
> We'll roast and eat you. [5]

Is there a connection between Lady Suro and King Suro? The two
names are written in different Chinese characters, but since they are
homophonous they might have been the same Korean name (this
often occurs in the early records). We simply do not know.

Another puzzling question has to do with the cow led by the old
man. Is it just a cow, or do the cow and the old man together
perhaps represent an important symbol of Sŏn (Zen) Buddhism,
as has been suggested?[6] Since neither the *Samguk yusa* nor any
other historical records supply satisfactory explanations to these
questions, we are left mostly to our own imagination. But it is partly
these unanswered and unanswerable questions that make this ancient
four-line poem so appealing, for its very mysteriousness makes it so
much more suggestive.[7]

It has been suggested that most of the extant hyangga are Buddhist in theme and inspiration. But in fact they contain a broad
range of themes, perhaps hinting at an even greater range in the
early Korean poetry that has not survived. The shortest of the
hyangga sound like folk songs, perhaps popular among ordinary
people and orally transmitted for long periods until they came to be
written down in the *Samguk yusa*. I am thinking specifically of the
three four-line poems "Song of Mattung," "Ode to Yangji," and
perhaps "Tonnorae: Dedication." There are also moving elegies,
some dedicated to heroic hwarang knights[8] by their former friends
and followers: "Ode To Knight Chukchi" and "Ode To Knight
Kip'a" as well as a "Requiem" for a deceased sister. There is also a
didactic poem ("Statesmanship"), a shaman exorcism ("Song of

Ch'ŏyong"), and the longest piece, a Buddhist prayer-poem in eleven verses by Great Master Kyunyŏ.

The "Song of Ch'ŏyong" is perhaps one of the easiest to decipher but also one of the most puzzling of the hyangga. Traditionally the poem has been read as a song of exorcism supposed to be effective in warding off evil spirits. This reading of the poem was derived from the account of Ch'ŏyong given in the *Samguk yusa:*

King Hŏngang [of Shilla: r. A.D. 876–886] took a pleasure trip to Kaeunp'o. When he stopped for a rest by the sea on the way back, suddenly clouds and fog thickened so much that the king nearly lost his way. Amazed, the king asked his subordinates what was happening. The weather official told him that it was the doings of the Dragon of the East Sea, and propitiatory offerings were in order. The king ordered the appropriate officials to erect a Buddhist temple in the vicinity for the dragon. As soon as the king's order was given, the clouds and fog cleared. . . . Much pleased, the Dragon of the East Sea appeared before the king with his seven sons and provided music and dance in praise of the king's virtue. One of the sons, whose name was Ch'ŏyong, remained with the king, following him to the capital, and assisted him in the work of governance. The king bestowed on him an official rank and gave him a beautiful woman in marriage in order to make him stay. Because Ch'ŏyong's wife was very lovely, an evil spirit transformed itself into a man, stole into the house at night, and lay with her. Returning home, Ch'ŏyong found them lying together in bed. He sang and danced this song and withdrew.

> Having caroused far into the night
> In the moonlit capital,
> I return home and in my bed,
> Behold, four legs.
>
> Two were mine,
> Whose are the other two?
> Formerly two were mine:
> What shall be done now that they're taken?

Then the evil spirit reappeared in its own shape, and kneeling before Ch'ŏyong it said: Even though I've violated your wife in lust, you have not shown anger. I am impressed and find you admirable. I swear therefore to never violate henceforth any place where even your likeness is displayed. From this comes the custom of people's warding off evil spirits with the likeness of Ch'ŏyong on their gates.[9]

Now what does this prose account tell us about the "Song of Ch'ŏyong"? Even though the *Samguk yusa* ties the poem to the wondrous story about Ch'ŏyong, one of the Sea Dragon's sons, who came on land to serve the king, the story does not explain the mystery of the poem itself. Is it a riddle? Could it be some sort of prehistoric incantation or formula that was inserted into the story of the Dragon of the East Sea? Various theories have been advanced by Korean scholars. One scholar has even suggested that the Ch'ŏyong of the poem might have been an Islamic merchant who came through one of Korea's harbors on the East Sea, which were then open to international trade.[10]

As with the other hyangga in the *Samguk yusa,* the "Song of Ch'ŏyong" can best be understood if read as part of the prose account accompanying it. In his suggestive reading of the poem Hyŏn Yong-jun has identified some of the main legends and folk beliefs that inform the poem and its accompanying prose account:

1. an early legend concerning the origin of the place name Kaeunp'o;
2. a belief widely held by the Shilla people that the Dragon of the East Sea was their guardian spirit;
3. a popular belief that evil spirits could transform themselves into human forms in order to ravish beautiful women, thereby causing sickness and calamity;
4. a popular belief in the gate guardian, a deity that could ward off all evil spirits at the entrance to a residence.[11]

Professor Hyŏn sees the first half of the *Samguk yusa* prose account woven out of the legend concerning the place name

Kaeunp'o ("harbor where the mists and clouds clear up"). There the local people had long performed rites to placate the Dragon of the East Sea so that the coast would clear of mists and clouds. This legend, combined with the local people's long-held belief in the Dragon of the East Sea as their guardian spirit, had long since produced the legend of Ch'ŏyong, who comes on land to act as a sort of resident guardian of the local people. It is this legend of Ch'ŏyong at Kaeunp'o that, appropriated by the *Samguk yusa,* becomes the story of King Hŏngang's encounter with the Dragon of the East Sea at Kaeunp'o. The Buddhist and nationalistic touches in the *Samguk yusa* version—King Hŏngang's command to erect a Buddhist temple—were probably added by Iryŏn, the Buddhist author of the *Samguk yusa.*

What is the significance of Ch'ŏyong's coming on land to serve the king? As Cho Tong-il has suggested, assisting the king in governance would naturally mean helping him strengthen the nation and avoid calamities.[12] And how better to do that than to fend off evil spirits, especially the evil spirit of sickness and calamity (the *yŏkshin*) of the poem? Now we begin to better understand the connection between the poem and the accompanying prose account.

According to Professor Hyŏn, the poem represents a shaman rite of exorcism, combining song and dance, performed by Ch'ŏyong at the most critical juncture in the episode. Returning home late at night, Ch'ŏyong finds his beautiful wife being assaulted by the evil spirit. It is precisely at this point, we are told, that Ch'ŏyong "sang and danced this song and withdrew." The singing is accompanied by dancing and some other dramatic movements, because it was believed that in order for an exorcism to be sacred and powerful it had to be accompanied by dramatic, measured movements such as dancing.

The prose passage that directly follows the poem seems to bear out Profressor Hyŏn's reading. Humbled by Ch'ŏyong's show of grace and superiority, the evil spirit withdraws, swearing "to never violate henceforth any place where even your likeness is displayed." And, of course, it is this pledge that brings Ch'ŏyong to the next stage of his career on land. Until now a guardian spirit of the Shilla people, Ch'ŏyong is now transformed into the gate guardian, whose function is to safeguard the entrance to a residence, protecting the household from all evil spirits.[13]

Illuminating though it is, Professor Hyŏn's reading seems to leave one critical question unanswered. Why does Ch'ŏyong resort to an exorcism that involves only a show of grace and superiority rather than violence or a threat of violence toward an evil spirit attacking his own wife—the one person he should be most anxious to safeguard? The exorcism succeeds only because the evil spirit voluntarily withdraws. But what if the evil spirit had not been so yielding? And doesn't it seem rather strange that an *evil* spirit should be so yielding?

Other details are even more troublesome. According to the *Samguk yusa,* Ch'ŏyong "sang and danced this song and *withdrew*" [emphasis added] when he found his wife bedded by the evil spirit. Doesn't this passage seem to suggest resignation or, worse, admission of defeat, rather than determination to expel and destroy the evil spirit? The second stanza of the poem reads:

> Two were mine,
> Whose are the other two?
> Formerly two were mine:
> What shall be done now that they're taken?

These lines together with the prose passage immediately preceding them—"He sang and danced this song and withdrew"—seem to suggest that Ch'ŏyong has lost his will and also his power to protect the Shilla people from the evil spirit. For if he could not protect his own wife from the evil spirit, how could he be expected to protect the Shilla people? As Cho Tong-il has suggested, the exorcism is more likely an admission by Ch'ŏyong of his own defeat, which seems to bode ill for the people of Shilla, of whom Ch'ŏyong is supposedly the guardian spirit.[14] The potential for national tragedy implied in the image of the weakened Ch'ŏyong seems confirmed a little later in the *Samguk yusa* when we are told that Shilla fell because its rulers continued to indulge themselves in pleasures and neglected the warnings the various guardian spirits had given them.

Though not entirely satisfactory, Professor Hyŏn's reading nevertheless helps to clarify the connection between "Song of Ch'ŏyong" and its accompanying prose account. Still, it is the very mystery of this poem that continues to draw us to it. Because it gives us no more than fleeting glimpses into the shadowy world of long ago, a world whose dim outlines are veiled by time, we are forever drawn to this world.

Even in translation the most poetic of the hyangga possess this exquisite suggestiveness. They seem perfectly poised between an apparent simplicity of language and an underlying sense of mystery. The poem that perhaps best exemplifies this quality of the hyangga is "Che mangmae ka" (Requiem), supposedly composed by Master Wŏlmyŏng in remembrance of his deceased sister:

> On the hard road of life and death
> That is near our land,
> You went, afraid,
> Without words.
>
> We know not where we go,
> Leaves blown, scattered,
> Though fallen from the same tree,
> By the first winds of autumn.
>
> Abide, Sister, perfect your ways,
> Until we meet in the Pure Land.[15]

Here the uncertainty and evanescence of our lives are compared to the leaves blown away by the first gusts of autumn. The first two lines of the poem are especially suggestive—"On the hard road of life and death / That is near our land" (a more literal translation would be something like "The road of life and death / Is here and now").

What do these lines mean? That we are constantly shadowed

by the prospect of death, and that this shadow of death enhances the light that is our life? The poem seems perfectly poised between the world it reveals and the world it veils; the feeling of deep and genuine sorrow it elicits is perfectly balanced by the sense of wonder we feel for the world hidden behind the words and their silence. It is this perfect balance between the seen and unseen worlds that gives an added poignancy as well as mysteriousness to the poem. The sense of mystery is heightened by the uncertain meaning of some of the words and phrases in the original.

As I peruse the original versions of the hyangga I see formidable chasms separating the various stages of their transformation from hyangch'al to modern Korean and English. Examining each stage of this long, painstaking, and complex transformation, I am struck as much by the process itself as by the final polished versions in modern Korean or English. And I cannot help but wonder what relation the original poems actually bear to these Korean or English renditions, especially since portions of several hyangga still await full deciphering. This is why an appreciation of the hyangga cannot be separated from an appreciation of the process of deciphering, transcribing, and translating them. For only then do we fully understand how uncertain and how provisional these verse transcriptions and translations really are.[16] These often enigmatic verses offer only blurred glimpses of a people and world that vanished more than a thousand years ago. Yet it is precisely this shadowiness and incompleteness that continues to draw us to the hyangga.

Notes

1. Chang Tŏk-sun, *Hanguk munhak sa* (A History of Korean Literature) (Seoul: Tonghwa munhwa sa, 1987), 3.

2. *Samguk yusa wa munyejŏk kach'i haemyŏng* (The *Samguk yusa* and Analyses of Its Literary Value), ed. Kim Yŏl-gyu and Shin Tong-uk (Seoul: Saemun sa, 1980), III:53–54.

3. Peter H. Lee, *Poems from Korea: A Historical Anthology* (Honolulu: University Press of Hawaii, 1974), 36–37.

4. Peter H. Lee, *Korean Literature: Topics and Themes* (Tucson: University of Arizona Press, 1965), 2.

5. Ibid., 2.

6. Cited in *Samguk yusa wa munyejŏk kach'i haemyŏng*, ed. Kim Yŏl-gyu and Shin Tong-uk, 1:10.

7. That the poem has so stirred the imagination of its readers is attested to by the many twentieth-century poems and stories based on it. The most provocative example is perhaps Sŏ Chŏng-ju's poem "Noin hŏnhwa ka" (An Old Man's Flower Dedication Song), which has been translated into English both by David McCann, of Cornell University, and by Brother Anthony, of Sŏgang University in Seoul.

8. Hwarang knights were young men from elite Shilla families who, after long training periods, became military and artistic leaders of the nation.

9. My English translation of this passage is based on the revised edition of Yi Pyŏng-do's Korean translation of the *Samguk yusa* (Seoul: Kwangjo sa, 1979), 256–57. The translation of the poem itself is by Peter H. Lee; this latest version is quoted by permission of the translator. There is some debate as to how the sentence "He sang and danced this song and withdrew" should be read. Is it Ch'ŏyong who withdrew, or did he succeed in making the evil spirit withdraw? One's reading of this passage would depend, I think, on how one interprets the entire episode given in the *Samguk yusa*.

10. Yi Yong-bŏm, "Ch'ŏyong sŏlhwa ŭi il koch'al" (A Consideration of the Ch'ŏyong), *Kungmunhak nonmunsŏn* (Selected Essays on Korean Literature) (Seoul: Minjung sŏgwan, 1977), 1:314–19.

11. Hyŏn Yong-jun, *Musok shinhwa wa munhŏn shinhwa* (Shaman Myths and Recorded Myths), (Seoul: Chimmundang, 1991), 379–419.

12. Cho Tong-il, *Hanguk munhak t'ongsa*, 2nd ed. (Seoul: Chishik sanŏp sa, 1989), 1:214.

13. Hyŏn, *Musok shinhwa wa munhŏn shinhwa*, 379–419. This part of Professor Hyŏn's reading is especially helpful in explaining the masked-dance version of the Ch'ŏyong story that appears later in Koryŏ and Chosŏn court music.

14. Cho Tong-il, *Hanguk munhak t'ongsa*, 1:215.

15. Trans. Peter H. Lee in *Anthology of Korean Literature*, 19.

16. See Richard Rutt's comments on the hyangga in his fascinating essay on the *hwarang*, "Flower Boys of Shilla," *Transactions: Korea Branch of the Royal Asiatic Society*, 38 (1961): esp. 51–52.

3

The Incomparable Lyricism
of Koryŏ Songs

The Koryŏ songs are in a sense the earliest surviving vernacular Korean poetry. For although the earliest of the Shilla hyangga poems predate the Koryŏ songs by several centuries, those earlier poems do not survive as poetry in the full meaning of the word, that is, both in sound and in sense. By deciphering hyangch'al, the hybrid writing system in which the hyangga were composed, we can grope toward the sense of each of the twenty-five surviving hyangga poems, but as to their exact sound we have much less to go on. With the Koryŏ songs, however, it is an entirely different matter. Because they come down to us in their later transcriptions into hangŭl, we have not only their sense but their sound as well. As we shall see, that sound is an integral part of the Koryŏ songs and the fascination they hold for us.

As with the earlier hyangga, the Korean-language songs surviving from the Koryŏ period (A.D. 918–1392) are extremely few. Only twenty-one are known to us.[1] This paucity has two main causes. First, there was no indigenous writing system during the Koryŏ period and it was therefore necessary to rely on oral transmission of these vernacular verses. Second, even among those few Korean-language poems that survived through oral transmission from the Koryŏ to the Chosŏn period, some were lost by virtue of being excluded for one reason or another from anthologies of Korean-language poems compiled by Chosŏn Confucian scholars or expunged from existing anthologies because they were considered improper or indecent.

All twenty-one surviving Koryŏ songs are fascinating and valuable in their own way, although they vary widely in poetic quality. They range from "Hallim pyŏlgok," also known as "Kyŏnggich'e ka,"[2] to those verses consisting entirely of a series of patterned but nonsense syllables believed to be shaman chants,[3] and finally to about a dozen poems of exquisite lyricism such as "Samo kok," "Isang kok," and "Kashiri." It is this last group, variously named *changga, Koryŏ kayo, sogak kasa,* or *ko sokka,* that deserve our careful study and appreciation.

These Koryŏ vernacular poems are preserved in three music books compiled during the early Chosŏn dynasty: *Akhak kwebŏm, Akchang kasa,* and *Shiyong hyangak po.* Most of them are anonymous secular songs of the Koryŏ court that were transmitted orally and then written down during the late fifteenth and early sixteenth centuries after the invention of hangŭl in 1446. Because they were not committed to paper until after the invention of hangŭl, we do not know if we have them today exactly as they were during the Koryŏ period. Some of the poems may have been altered by Chosŏn anthologists, especially the love lyrics, which were considered indecent by Chosŏn Confucian scholars. Still, as the earliest and finest examples of Korean vernacular poetry that have survived in both sound and sense, these Koryŏ poems form an invaluable part of Korea's literary and musical heritage.

The key to our appreciation of these poems lies, I believe, in what Cho Tong-il has called the dual character of their origin and composition.[4] Although they have survived as Koryŏ court music, most of these verses originated in orally transmitted folk songs. This origin is most apparent in their folk song rhythm (three or four phrase groups to a four-beat line), the simplicity of their diction, and especially their refrains. To these folk elements the professional court musicians and poets probably added refinements in diction and music. The incomparable lyricism of the best Koryŏ songs comes from the interplay of these two very different elements. When folk and court elements are in perfect harmony, we have poems such as "Samo kok," "Isang kok," and "Kashiri," which display not only the lively rhythm and splendidly musical refrains of the folk song but also the exquisitely refined poetic diction and music contributed by court musicians and poets. Along with these three poems let us discuss two others, "Manjŏnch'un pyŏlsa" and "Ch'ŏngsan pyŏlgok," two works that are at once fascinating and problematic.

"Samo kok," is one of the briefest of those Koryŏ songs that appear to effectively combine both folk and court elements. Here is my literal translation of the poem:

> Though a hoe too is an edged blade,
> It does not cut like a scythe.
> Though father too is a parent,
> *Wi tŏngdŏ-tungshŏng,*
> Nobody loves like a mother.
> Please understand, my lord,
>   nobody loves like a mother.

According to Kim Hak-sŏng this brief poem was known by three different names, each representing a stage in its development into Koryŏ court music. It was first called "Mokchu," for the locality where the folk song originated. It was next called "Ŏnnorae" (Song of Mother). This change, according to Professor Kim, probably indicates that what had been a provincial folk song with limited dissemination had now spread widely enough to acquire a name of its own that represented its theme. Finally the song acquired its hanmun title, "Samo kok" (Song of Longing for Mother), simply a more formal title with little change in meaning.[5] It is as "Samo kok" that the poem has come down to us, indicating its elevation from the status of a folk song to that of Koryŏ court music.

What changes took place in the text of the poem as it changed from "Ŏnnorae" to "Samo kok"? Professor Kim believes that the text probably remained virtually unchanged except for the addition of the purely musical fourth line, "*Wi tŏngdŏ-tungshŏng,*" the placement of which, he believes, diminishes the lyricism of the song. As brief as the poem is, however, its fine diction and taut unity make me believe that more was done to the original folk song than simply adding a purely musical fourth line. First of all, the simple-seeming but subtle contrast between the not so sharply edged blade of a weeding hoe and paternal love seems much more refined, especially in phrasing, than what is generally encountered in a folk song. Furthermore, unlike Professor Kim, I find the placement of the fourth line—which probably represents the sound of the instrumental accompaniment—exactly right. As I read them, the musical syllables "*Wi tŏngdŏ-tungshŏng*" intensify the theme of the poem by slowing its unfolding. The first three lines of the poem only hint at its theme, that is, the uniqueness of a mother's love, without explicitly stating it:

> Though a hoe too is an edged blade,
> It does not cut like a scythe.
> Though father too is a parent,

The placement of "*Wi tŏngdŏ-tungshŏng*" in effect turns the third line into something like a question: "What is a father, really, even though we know he too is a parent?" As the flow of water, if temporarily dammed, gathers momentum, so does the statement of the theme gather intensity by being stopped midstream, so to speak. When the implied question is finally answered, the theme gains in intensity, not only through the interruption of the fourth line but also from the repetition in the fifth and sixth lines:

> **Nobody loves like a mother.**
> Please understand, my lord,
> **nobody loves like a mother.**
> [emphasis added]

Thus, even if the fourth line was the only alteration made by court musicians when "Ŏnnorae" became "Samo kok," we can see that what had probably been a relatively easygoing folk song was transformed into a tautly unified and more intensely lyrical work when it entered the Koryŏ court repertoire. Although no one can be sure of precisely what changes were made when "Ŏnnorae" became

"Samo kok," it is not difficult to imagine that along with the instrumental accompaniment the words of the folk song were probably pruned and polished, making the poem shorter, more coherent, and less repetitive.

What makes "Manjŏnch'un pyŏlsa," which Peter Lee translates as "Spring Overflows the Pavilion," so intriguing is not only its extraordinary first stanza but also its failure to achieve that harmony between the folk and court elements so essential to the best Koryŏ songs. Here is Peter Lee's translation:

> Were I to build a bamboo hut on the ice,
> Were I to die of cold with him on the ice,
> Were I to build a bamboo hut on the ice,
> Were I to die of cold with him on the ice,
> O night, run slow, run slow, till our love is spent.
>
> When I lie alone, restless,
> How can I fall asleep?
> Only peach blossoms wave over the west window.
> Ungrieved, you welcome the spring breeze.
> Welcome the spring breeze.
>
> I have believed those who vowed to each other:
> "May my soul follow yours forever."
> I have believed those who vowed to each other:
> "May my soul follow yours forever."
> Who, who persuaded me this was true?
>
> "O duck, O duck,
> O gentle duck,
> Why do you come
> To the swamp, instead of the shoal?"
> "If the swamp freezes, the shoal will do, the shoal
>   will do."
>
> A bed on Mount South,
> With Mount Jade as pillow,

> And Mount Brocade as quilt,
> And beside me a girl sweeter than musk,
> Let's press our hearts, press our hearts together!
>
> O love, let us be forever together![6]

In the original, the extraordinary vividness and intensity of the first stanza are due, first, to the concreteness of its simple and specific Korean words and phrases, such as "bamboo leaves," "ice," and "this love-steeped night," and, second, to the repetition of both the first two lines and a key phrase in the final line. Together they state the theme of the stanza with clarity, power, and poignancy: the passion of the lovers is so great that even if the woman and her beloved were to perish on the ice, she wishes for this love-steeped night to pass ever so slowly. Here is a more literal rendering of the first stanza:

> Lying on bamboo leaves spread upon the ice,
> Even if my lord and I were to freeze to death,
> Lying on bamboo leaves spread upon the ice,
> Even if my lord and I were to freeze to death,
> Let this love-steeped night pass slowly, pass slowly.

After this extraordinary first stanza, however, the song deteriorates poetically. For one thing, because the diction varies from stanza to stanza, alternating between lyrical Korean and formulaic Sino-Korean, the tone also changes from stanza to stanza. In the second stanza, for example, more than half of which is phrased in Sino-Korean, even though the sense of the words suggest sorrow and despair, the stanza as a whole sounds ironic and self-conscious because of its singsong cadence and formulaic diction. This is my literal translation:

> Lying alone in bed
> I cannot sleep.
> When I open the west window,

> The peach blossoms in full bloom,
>   unworried,
> Smile at the spring breeze, smile at
>   the spring breeze.

The passionate lyricism of the first stanza has been replaced by a melancholy weariness. The tone shifts again in the third stanza, and yet again in the fourth and fifth stanzas. Thematically, too, there is little coherence. Although the song as a whole appears to be concerned with various aspects of love, it is not at all clear how the stanzas are related. Even the gender of the narrator seems to undergo a change toward the end of the poem. From the first through the initial two lines of the fourth stanza, the voice of the poem appears to be that of a woman, but beginning with the last line of the fourth stanza, a male voice seems to take over.

Thus, although "Manjŏnch'un pyŏlsa" starts off powerfully, it slides into a confusing medley of voices of varying intensity and vividness, failing to achieve an overall unity of effect in either sound or sense. Perhaps this is why some scholars have speculated that the poem represents an unsuccessful effort to stitch together parts of various contemporary songs into a piece of court music.[7]

With the inimitable music of its lyrics and refrain, "Ch'ŏngsan pyŏlgok" (Song of Green Mountain) is surely one of the loveliest of Koryŏ songs. Here is Peter Lee's translation:

> Let's live, let's live,
> Let's live in the green mountain!
> With wild grapes and thyme,
> Let's live in the green mountain!
> *Yalli yalli yallasyŏng yallari yalla*
>
> Cry, cry, birds,
> You cry after you wake.
> I've more sorrow than you
> And cry after I wake.
> *Yalli yalli yallasyŏng yallari yalla*

I see the bird passing, bird passing,
I see the passing bird on the water.
With a mossy-plow
I see the passing bird beyond the water.
Yalli yalli yallasyŏng yallari yalla

I've spent the day
This way and that.
But where no man comes or goes,
How am I to pass the night?
Yalli yalli yallasyŏng yallari yalla

At what place is this stone thrown?
At what person is this stone thrown?
Here no one to hate or love,
I cry being hit by a stone.
Yalli yalli yallasyŏng yallari yalla

Let's live, let's live,
Let's live by the sea!
With seaweed, and oysters, and clams,
Let's live by the sea!
Yalli yalli yallasyŏng yallari yalla

I've listened as I went, went,
Turning the corner of the kitchen I've
    listened.
I've listened to the stag fiddling
Perched on a bamboo pole.
Yalli yalli yallasyŏng yallari yalla

I have brewed strong wine
In a round-bellied jar.
A gourd-shaped leaven seizes me.
What shall I do now?
Yalli yalli yallasyŏng yallari yalla[8]

The more lyrical a poem is in the original, the more difficult it is to translate into another language. So it is with "Ch'ŏngsan pyŏlgok." But even a quick glance at the first two lines of the original together with their literal translation is enough to give us a feel for their lyricism as well as their music:

> *Sarŏri sarŏri ratta*
> *Ch'ŏngsan e sarŏri ratta*
> (Live, let us live
> In the green mountain let us live)

In the original we see a succession of vowel harmony (*a*'s, *ŏ*'s, and *i*'s), alliteration (*s*'s and *r*'s), and even something like an end rhyme (*ratta*). A similar pattern of sound harmony runs throughout the original. This together with the refrain of each of the eight stanzas—*Yalli yalli yallasyŏng yallari yalla*—makes the poem one of the most invigorating, high-spirited, and musical of the Koryŏ songs. But there is a problem—an apparent discrepancy between the sense and the sound of the poem; what the words of the poem seem to say appears to belie the music of the poem. For instance, while the invigorating rhythm and cadence of the song sound a note of exhilaration, the words of the song suggest something quite different—crying from sorrow (second stanza), empty days and nights (fourth stanza), and fear and uneasiness (fifth stanza). "Ch'ŏngsan pyŏlgok" is thus a poem that sounds exhilarating but whose words suggest melancholy and sorrow. What is to be made of this discrepancy?

Cho Tong-il has suggested that the words of the poem might have been tacked on to an existing folk song refrain,[9] just as different sets of words have been tacked on to the same refrain in the folk song "Arirang." This explanation is persuasive if we consider another Koryŏ song, "Taeguk" (Great Kingdom). The refrain of this song—*Yalli yalli yalla yallasyŏng yalla*"—is very much like that of "Ch'ŏngsan pyŏlgok," although the themes of the two songs are entirely different. Therefore, it may well be that the refrain, derived from the folk song tradition, was attached to various court songs when they were adopted into the Koryŏ court repertoire.

Is "Ch'ŏngsan pyŏlgok," then, like "Manjŏnch'un pyŏlsa," an instance of a failure to harmonize the two very different elements of the Koryŏ songs? The question is complicated, for one thing, by the fact that there is too much in the poem we do not yet understand completely. For example, what does the line "Let's live in the green mountain!" mean? Is it about a scholar's longing to withdraw from society into the peace and quiet of country living? Or is it about a peasant family's flight to the mountains or seashore to escape the tyranny of landlords or depredations of Mongol invaders, both of which occurred during the Koryŏ period? The answer to these questions lies in part in how some of the other knotty passages are read. The third stanza, for example, has long posed difficulties and has not yet been deciphered to everyone's satisfaction. Literally translated, it reads:

> I see a bird flying by, a bird flying by.
> I see a bird flying by under the water.
> Holding a moss-covered plow,
> I see a bird flying by under the water.
> *Yalli yalli yallasyŏng yallari yalla.*

But since a bird cannot fly underwater, the second and fourth lines seem to require a different reading. It has been suggested that the phrase *kadŏn sae,* "bird flying by," might be a contraction of *kaldŏn sarae,* "furrows formerly cultivated." Thus reconstructed, the third stanza would read:

> I see the furrows, the furrows of my old field.
> I see the furrows of my old field way down the river.
> Holding a moss-covered plow,
> I see the furrows of my old field way down the river.
> *Yalli yalli yallasyŏng yallari yalla.*

Such a reading obviously changes the meaning of the song considerably. Another difficult passage is the third and fourth lines of the seventh stanza, which in Peter Lee's translation read: "I've listened to the stag fiddling. / Perched on a bamboo pole." A stag perched on a bamboo pole seems unlikely enough, but fiddling besides? According to a widely accepted reading, the stag here is actually an entertainer-acrobat (*kwangdae*) costumed as a stag.[10] And what about the sixth stanza? Are we to understand it as an expression of the singer's fervent wish to live by the sea, subsisting on seaweed, clams, and the like? While the music of the verse may suggest joyful expectancy of carefree living, surviving on seaweed, oysters, and clams does not necessarily mean a happy or carefree life.

Clearly these readings remain problematic, and yet it seems to me that these incompletely deciphered passages do not diminish our appreciation of this poem at once so wonderfully lively, melancholy, and puzzling. As with some of the hyangga, the tantalizing enigmas of "Ch'ŏngsan pyŏlgok" add to the overall power and beauty of the song. Could it be that the wonderful music and pure vernacular poetic diction are sufficient in themselves to make an indelible impression on the mind?

In its diction, imagery, and theme "Isang kok" (Frost-Treading Song) is one of the most vividly evocative Koryŏ songs.[11] Even though the surviving text of the poem provides no clear stanzaic divisions, most scholars see three stanzas. According to this reading, the first stanza takes up the first five lines while the second and third stanzas take up the next five and three lines, respectively.[12] The first stanza, which establishes the physical landscape of the song, is stunning in its structure, imagery, music, and diction. What is especially striking structurally is that its five lines are divided into two distinct two-line sections of sharply constrasting imagery and meaning, which are in turn bridged by a purely musical third line that reads "*Tarongdiushŏ madŭksari madunŏjŭse nŏuji.*" This interlude not only provides a pause in the narrative but also approximates either the sound of the instrumental accompaniment or the sound of feet treading on frost-covered ground.[13]

The first two lines of the song read and sound very much like a

couplet: they have an equal number of syllables (thirteen) and end
in two nearly rhyming words—*nal e* ("on the day") and *kil e* ("in
the path"). They also form the most beautifully concrete passage of
the entire poem, evoking a set of vivid images of the physical
landscape: a narrow, winding path in the woods; a crisp, rain-
cleansed day and snow-covered ground. Here is a literal translation
of the first two lines:

> Been raining   cleared up   much snow has fallen   on
>   this day
> Entangled over and over   a narrow winding path   in
>   the woods.[14]

The purely musical third line bridges these two lines and the next
two lines, which in sharp contrast with the first two evoke the inner
landscape of the narrator's anguish. The third line thus marks the
passage from an outer to an inner landscape. The fourth and fifth
lines, literally translated, read:

> Thinking of   my sleep-robbing lord
> Through the dawning path   will he come to stay
>   with me?

This first stanza, through its music and exquisite Korean diction,
transports us to the scene, where we join the narrator as she
sleeplessly awaits her lover, her eyes fixed on the narrow, winding path through the woods. But as the woodland path emerges
clear and empty in the light of dawn, she all but gives up hope of
seeing her lover that morning.

The second stanza, however, differs from the first both in diction
and in sound. The third and fourth lines double the first two
lines,[15] and there is considerable variation in diction: the first and
third lines are heavily Sino-Korean, the second, fourth, and fifth
very much Korean. Literally translated, this second stanza reads
as follows:

> Over and over struck by lightning   fallen
>   into hell
> Soon to perish   this my body,
> Finally struck by lightning   ah   fallen
>   into hell
> Soon to perish   this my body,
> Leaving my lord   dare I go   to another mountain?

While the Sino-Korean diction of the first line sounds quite formulaic, the second and fifth lines are delicately lyrical, reminding
us of the exquisiteness of the first stanza. The near repetition of
the first two lines appears to have two effects: it increases the
formulaic quality of the lines but also conveys a deepening sense
of the woman's despair. Thus, although the second stanza is cle-
ary less lyrical than the first, it is also more intense emotionally.
Is the narrator plunged into despair and fear of retribution—
"struck by lightning   fallen into hell / Soon to perish   this my
body"—because of her love affair, or because she now feels more
vulnerable to temptation, her lover having failed to appear? Her
vulnerability to temptation is suggested in the phrase "another
mountain." The question is left unanswered. But what is unam-
biguous in the stanza is the woman's unhappiness and uneasiness, and that seems to be why the final stanza stresses her
struggle to shore up her resolution.

The final three lines of the song are a mix of Korean and Sino-
Korean diction. The vivid and poignant lyricism of the first
stanza has all but vanished in favor of a series of quiet phrases
expressing uncertainty and uneasiness. The following is a literal
rendering:

> This way or that-a-way
> This way or that-a-way   dare I pledge?
> Nay, my lord, I wish to go where you go!

Although she struggles to firm up her resolution, it is her uncertainty that dominates, connecting this concluding stanza themati-

cally with both the heartbreak of the first stanza and the fear and vulnerability expressed in the second. The woman's uneasiness has perhaps been increased by the mutinous suggestion of another lover ("another mountain") in the final line of the preceding stanza, and as hard as she struggles to keep it out of her mind, the notion is not so easily dismissed. This struggle is effectively conveyed in the phrase repeated in the first two lines: *"iröch'ö dyöröch'ö"* ("this way or that-a-way"). The rest of the stanza seems to show her struggling to suppress this fearful suggestion by reaffirming her pledge to the absent lover.

Ultimately, what makes "Isang kok" so stunning is not only the exquisite music and Korean diction but also the contrast so clearly and poignantly drawn between the vivid images of the physical landscape and those of the woman's anguish and struggle throughout the poem.

"Isang kok" and "Kashiri" are connected by a common theme, one that recurs in many classical Korean love lyrics. It is the theme of a lover's sorrow arising either from a futile expectation that the beloved will return or, as in "Kashiri," from the struggle to hold on to the beloved, who is about to leave. But obviously there is much more to "Kashiri," for it is the most extraordinary of the Koryö songs. What gives it such extraordinary resonance, which defies simple or logical explanation? Perhaps it has something to do with its rhythm and pure Korean diction, which seem to touch the heart of the Korean people. In some inexplicable way the line *"Kashiri kashiri itko nanŭn,"* which is at least half a millennium old, has a magically evocative effect even on the twentieth-century Korean reader. It is as if its rhythm and diction well up from the deepest part of our mind.

"Kashiri" is a poem of only four three-line stanzas. The third line of each stanza is a refrain made up of two half-lines of no apparent meaning, added for sound harmony only: four syllables of purely musical sound—*"Wi chŭngjŭlga"*—make up the first half-line, and a phrase signifying "an age of great peace and prosperity" the second half-line. This second half-line, however, sounds just as nonsensical as the first, since it appears totally unrelated to the theme of the poem. The following is Peter Lee's translation of the poem (which he titles "Will You Go?"):

Will you go away? *nanŭn*
Will you forsake me and go? *nanŭn*
Wi chungjŭlka O age of great peace and plenty!

How can you tell me to live on
And forsake me and go away?
O age of great peace and plenty!

I could stop you but fear
You would be annoyed and never return.
O age of great peace and plenty!

I'll let you go, wretched love,
But return as soon as you leave.
O age of great peace and plenty![16]

The more lyrical a poetic work, the more difficult it is to translate into another language, for what makes the work so lyrical in the original is precisely what cannot be carried over into a different language. Hence the sheer impossibility of rendering in English the qualities that make "Kashiri" sing in Korean.

What makes this poem so exquisitely lyrical in the original? In part it is the delicately phrased plea of the singer to the departing lover, a plea at once loving, worshipful, and deeply distressed. We hear and feel its poignancy especially in the first two lines of the first stanza and the final two lines of the last stanza:

Kashiri kashiri itko nanŭn
Parigo kashiri itko nanŭn

.   .   .   .

Shyŏron nim ponae opnani nanŭn
Kashinŭn tŭt toshyŏ oshioshyŏ nanŭn

The last line, so poignantly delicate, literally means "In the manner you're leaving, please return." Part of the magic of these lines comes from the use of the honorific form of the words for "go away" and "come" (*kashi* and *ohsi,* respectively), especially in the final line. The alliterative *s*'s (part of what makes the words honorific) in both halves of the line heighten the effect of the singer's plea to the departing lover by making it at once so urgent and loving. We could perhaps call it loving grief, or intense sorrow balanced by equally intense loving solicitude. The line-ending *nanŭn,* recurring throughout the poem, adds still further to the poignancy of the appeal. For even though it is supposedly added for the sake of sound harmony only, the word—which literally means "me"—repeatedly accents the pathos of abandonment and the lover's grief.[17]

For the modern Korean reader, the powerful and insistent resonance of the poem probably also derives from its close link in rhythm, diction, and theme to the other long-treasured love songs and poems of the Korean people. The first and most obvious link that comes to mind is "Arirang," that best-loved of all Korean folk songs. No one seems to know exactly how old "Arirang" is. Some trace it back as far as the Three Kingdoms period; others see it originating as recently as the late nineteenth century. What is indisputable, however, is that its melody and words, which sing of the heartbreak of abandonment or forced separation, seem almost as old as the collective memory of the Korean people. The most poignant passage in "Arirang" closely resembles that of "Kashiri":

> *Na rŭl pŏrigo kashinŭn nim ŭn*
> (My lord   going away   abandoning me)
>   (from "Arirang")

> *Kashiri kashiri itko nanŭn* (Going, going away,
>   are you?)·
> *Parigo kashiri itko nanŭn* (Leaving me,
>   are you going away?)
>   (from "Kashiri")

The rhythm and diction of both "Kashiri" and "Arirang" are also sounded by Korea's best-loved modern lyric poet, Kim Sowŏl, in his "Chindallae kkot" (Azaleas)," also a poem about struggling to hold on to a lover who is leaving. The most insistently resonant passage in this twentieth-century poem echoes the key passages of both "Kashiri" and "Arirang":

> *Na pogi ka yŏggyŏwŏ* (Weary of seeing me,)
> *Kashilttae enŭn* (When you go away)[18]

There is still more. The most unforgettable love lyrics left us by Hwang Chini (an early-sixteenth-century *kisaeng* poet) also seem to echo the rhythm, diction, and motif of "Kashiri" and "Arirang." Obviously, coming together and parting are central yet contrary activities of lovers. And in Korean these contrary actions are represented by *kashi* and *oshi,* a pair of words that in their honoric form are strikingly similar yet contrasting in sound. In her best-known shijo Hwang Chin-i plays on this poignant similarity and contrast. The poem, which is set on a long, midwinter night, pivots on this pair of words both in sound and in sense. Even though the word *kashi* does not appear in the poem, it is there in the background, silent but insistent, for the poem is utterly focused on the night the departed lover (*kashin nim*) will have returned: "*nim oshin nal pam*" (literally, "the night of the day the lover has returned").

We find in "Kashiri" the earliest example of the theme of parting and loss combined with the most exquisite Korean poetic diction and rhythm. It is this combination that links it not only to "Arirang," the most popular Korean folk song, and to Kim Sowŏl's "Chindallae kkot," perhaps Korea's most beloved lyric poem of the twentieth century, but also to one of the finest classical shijo, by Hwang Chin-i. Why has the theme of parting and loss together with the lyrical phrasing of that theme touched the Korean heart so deeply, so insistently, and for so long? Is it because parting and loss have been a bitter yet central experience through much of Korean history? To be Korean has been to experience the sorrows of parting and loss, for the many national calamities—the Mongol, Japanese, and Manchu invasions, the Japanese occupation, and the Korean War, to name just the most obvious examples—have invariably meant the loss of, separation from, or abandonment by loved ones.

Would this not have been especially true for Korean women, countless numbers of whom died during the various invasions of the Koryŏ and Chosŏn periods? Many others were kidnapped to China, Japan, or elsewhere,[19] and those who managed to return to Korea found themselves repudiated by their husbands' families for having been "dishonored." Even a royal decree proclaiming them cleansed of all stains once they had ritually bathed themselves at Hongjewŏn (a place north of the capital) could not reinstate them in their husbands' families. Anyone who watched the latest chapter of this story—the joyful but also frequently traumatic reunions of family members long separated by the Korean War—played out on Korean national television perhaps understands better why this theme of parting and loss has so long preoccupied the poetic imagination of the Korean people.

There is perhaps another dimension to this best-loved of Koryŏ songs—that of rhythm and diction. If, as Bob Hass has pointed out, "rhythm has direct access to the unconscious,"[20] so too must poetic diction, since diction is as central to song and poetry as rhythm is. Thus rhythm and diction together express the deepest part of ourselves as a people, tapping long-accumulated reservoirs of conscious and unconscious memories. Why else would "Kashiri" remind us of "Arirang" and "Chindallae kkot," and vice versa? It is certainly not because Kim Sowŏl modeled his poem on the Koryŏ songs—he probably didn't know of their existence. Rather, all three of these poems have tapped Korea's most enduring poetic rhythm, that of the folk song, and they utilize poetic diction that is both quintessentially Korean and utterly lyrical. And when this most Korean of rhythm and diction are coupled with the theme of parting and loss, do we not have the most Korean of poetry?

Half a dozen of the remaining Koryŏ songs deserve study and appreciation. Three of these are especially interesting, in part because they are not merely songs but what Cho Tong-il calls *nori-*

norae (song and play):[21] "Ssanghwa chŏm" (The Dumpling Shop), "Ch'ŏyong ka" (Song of Ch'ŏyong), and "Tongdong" (Song of the Year).

"Ssanghwa chŏm" is perhaps the easiest to understand as well as to translate. Because the poem is more comic and satirical than lyrical, its prose content is straightforward and clearly defined. Its earthy language and unabashed celebration of lust form a sharp contrast with the intense love and longing exquisitely represented in the Koryŏ love songs. Here is the opening verse of this four-stanza poem, translated by Marshall R. Pihl:

> I went to the dumpling shop to buy myself some
>   dumplings
> Then a Muslim codger caught me by the wrist!
> If word is spread beyond this shop,
> *Tarorŏ kŏdirŏ*
> I'll say you're telling lies, you little actor's mask!
> *Tŏrŏtungshyŏng tarirŏ tirŏ tarorŏ kŏdirŏ tarorŏ*
> I too will go to lay me in that place
> *Wi wi tarorŏ-kŏdirŏ tarorŏ*
> There was ne'er a place so scruffy as where
>   I slept.[22]

In the remaining three stanzas the woman narrator goes to a Buddhist temple, a village well, and a tavern and has a similar encounter in each place. If, as has been suggested, the dragon in the village well in the third stanza represents the king, we can see that the poem paints a relaxed moral atmosphere in nearly every level of Koryŏ society, including both secular and religious institutions, but without explicit moral disapproval. The prevailing tone of the poem thus appears to be affirmation and acceptance of the human comedy. According to the *Koryŏ sa* (History of Koryŏ), "Ssanghwa chŏm" was performed at the court by a troupe of singers and dancers. Unlike most of the other Koryŏ songs, which were derived from the popular folk songs of the times, "Ssanghwa chŏm" is believed to have been composed by one or two courtiers of King Ch'ungnyŏl (r. 1274–1308),[23] a monarch known to have been excessively fond of having singers, dancers, and actors perform at the court.

The Koryŏ "Ch'ŏyong ka" is extremely complex and difficult, more a masked dance and play than a poem. The Shilla hyangga of the same name is much shorter. That earlier poem, without its last two lines, forms part of this Koryŏ version. Here Ch'ŏyong—called Father Ch'ŏyong—is presented as a resplendent and powerful gate guardian whose mere appearance frightens the plague spirit (*yŏkshin*) into a hasty flight: "Be it mountain or field—to a place one thousand leagues away, / I want to get away from Father Ch'ŏyong!"[24]

The most exciting of these three *nori-norae* is "Tongdong."[25] As we have seen, the Koryŏ songs achieved poetic perfection when they combined folk and court elements in exquisite harmony. "Tongdong" is another instance of this harmony. Although it is now impossible to clearly separate the elements of these two traditions, it is noteworthy that the poem appears to consist of two distinct parts: the opening stanza and the remaining twelve stanzas. Not only does the opening stanza differ thematically from the rest of the poem, but according to the explanatory notes accompanying the poem it was also sung differently.[26] This first stanza is clearly dedicatory and may have been composed when an earlier folk song was adapted to court music. Literally translated, the opening verse reads as follows:

> Virtue we offer to the spirits
> Blessings we offer to our lord.
> What we call virtue and blessings,
> Step forward to offer them up.
> Ah, *tongdong tari!*[27]

According to the accompanying notes, two female singers step forward from the troupe of performers to sing this dedication, followed by several additional female singers as well as the rest of the troupe.[28] In this manner the performers offered virtue and blessings to the king.

The twelve stanzas that follow seem quite different thematically. They appear to be a love song of folk origin delineating month by month and season by season the ever-changing mood and relationship of a woman and her lover. What is so exciting about this cycle of twelve calendrical verses—despite the difficulties and obscurity of some of the passages—is the startling exquisiteness of their diction and imagery, which are comparable to the best of the Koryŏ songs.

It is not quite clear who the object of the woman narrator's adoration is. He is, we are told in the third stanza, bright like the brightly lit lantern of February 15. Literally translated, the stanza reads as follows:

> On the fifteenth of the second [lunar] month,
> Ah, [you] are like the light of a lantern
> Brightly lit high above
> Shining light on all persons.
> Ah, *tongdong tari!*

Is the object of adoration the full moon of February, as Professor Pihl seems to believe? The woman's lover, as the rest of the poem seems to suggest? The king, to whom the entire performance is supposedly dedicated? The answer is not given in the poem. Yet because the music and poetry of this thirteen-verse poem are so lovely, such obscurities are all the more beguiling, drawing us further into the poem.

Although every one of the thirteen verses—the last twelve corresponding to the months of the lunar year—is exquisite, the loveliest and most poignant is perhaps the second stanza. This verse sings of the lunar month of January, the Janus-faced month of passage from the end of winter to the beginning of spring when all things in nature are in a state of flux. Literally translated, the stanza reads as follows:

> The stream of January
> Ah, it freezes, melts; freezes and melts.
> This body, born in this world,

Lives all alone.
Ah, *tongdong tari!*

In the original the poignancy of the narrator's heart-wrenching cry is heightened by the constrast in both sound and meaning of *ŏjŏ* ("freezes") and nokjŏ ("melts") as well as the similarity in sound of *narit* ("stream") and *nurit* ("world"). The narrator's sense of aloneness in the world is deepened by her awareness of the temporalness of life and nature, which in turn heightens the preciousness of her few moments of joy in this world of never-ceasing change and passage of time. In the verse for August, she cries out:

August fifteenth is
Ah, of course a festival day.
But today is a festival day,
For today I'm with my lord.
Ah, *tongdong tari!*

It is such passages that make "Tongdong" an unforgettable, incomparably lovely poem.

Notes

1. Pak Pyŏng-ch'ae, *Koryŏ kayo ŭi ŏyŏk yŏngu* (A Study of Koryŏ Kayo: Words and Meaning) (Seoul: Iu ch'ulp'ansa, 1975), 27. In addition to the twenty-one surviving songs, we have the titles of thirty-nine pieces whose lyrics have been lost.
2. The name comes from the refrain that ends each of its verses: "*Kyŏnggi kŭi ŏttŏhari.*" These are poems composed by the literati for the literati, and their diction is heavily Sino-Korean.
3. For example, the first verse of "Kunma taewang" (The Great King War Horse), goes as follows: "*Rirŏru rŏrirŏru rŏllŏ riru / Rŏru rŏrirŏru / Rirŏruri rŏriro / Rori rorari / Rŏrirŏ rirŏru rŏllŏ riru / Rŏru rŏrirŏru / Rirŏruri rŏriro.*
4. Cho Tong-il, *Hanguk munhak t'ongsa* (A Comprehensive History of Korean Literature), 2nd ed. (Seoul: Chishik sanŏp sa, 1989), II:127.
5. Kim Hak-sŏng, *Kungmunhak ŭi t'amgu* (Explorations in Korean Literature) (Seoul: Sŏnggyungwan taehakkyo chŭlp'ansa, 1987), 30–34.
6. Peter H. Lee, the latest revision quoted by permission of the translator.
7. Kim Hak-sŏng, *Kungmunhak ŭi t'amgu*, 37–39.

8. Lee, the latest revision quoted by permission of the translator.

9. Cho Tong-il, *Hanguk munhak t'ongsa,* II:152–53.

10. Ibid.

11. According to Yi Im-su, in classical Chinese literature a woman's pain and anguish are often represented by the image of frost. The term for a young or teenage widow, for instance, includes the Chinese character for frost, and hence the connection between the title and the theme—a woman's heart-break—of this song. Yi Im-su, *Yŏga yŏngu* (A Study of Koryŏ Songs) (Seoul: Hyŏngsŏl chŭlp'ansa, 1988), 218–19.

12. Ibid., 214–15; Cho Tong-il, *Hanguk munhak t'ongsa,* II:142–43.

13. Yi, *Yŏga yŏngu,* 219.

14. A slightly different reading of this line is given by Pak Pyŏng-ch'ae in his *Koryŏ kayo ŭi ŏyŏk yŏngu* (A Study of Koryŏ Kayo: Words and Meaning), rev. ed. (Seoul: Kukhak charyowŏn, 1994), 297. The reading of this line remains problematic.

15. The third line varies slightly from the first: one *chong* instead of two, and the addition of *a* ("ah"). See Pak No-jun, *Koryŏ kayo ŭi yŏngu* (A Study of Koryŏ Songs) (Seoul: Saemun sa, 1990), 208–14.

16. Lee, the latest revision quoted by permission of the translator.

17. Cho Tong-il, *Hanguk munhak t'ongsa,* II:148.

18. Translation by David R. McCann in his *Form and Freedom in Korean Poetry* (Leiden: E.J. Brill: 1988), 83, 87.

19. In 1253 alone, during the Mongol occupation of Korea, over 200,000 Korean men and women were taken away by the Mongols. See *Samguk yusa yŏngu nonsŏnjip* (Selected Essays on the *Samguk yusa*) (Seoul: Paeksan charyowŏn, 1986), I:167.

20. Robert Hass, *Twentieth Century Pleasures* (New York: Ecco Press, 1984), 108.

21. Cho Tong-il, *Hanguk munhak t'ongsa,* II:133.

22. Marshall R. Pihl, ed., "A Reader in Traditional Korean Literature: From Myth to Oral Narrative" (unpublished manuscript, 1993), 63.

23. Pak Pyŏng-ch'ae, *Koryŏ kayo ŭi ŏyŏk yŏngu,* 245.

24. Pihl, ed., "A Reader in Traditional Korean Literature," 59.

25. "Tongdong" is believed to represent the sound of the drum accompaniment as well as the movement of lovers in perfect harmony. Pak Pyŏng-ch'ae, *Koryŏ kayo ŭi ŏyŏk yŏngu,* rev. ed., 66.

26. Ibid., 53–54.

27. For the full text of "Tongdong," see Ibid., 51–53.

28. Ibid., 53–54.

4

Notes on the *Samguk sagi* and *Samguk yusa*

Two of the oldest and most important works containing Korean hanmun prose literature are the *Samguk sagi* (History of the Three Kingdoms) and *Samguk yusa* (Memorabilia of the Three Kingdoms). The first is an official history of the Three Kingdoms in annalistic form compiled in 1145 by Kim Pu-shik (1075–1151). The second, as the title implies, is an unofficial chronicle of historical occurrences, myths, legends, and folklore compiled in 1281 by the Sŏn (Zen) priest Iryŏn (1206–1289). The *Samguk yusa* has long been valued far more than the *Samguk sagi* by Korean scholars of literature. For while the *Samguk sagi* concerns itself mostly with dynastic histories and biographies of kings and other persons of historical importance, the *Samguk yusa* is a repository of the earliest Korean legends, folklore, and myths, most notably the Tangun myth as well as the other foundation myths of the Korean people, all recorded for the first time in this volume. One could easily devote a lifetime of study to these two early histories. What follows are some brief observations based on my initial readings of them.

While the two works are very different, they do have some similarities. Both are histories of the Three Kingdoms by Koryŏ men of learning who believed the Koryŏ dynasty to be the inheritor of the Shilla, rather than Koguryŏ, tradition. This is why in content as well as in sympathy both histories appear heavily weighted in favor of the Shilla. For example, not only does the *Samguk sagi* begin with the founding of the Shilla kingdom, claiming Shilla to be the most ancient of Korea's Three Kingdoms; it also includes more Shilla lives in its *yŏlchŏn* (biographical) section than any other. Of the eighty-six lives, fifty-six are from Shilla, ten from Koguryŏ, and only three from Paekche.[1] The preponderance of the Shilla material is even greater in the *Samguk yusa,* since most of its Buddhist legends and folklore derive from the Shilla period and Shilla sources. (An obvious reason for this preponderance is the great disparity among the documentary resources surviving at the time the two histories were written. Documents for Shilla were much more plentiful; the historical records for Koguryŏ and Paekche had mostly been destroyed in the fall of those kingdoms.)

Another similarity is that both histories appear to have many sources in common, particularly the now lost *Ku Samguk sa* (Old History of the Three Kingdoms) along with other Korean and Chinese histories. Besides, it is evident that Iryŏn, compiler of the *Samguk yusa,* drew on the *Samguk sagi,* especially for comparison and contrast, as he compiled his own history.

Consider, for example, the accounts of the fall of King Ŭija, the last king of Paekche, given by the two histories. Both accounts emphasize the moral decline and misrule of King Ŭija, who had been exemplary as son and crown prince. Both detail the same omens of the impending doom of the Paekche kingdom: a Cassandra-like ghost that appears in the royal palace and cries out, "Paekche will fall!"; a white fox that sits in the spot reserved for one of the ministers; a chicken that copulates with a sparrow; a tortoise whose back bears an inscription saying that Paekche is like the full moon—and therefore about to wane—while Shilla is like the new moon; and finally King Ŭija's execution of the shaman for his honest but unwelcome reading of the inscription, an act clearly showing that the king, self-indulgent in his delusion, is unable to confront the truth. The similarities in this account suggest that both the *Samguk sagi* and *Samguk yusa* not only relied on a common source but also shared a pro-Shilla bias, since both histories attribute the fall of Paekche principally to the moral failure of its last king while downplaying external pressures brought on by the united military power of T'ang China and Shilla.

But the differences between the two histories are even greater and more significant. Because Kim Pu-shik, principal compiler[2] of the *Samguk sagi,* was a Confucian scholar-statesman while Iryŏn was a Sŏn Buddhist priest, they looked at history very differently. Whereas Kim Pu-shik was a Sinophile and a rationalist, Iryŏn, a devoted Buddhist and a fervent nationalist, had a more religious and mythopoeic approach to history. The two men appear also to have differed markedly in their understanding of Korea's relation to China. Kim Pu-shik's was a Sino-centric world view intellectually, morally, and culturally, Iryŏn's a Buddhist and Korea-centered world view.

These were significant differences. From a Buddhist's point of view, unlike a Confucianist's, both China and Korea belonged to the larger Buddhist world and hence were more or less equal members of the worldwide Buddhist community. Furthermore, because Iryŏn lived at a time when Korea's very existence was imperiled by Mongol invasions, he felt a deep need to assert Korea's cultural independence and worthiness. Hence his lifelong effort to rediscover and promote all that was Korean, and his decision to put the founding of the earliest Korean kingdoms on an equal footing with that of the Chinese kingdoms. Perhaps this was also his reason for beginning the *Samguk yusa* with the Tangun myth—the foundation myth of Korea—which had been left out of the *Samguk sagi.*

Iryŏn's inclusion of the Tangun myth in the *Samguk yusa* forms an implicit challenge to Kim Pu-shik's exclusion of it in the *Samguk sagi.* Iryŏn includes not only the Tangun myth but also the various other native myths and legends, and in particular the Buddhist legends and tales left out of the *Samguk sagi* altogether. He even sought out local legends and tales by making on-site visits and investigations.[3] His inclusion of native myths and legends therefore posed a nationalistic and Sŏn Buddhist challenge to Kim Pu-shik's Sino-centric and Confucian-rationalist view of history.

An essential part of Iryŏn's nationalism was his belief that Korea, too, was a Buddhist holy land, the sacred ground of many of the Buddha's earlier incarnations.[4] From this conviction had naturally followed his belief that Korea was one of the Buddha-lands where many bodhisattvas and miracles would appear, as foretold in Buddhist legends and folklore. For Iryŏn, early Korean myths such as the Tangun foundation myth were therefore no less real than this wondrous Buddhist lore. In his preface to the section on the "strange and wondrous," which begins the narrative part of the *Samguk yusa,* Iryŏn explains the strange and wonderous occurrences that accompanied the founding of the Korean nation:

> The rise of emperors and kings, accompanied by heavenly signs, is different from that of ordinary men. . . . Thus, there is nothing strange about the founders of the Three Kingdoms having been born in a supernatural manner. Such is the meaning of the strange mysteries set forth at the start of these chapters.[5]

For, as Iryŏn points out in the same passage, hadn't the founding emperors of China had supernatural births? If one believed this, then why not believe the same for the founders of the Koguryŏ, Paekche, and Shilla kingdoms? This was reason enough for Iryŏn to believe that the founder of the Korean nation was just as godlike as the founders of the Chinese kingdoms. In fact, he traces Tangun's lineage directly to heaven, thus making him a son of Heaven.[6]

We can perhaps better see the differences in focus and emphasis between the *Samguk sagi* and *Samguk yusa* by examining how they deal with a common subject. For example, Kim Yu-shin is clearly the most exemplary patriot-warrior-statesman of Shilla for both Kim Pu-shik and Iryŏn. Yet his life is dealt with very differently in the two histories. Not only does the *yŏlchŏn* (biographical) section of the *Samguk sagi* begin with the life of Kim Yu-shin, it also devotes the most space to him—an extraordinary amount of space, in fact, compared with that allocated to the other lives. Whereas a single chapter of the *yŏlchŏn* typically includes from two to half a dozen lives, three whole chapters are devoted to the life of Kim

Yu-shin, although these chapters also include details about his sons and grandsons.

What makes these chapters so extraordinary are the vividly re-created episodes of Kim Yu-shin's long life, during which he was called upon so often to lead the Shilla nation in times of extreme crisis. In one striking vignette, for example, Kim returns to the capital from two consecutive military expeditions to repel the enemy, but even before he can return home he is ordered once again to march out to battle. As he and his troops pass by his residence the members of his household are lined up in front of the gate to welcome him. But he marches on without a backward glance. Fifty steps later he stops and sends a man to fetch water from his house. "The water at my house tastes the same as before,"[7] he is reported to have said before marching on to the western front.

In reflecting Kim's selfless devotion to the cause of his nation, the biography shows him to be a splendid warrior-statesman and a wise and shrewd human being. It is a multidimensional portrait of a clearly extraordinary man. But above all else the portrait sets up Kim as a model of dedication to the Shilla nation, warrior-statesman for all to emulate, especially for the strife-torn Koryŏ aristocrats of Kim Pu-shik's own time.

By comparison the section on Kim Yu-shin in the *Samguk yusa* is brief, consisting mostly of an account of his rescue by three local guardian spirits of the Shilla countryside from a trap set by a Koguryŏ agent. It is probable, as most Korean scholars have conjectured, that Iryŏn included in his account only what had been left out of the *Samguk sagi* account. But that couldn't be the whole story. Iryŏn must have chosen this specific anecdote not so much for its wondrousness as for its effectiveness in illustrating both halves of an important theme enunciated in the *Samguk yusa:* not only was Shilla protected by the gods, but Koguryŏ, on the contrary—as was Paekche under King Ŭija—was doomed to destruction by the moral failure of its king and queen. The rescue of Kim Yu-shin through the intercession of Shilla's three local guardian spirits illustrates the first half of this theme. On the other hand, the part of the account that deals with the Koguryŏ shaman Ch'unam, who is put to death for revealing unnatural sexual behavior between the Koguryŏ king and queen, seems to illustrate the other half of the theme, that is, the inevitability of Koguryŏ's fall because of the moral degeneration of its leaders. According to the *Samguk yusa,* just before Ch'unam was put to death he swore he would be reborn as a Shilla general in order to destroy Koguryŏ. And in a dream that very night the Koguryŏ king saw the unjustly executed shaman enter the body of Kim Yu-shin's mother.[8]

Both the *Samguk sagi* and the *Samguk yusa* include lives, legends, and stories that defy categorization as either history or literature. Some seem more literature than history. But however we regard them they are significant because they deal in one way or another with life's central questions, such as the nature of justice, love, loyalty, responsibility, true wisdom, and so on. If there is one essential difference, however, between the lives, legends, and stories of the *Samguk sagi* and those of the *Samguk yusa,* it is in the degree of moral and religious bias. The accounts in the *Samguk yusa* have clear-cut moral and religious—that is, Buddhist—themes. On the other hand, the *Samguk sagi* accounts are clearly not religious, and while many of them have a didactic ring, it is not always clear what their message is. This may be in part because the *Samguk sagi* must keep faith not only with the moral vision of its compilers but also with their sense of fidelity to historical truth. As one scholar has put it, we enter a world of myths and legends in the *Samguk yusa,* but in the *Samguk sagi* we enter a world of history.[9]

Although most of the lives, legends, and stories in the *Samguk sagi* are found in the *yŏlchŏn* section, a few of them appear in the annals section. Although they are supposedly historical accounts, some seem woven as much out of imagination as out of historical facts. The best known of these accounts is perhaps the tragic story of Princess Nangnang (in Chinese, Princess Lo-lang) of the Nangnang colony and Prince Hodong of Koguryŏ. The brief passage in the annals section reads as follows:

In April when Prince Hodong was traveling in the Okcho area, Ch'oe I, governor of Nangnang Colony, saw him while on one of his outings.

"Judging by your face, you're not an ordinary person. Are you by any chance the son of King Shin of the Northern Kingdom?"

And the governor took him home and gave him his daughter in marriage.

Some time afterwards Hodong returned to his own country and through a secret messenger sent word to Governor Ch'oe's daughter: "Unless you enter the armory of your country and destroy the drum and horn [musical instruments of the military], I will not receive you as my wife."

This was because the mysterious drum-and-horn set in Nangnang Colony sounded by itself at the approach of enemy soldiers. The governor's daughter, entering the armory with a sharpened knife, destroyed both the drum and horn, and sent word to Hodong. Hodong advised the king to launch a sudden attack on Nangnang Colony. Ch'oe I, the governor, was caught completely by surprise because the drum and horn had not sounded. Only when the Koguryŏ forces suddenly appeared at the foot of the fortress did he realize the drum and horn had been destroyed. So, after putting his daughter to death, he came out and surrendered.

In November Prince Hodong committed suicide. Hodong was the king's secondary consort, that is, born of the granddaughter of King Kalsa. Hodong was handsome and much loved by the king. That was why he was called Hodong [literally, "handsome lad"]. The queen, fearing the king might make Hodong his heir instead of her own son, falsely accused Hodong: "Hodong does not treat me with courtesy, and I fear he probably intends to violate me."

The king replied, "Isn't it that you hate him because he is born of my other wife?"

The queen, fearing calamitous consequences since the king did not believe her words, said to him weeping, "I request that your highness observe us in secrecy, and if my words should prove baseless, I'll gladly accept punishment." At this the king could not help but suspect Hodong, and he planned to punish him.

A certain person asked Hodong why he did not vindicate himself. The prince replied, "If I should vindicate myself, it would then expose the queen's evil, thus adding to the king's many cares. How could that be consistent with a son's filial duty!" And soon afterwards he killed himself by falling on his own sword.[10]

What is the meaning of this story, which seems based as much on poetic imagination as on historical facts? For example, according to Yi Pyŏng-do, respected historian and a translator of the *Samguk sagi,* Ch'oe I does not appear in any of the Chinese historical records.[11] What, moreover, do we make of the drum and bugle that supposedly had the magical power of forewarning the approach of an enemy? Do they represent supernatural powers provided by the guardian spirits of Nangnang Colony? And why do they have to be destroyed by none other than the governor's virgin daughter, who falls in love with a handsome prince from a neighboring but hostile nation? The story seems richly suggestive but its message is not entirely clear.

Obviously, Prince Hodong is clever but also brutally manipulative. Born of a secondary consort—like Edmund in *King Lear*—he has to be more clever and scheming in order to have a chance at the succession. At first he is successful but in the end he is outsmarted by the queen. What is puzzling is that he should resign himself meekly to the queen's stratagem; it seems out of character for one who had so cruelly exploited Princess Nangnang's love-born weakness. Wouldn't such a man have fought back and tried to outmaneuver the queen? For Hodong is a person who would have had to be driven to suicide by superior force, and not by a sense of filial obligation to his father, and especially not in deference to a queen who is not his mother.

Doesn't the story seem to raise moral questions that transcend political and military success or failure, questions that go to the heart of human relationships? Prince Hodong succeeds by taking advantage of Princess Nangnang's love for him to advance his prospects for succession to the Koguryŏ throne and make up for being the son of a secondary consort. Princess Nangnang, on the contrary, had failed utterly in her love and duty to her father as well as her nation. A foolish woman, she falls easy prey to Prince Hodong's cold manipulation and loses everything for nothing. Interestingly, the *Samguk sagi* account balances the tragic story of Princess Nangnang with the tragedy that overtakes Prince Hodong. In the first half of the account Hodong, victorious in love and war, appears to gain the upper hand in the succession struggle. But it is precisely his successes that seem to sow the seeds of his own destruction, for they mobilize his rivals to bring him down. It is this juxtaposition of his initial success with his subsequent fall that seems to bring into focus the question about the meaning of this story. On the surface the story appears to be part of the chronology of events during the reign of King Taemushin of Koguryŏ (A.D. 18–44), a story of how the Koguryŏ forces vanquished Nangnang Colony and how in jockeying for power Prince Hodong was undermined by his own successes.

Although the *Samguk sagi* account does not explicitly connect Princess Nangnang's tragedy to Prince Hodong's, the connection seems to be suggested in the series of events that lead to his suicide. True, there is no suggestion in the account that the queen is anything like a moral agent of Heaven—the "scourge of God"—avenging the wrongs done to Princess Nangnang by Prince Hodong. But most of us as we read this story are moved to feel, as Cho Tong-il has suggested, that "while Hodong's death is sad and regretful in one sense, by the same token it is appropriate in another sense. Princess Nangnang must bear responsibility for her own tragedy, and the same is true of Hodong and his tragedy. While we pity Princess Nangnang's error, Hodong's deserves our condemnation."[12]

As I have mentioned, however, the *Samguk sagi* account does not make a clear moral connection between the two tragedies. One could very well argue that the story is simply a factual account of the triumph of the clever, strong, and unscrupulous over the naive and weak. The queen sacrifices Hodong for her own ends just as Hodong sacrificed Princess Nangnang for his. There seems to be neither a triumph of good over evil nor a clear moral theme, but only a sort of grim historical reality where events are played out to their inexorable end. Although Kim Pu-shik is unhappy enough with the behavior of the Koguryŏ king and Prince Hodong to append his own criticism to the historical account, the narrative itself seems to acknowledge the helplessness of men and women caught in the amoral procession of history. Perhaps it is this helplessness that invests the account of Princess Nangnang and Prince Hodong with a sense of the tragedy of life.

The *yŏlchŏn* section of the *Samguk sagi* gives an even stronger sense of this inexorableness of human history. For example, even in the life of the splendidly triumphant Kim Yu-shin we find a strangely disturbing episode about his second son, Wŏn-sul. Toward the end of Kim Yu-shin's glorious career Wŏn-sul is involved in a losing battle against the T'ang forces and returns home alive but in dishonor. The account makes it clear that it was through no fault of his own that Wŏn-sul had failed to die in defeat: he had been prevented from doing so by his attendant so that he might vindicate himself on another day. Nevertheless, Kim Yu-shin advises the king that Wŏn-sul should be beheaded since he has disgraced not only the nation but also his own family. Understandably, the king pardons him instead. But Wŏn-sul's own parents are unable to forgive him and they disown him irrevocably. Even after his father's death Wŏn-sul's mother refuses to see him. Vindication finally comes years later when Wŏn-sul distinguishes himself in another battle, but still his mother refuses to see him. Because of the shame he has brought on his parents, Wŏn-sul withdraws permanently from public life.

Though this episode seems oddly out of place in the biography of the heroic Kim Yu-shin, it is understandable in a way. For Kim Yu-shin is presented throughout his long life as an utterly selfless patriot and public servant: his public life does not exist except in the service of the national good. Besides, the code of the warrior stipulated that one should never retreat in battle, and Wŏn-sul, son of the nation's most celebrated warrior-statesman, would have understood this as well as anyone in Shilla. Thus, it is perfectly understandable that Kim Yu-shin should have disowned him.

At the same time, what comes through so poignantly in this episode is the private side of the family story: an instance of failure amidst heroic accomplishments, an instance of tragedy amidst the unmatched triumphs of Kim Yu-shin and his family, an instance that casts a shadow over Wŏn-sul and also Kim Yu-shin and his wife. Did Kim's unmatched fame and honor make it impossible for him and his wife to display their personal and human side as parents? Was that the price of great public achievements? Or is the *Samguk sagi* simply being true to history in this case? Whatever the message, the Wŏn-sul episode seems to point to the inevitability of tragedy even in the midst of great triumphs. As defeat is the other side of victory, so is tragedy the flip side of success. Such seems to be the grim but historical realism of the *Samguk sagi,* which is one of the significant differences between it and the *Samguk yusa.*

One more example from the *yŏlchŏn* should suffice to make the point. In a brief section on the life of Chukjuk, we encounter another episode that seems to reveal a darker side to the official account. Chukjuk is a low-ranking staff officer posted to Taeyasŏng (present-day Hapch'ŏn, Kyŏngsang Province), a major Shilla fortress. There he serves under Kim P'um-sŏk, commandant of the fortress and son-in-law of Kim Ch'un-ch'u (who later becomes King Muyŏl, the twenty-ninth king of Shilla). P'um-sŏk is thus a wellborn and well-connected member of the Shilla aristocracy. In 642 when the fortress is under siege by the Paekche general Yunch'ung, P'um-sŏk decides to surrender without a fight despite a strong protest by Chukjuk. When the gate is opened and the Shilla soldiers go out to surrender, they are ambushed and massacred. Informed of what has occurred, P'um-sok puts his wife and children to death, then kills himself. Chukjuk, gathering what is left of the Shilla defenders, decides to fight to the death. Told by one of his comrades that it would be better to save themselves for another day, he replies: "I admit the justice of your words. But my father named me Chukjuk [the name consists of a doubling of the Chinese character signifying bamboo] in order to make me unbending even in the depth of cold winter as well as unyielding even when badly bent. How could I, fearing death, surrender in order to live?"[13] Chukjuk and the others all perish fighting to the end.

If we assume that this episode is mainly about Chukjuk—it is after all named after him—its theme seems to be the patriotism and valor of Chukjuk, who is posthumously promoted and whose wife and children are handsomely rewarded by the grateful king. It is this low-ranking official of exemplary courage and devotion who is glorified, rather than the wellborn and well-connected commandant. A splendid story, indeed. But is that what this episode is really about? Closer examination of a few details indicates that the focus is actually on P'um-sŏk rather than Chukjuk. For one thing, the death of P'um-sŏk and his wife, daughter of the future king of Shilla, seems to have been a notable event. It is mentioned three more times in the *Samguk sagi*—twice in the lengthy biography of Kim Yu-shin and once in the annals section on King Muyŏl in connection with Pŏmmin, the crown prince; in all three instances it is treated as an event of great importance.

In the first instance we are told that Kim Ch'un-ch'u, the future king, heartsick at the death of his daughter, undertakes a dangerous mission to Koguryŏ to seek that kingdom's help against Paekche. In the second, we learn that after a great victory against Paekche, Kim Yu-shin exchanges eight captured Paekche generals for the bones of P'um-sŏk and his wife. And in the third instance we are told that when Paekche is defeated by the combined forces of T'ang and Shilla, Crown Prince Pŏmmin spits on the prostrate Paekche crown prince, cursing him for the Paekche king's responsibility for the death of Pŏmmin's own sister (P'um-sŏk's wife) some twenty years earlier. It is clear from these references that the death of P'um-sŏk and his wife at Taeyasŏng was a bitter and painful memory for the Shilla court, and especially King Muyŏl, the crown prince, and Kim Yu-shin.

Now let us return to the Chukjuk section of the *yŏlchŏn* and examine the few key details concerning P'um-sŏk, his character, and his behavior as commandant of the fortress. We are told of an important incident that occurred before the Paekche forces attacked the fortress in 642:

P'um-sŏk, noticing the beauty of the wife of one Kŭm-il, a low-ranking official at the fortress, had taken her away [from her husband]. Kŭm-il, bitter and angry, collaborated with the enemy and torched the storehouse at the time [of the Paekche attack], putting the fortress into confusion and thus making it extremely difficult to defend it securely.[14]

The *Samguk sagi* is silent on any effort P'um-sŏk might have made to rally the defenders against the attack. It merely says that P'um-sŏk, following the advice of a gullible subordinate, decided to surrender to the Paekche forces.

Don't these details seem to reveal not only that P'um-sŏk was incompetent and cowardly, and therefore totally unfit for the high post entrusted to him, but, more seriously, that he was immoral and unjust to his subordinates? It was P'um-sŏk's immorality coupled with his incompetence and cowardice that brought about the fall of the Shilla fortress. How was it that a person of such failings was placed in a post of critical importance? The *yŏlchŏn* is silent on this.

Reexamining the story in this light suggests that the real focus of this *yŏlchŏn* section is P'um-sŏk's failings rather than Chukjuk's valor and patriotism. Doesn't the failure of a well-born and well-connected Shilla aristocrat loom much larger than the exemplary conduct of Chukjuk, the purported theme of this episode? In other words, isn't the real theme of this episode the moral weakness and institutional wrongdoing at the top of Shilla society, failings that undermined the loyalty of a low-ranking official? Thus there seems to be a gap between the purported and the real themes of the Chukjuk episode. The heartening story of patriotism and valor is overshadowed by a darker story of abuse of power and betrayal, a story that reveals a more complex and perhaps more human underside of history. As Cho Tong-il has pointed out, there appears to be two sides to some of the lives in the *yŏlchŏn*, the outer, public side and an inner private side.[15]

The Chukjuk episode would thus seem to be another illustration of the grim, complex realism of the *Samguk sagi,* whose stories are invested with a sense of the tragedy of life. And for a history supposedly modeled on Sima Qian's great *Shi ji* (Book of Historical Records), this is not surprising at all, since the *Shi ji* is suffused from the very beginning of its biographical section with a profound sense of the inscrutability of the ways of Heaven. I find this aspect of the *Samguk sagi*—this sense of the tragedy of life— especially significant, because it is largely absent in the legends and stories of the *Samguk yusa*.

Kim Pu-shik and Iryŏn, compilers, respectively, of the *Samguk sagi* and *Samguk yusa,* lived in times of stark contrast in terms of Korea's relations with its neighbors. Kim lived during the first half of the Koryŏ dynasty, Iryŏn during the waning years of the dynasty. More important, whereas Kim lived during a time when Korea was independent of its northern neighbors, Iryŏn lived most of his adult life during the years of the Mongol domination. For over half a century, from the year 1231, when he was twenty-five, Iryŏn witnessed the unspeakable depredations of the Mongol forces in Korea. In the year 1253 alone an untold number of Koreans were killed by the invading Mongol army and an estimated 206,800 more were taken away as prisoners. According to a contemporary account, "the fields were covered with the bones of the dead; the dead were so many that they could not be counted"; wherever the Mongol army had passed, "the inhabitants were all burned out, so that not even dogs and chickens remained."[16] Even after Korea formally capitulated, not only were commodities such as horses, clothing, skins, gold, silver, and precious stones plundered, but hundreds of young men and women had to be sent off to the Mongol court as tribute. During the years 1274 and 1279, 1,200 warships had to be built and equipped by Koreans for the unsuccessful Mongol expeditions against Japan.[17] And not only were Koryŏ's crown princes obligated to marry Mongol princesses, they had to wear their hair in the Mongol style. Koreans were even forbidden to wear their customary white clothes.[18]

No wonder Iryŏn devoted himself to preserving the cultural and spiritual heritage of his native land. Having witnessed his people enduring extreme humiliation and suffering, Iryŏn became deeply

devoted not only to Buddhism but also to a kind of Korean nationalism. This dual devotion is perhaps most clearly revealed in
his efforts to preserve in the *Samguk yusa* all the tales and legends that seemed to him culturally and historically indigenous to
Korea as well as those that seemed to represent the best of Buddhist teaching.

It is in this light that we must see Iryŏn's inclusion of the
hyangga in the *Samguk yusa*—the oldest surviving indigenous
poetry—which the other chroniclers had ignored. In incorporating hyangga recorded in hyangch'al, he went as far as he could at
the time to preserve what was Korean in the closest thing to a
Korean writing system. Nor did he hesitate to write hanmun that
seemed more Korean in syntax and diction than classical Chinese, in an attempt to lessen the gap between the spoken and
written languages in Korea.

Perhaps the clearest example of Iryŏn's nationalism is his inclusion in the *Samguk yusa* of not only the Tangun myth but also
the foundation myths of the Three Kingdoms, the various legends
and tales related to Shilla's unification of the Three Kingdoms,
and the legends concerning remarkable place names, temples,
monks, and cults. As a result, much of what had existed until
Iryŏn's time as part of the oral tradition was written down for the
first time. Therefore, despite its Buddhist slant, the *Samguk yusa*
is the main repository of the oldest surviving Korean myths, legends, fables, tales, and poetry.

The most significant of the foundation myths is, of course, the
Tangun myth, perhaps the oldest of the various foundation myths
about the establishment of prehistoric Korea (Ko Chosŏn). The
essentials of the myth are as follows: Hwanung, a son of Hwanin,
with the blessings of his heavenly father and accompanied by
three thousand followers, descends to T'aebaek Mountain to rule
over the people. There in a cave he meets a tiger and a bear, both
of whom desire to become human. They are told by Hwanung
that if they subsist on mugwort and garlic and avoid the sunlight
for one hundred days they will be transformed into human be-
ings. The tiger fails in this ordeal but the bear is successful. After

twenty-one days she becomes a woman. Subsequently she is married to Hwanung and out of their union is born Tangun Wanggŏm, the mythic founder of the prehistoric Korean state.[19]

What does this myth mean? It is generally agreed that Hwanung, who descends from heaven with his followers, likely represents the leader of a group of recent arrivals on the Korean peninsula, probably a northern people whose superiority in warfare and technology allowed them to impose their rule on the native people. The bear was presumably the totem of the native people and might also represent the earth goddess of the place they occupied. The timeless pattern of human history played out between the immigrant and native peoples—encounter and struggle ending in some sort of mutual accommodation—is mirrored in most foundation myths. Since Koreans are part of the large group of East Asian peoples whose totem is the bear, it is not difficult to understand why it is the bear rather than the tiger that passes the ordeal and is transformed into a woman. The marriage between Hwanung and the bear-woman thus represents accommodation between the new arrivals and the native people: a union between the native earth goddess and the patron god of the immigrant people. As the scion of Hwanung and the bear-woman, Tangun Wanggŏm, the mythic founder of prehistoric Korea, is properly invested with legitimacy as ruler, since he represents both the new arrivals and the native people. The myth also seems to suggest that a period of hard struggle—represented by the bear-woman's twenty-one days of ordeal in the sunless cave—was necessary before the native people could amalgamate with the new arrivals.[20]

Among the foundation myths the next in significance and age is probably that of Koguryŏ.[21] In this myth Haemosu, like Hwanung, is a son of God who descends to earth. After besting the River God in a hard-fought test of magic, he marries the River God's daughter, Yuhwa. But unlike Hwanung of the Tangun myth, Haemosu returns to heaven alone, leaving his wife to suffer many ordeals on earth. Yuhwa gives birth to an egg out of which is born Chumong, who after many harrowing adventures and hardships founds the state of Koguryŏ. What is especially intriguing about this foundation myth is that the hero is born of an egg,[22] that the egg is abandoned for a period, and that the hero should undergo a long struggle before he succeeds in founding the new state. Some or all of these details are repeated with slight variations in the foundation myths of the neighboring states of northern China as well as the other Korean states.[23]

The foundation myth of Shilla, especially the part dealing with the birth of its founder, Pak Hyŏkkŏse, seems to differ significantly from both the Tangun and Koguryŏ myths. The central passage of the Shilla myth as it appears in the *Samguk yusa* is as follows:

> When they [the six chiefs of Chinhan, which became Shilla] climbed to a height and looked southward they saw an eerie lightning-like emanation by the Na Well under Mount Yang, while nearby a white horse kneeled and bowed. When they reached the spot they found a red egg; the horse neighed and flew up to heaven when it saw men approaching. When the people cracked the egg open, they discovered within a beautiful infant boy with a radiant visage. Amazed by their discovery, they bathed the infant in the East Spring, then he emitted light. Birds and beasts danced for joy, heaven and earth shook, and the sun and moon became bright. They named the child King Hyŏkkŏse, or Bright, and titled him *kŏsŭrhan*, or king.[24]

According to Cho Tong-il, the white horse kneeling and neighing probably indicates that Pak Hyŏkkŏse, the Shilla founder, arrived with a horse-mounted people who had ridden into the Korean peninsula boasting of their descent from heaven and placed themselves above the native people, as had earlier immigrant groups from the north. Two additional features seem to set this Shilla myth apart from the other two we have discussed. First, Pak Hyŏkkŏse undergoes hardly any ordeal in establishing himself as the founder of a new state. Even more intriguing is the second feature, the absence of a father figure like Hwanung in the Tangun myth or Haemosu in the Chumong myth. Professor Cho, noting this curious absence, mentions an earth goddess called the

Goddess of Fairy Peach Mountain (*Sŏntosan sŏngmo*), who is supposed to have given birth to both Pak Hyŏkkŏse and his queen, Aryŏng.[25] In any event, it may be that the absence of the father figure is related to the fact that Shilla alone of the three kingdoms had three reigning queens.

Perhaps what distinguishes the *Samguk yusa* from the *Samguk sagi* even more than these myths, making it so absorbing as literature, are the wonderfully human stories embedded in its Buddhist tales and legends. Iryŏn presents several kinds of legends and tales to illustrate his themes. To this end the most central are those in which Iryŏn seems to challenge aristocratic Buddhism, the mainstream Buddhism of Shilla and Koryŏ, which achieved the status of a state religion by focusing on the divine protection of the state and its ruling classes. Iryŏn, on the contrary, following the lead of Great Master Wŏnhyo, focuses on the everyday lives of the common people. He understood that we cannot seek the sacred and true apart from everyday things and people. Therefore, contradictory as it might seem, only by living in this world with the things of this world can we transcend everyday life and achieve enlightenment and salvation. His is thus the Buddhism of the people much more than that of the state and its leaders.

Thus in these legends and tales we encounter the embodiment of the Buddha or a boddhisatva more often than not among the most despised or lowly persons, the meanest of beggars, servants, or the most ordinary-looking country people or children. The bodhisattva one has been looking for turns out to be none other than a peasant woman washing her blood-soaked undergarments or a child monk with a torn earlobe.[26] These stories shock us out of our complacency and help us achieve a way of seeing things that is contrary to the traditional, more widely accepted views of the world. For instance, there is the story of Ungmyŏn, a bond-servant who persists in attending a temple service despite all the obstacles placed in her way by her mistress. At the end of the story we see her literally airborne, flying away toward the Buddha land.[27]

Iryŏn tells some of his most suggestive stories through the life

and teachings of Great Master Wŏnhyo. One such story involves
an encounter between Wŏnhyo and Hyekong, a great but eccentric monk. When Hyekong was at Hangsa Monastery, we are
told, Wŏnhyo would visit him to discuss doctrinal matters or
simply to have some fun together. One day the two go fishing in
a stream and after eating their catch they defecate on a rock.
Pointing to the excrement, Hyekong tells Wŏnhyo, "Your fish is
my shit."[28] What do we make of this peculiar episode? Interestingly enough, the story reminds me of the graveyard scene near
the end of Shakespeare's *Hamlet,* when Hamlet comes to realize
that even the greatest heroes of antiquity, such as Caesar and Alex-
ander, are finally no more than a handful of earth that goes to plug
up "a bunghole." For like every other creature on earth they too
must turn to dust, out of which grow plants that in turn make animal
and human life possible. This interconnectedness of all things is of
course what Hamlet is referring to when he tells Claudius the king,
"A man may fish with the worm that hath eat of a king, and eat of
the fish that hath fed of that worm" (*Hamlet,* 4.3.27–28).

Similarly, according to the Buddhist doctrine everything is
connected to everything else in the eternal cycle of nature, of
which each one of us is a part both in life and in death. Isn't this
the meaning of Hyekong's "Your fish is my shit"? There is no
difference between "your fish" and "my shit," for, understood
correctly, each is no more than the shape it momentarily assumes
in the eternal cycle of nature. To understand this is to understand
the truth essential to salvation.

Perhaps the most memorable of the Buddhist tales and legends
in the *Samguk yusa* are those that provide vivid glimpses of the
lives of ordinary people of earlier times, lives exposed to all the
vicissitudes of worldly existence. Let's look at four of these mar-
velously human stories. The first two are especially remarkable
because of their implied criticism of certain aspects of institutional Buddhism.

The incident in the first tale, we are told, occurred during the
reign of King Shinmun of Shilla (681–692):

One day Great Master Kyŏnghŭng, on horseback and attended by many followers, was about to enter the royal palace. Since the company looked quite resplendent in their clothing and equipage, the passersby in front of the East Gate yielded the right of way to them. A Buddhist monk with a cane, clad in rags and carrying a basket on his back, however, was found resting where the Master was to alight from his horse. The followers of the Master, finding the monk was carrying dried fish in the basket, scolded him loudly: "You who wear a monk's clothes, how dare you carry what is forbidden by our religion?"

The monk replied, "Isn't it better to carry dried fish from the market than carry a piece of living meat between your legs?" So saying he stood up and left. . . .

Master Kyŏnghŭng, told of this incident, took it to be a warning from the Buddha against horseback riding, and he never rode a horse again.[29]

The second tale, almost modern in tone, also warns of the *rigor mortis* to which prosperous institutions, even religious institutions, were susceptible. That this story of Indian origin was included in the *Samguk yusa* shows how appropriate it must have seemed to the Korean situation.

Thus recorded in the fourth book of Chiron [a Buddhist sutra]: Long ago a learned priest traveling among the monasteries arrived at Ilwang Temple, where a great assembly was taking place. But because the priest was dressed in rags, the gatekeeper shut the gate and refused to allow him into the temple. The priest tried several times to gain admittance, but he was prevented each time because of his tattered clothes. So he hit upon the scheme of dressing in nice-looking clothes, and this time the gatekeeper did not bar him from entering. Seated at a table and served many tasty foods and drinks, he offered them first to his clothes. People observing him asked why he did so. He replied, "Even though I tried to enter several times, each time I was barred. Only when I put on these clothes was I able to enter and be seated at this table and receive all this food and drink. So isn't it right that I offer the food and drink to the clothes?"[30]

The third tale is perhaps the most touching and human:

> It was during the reign of the fortieth king, Aejang [Shilla, 800–809], when the monk Chŏngsu was at Hwangnyong Temple. Late one winter evening when the snow lay deep everywhere, Chŏngsu was returning from Samnang Monastery and passed by the gate of Ch'ŏnŭm Monastery. There in front of the gate he saw a beggar woman lying nearly frozen to death with an infant she had just given birth to. Taking pity on the woman, he enfolded her in his arms, and she revived shortly afterward.
>
> Then he stripped off all his clothes, covered the woman and infant with them, and returned to his monastery totally naked. He spent the rest of the night covering himself with rice straw. In the middle of the night a voice from Heaven was heard within the king's palace. It said the monk Chŏngsu of Hwangnyong Temple should rightly be appointed royal mentor. Quickly people were sent out to look into the matter, and the king was informed of all the facts. With appropriate honor and ceremony the king received Chŏngsu into the palace and appointed him to the post of Great Mentor of the Nation.[31]

The last tale, popularly known as "Choshin's Dream," is perhaps the most literary of the Buddhist stories. Framed as an account of a dream, the story is supposed to convey the Buddhist theme that the joys of this world are vain illusions of a flickering moment, a mere fleeting dream, and thus not worth pursuing. But its details are so vividly conceived and realized that the story seems to convey to the reader an affirmation rather than a negation of life. Certainly, Choshin's is a strenuous, even a tragic life, but we come away from his story with a vivid sense of having lived a life rather than experiencing illusoriness or emptiness. A strenuous or tragic life is not necessarily a worthless life. "Choshin's Dream," therefore, is a distillation of human life, a rich mixture of varied experiences whose meaning cannot be reduced to a simple religious or philosophical creed. Herein perhaps lies the enduring appeal of the story.

During the days of Shilla, a monk named Choshin was sent out from his home monastery at Sedal Temple in Kyŏngju [the Shilla capital] to manage an estate in the countryside. There he fell hopelessly in love with the daughter of the provincial magistrate. For years he went in secrecy before the image of the bodhisattva Kwanŭm to prostrate himself and beg for assistance in his love for the magistrate's daughter. But it all turned out to be in vain. Within a few years the magistrate's daughter was married off to another man.

Again Choshin went before the image of the bodhisattva Kwanŭm, this time to complain bitterly and sorrowfully of his unrequited love. He was still crying as the sun set, and, exhausted by his sorrow and longing, he dozed off for a brief moment. Suddenly in his dream he saw the magistrate's daughter walk in through the door. Smiling at him lovingly she said, "I've loved you secretly ever since I first saw your face, and never for a moment have I forgotten you. But I couldn't oppose the wishes of my parents and I allowed them to marry me off to another man. But now I've come to spend my life with you."

Choshin was beside himself with happiness. They returned home and lived together for forty years, producing five children between them. But eventually they were overcome by poverty. Lacking a place to sleep or even enough food to keep themselves alive, they drifted from place to place, barely surviving by begging. After they had lived this way for ten years their clothes were so torn and ragged they scarcely covered their nakedness. When their eldest son, fifteen years old, perished suddenly from starvation as they were crossing Haehyŏn Pass in Myŏngju, they buried him by the roadside. With their remaining four children they drifted on till they came to a small roadside straw hut in Ugok County. By this time Choshin and his wife were too old, sick, and exhausted to go out begging, so they survived on the alms brought by their ten-year-old daughter.

One day, the daughter came home weeping in great distress and lay down in tears beside them. She had been bitten by a village dog on her begging rounds. Choshin and his wife wept in grief, bitterly lamenting their lot. Then his wife sat up straight, wiped away her tears, and said to Choshin, "When I first met you we were young and handsome and had plenty of nice clean clothes. Our love for each other was such that it was enough to have one bowl of rice and one piece of cloth to share between us. Thus we lived in happiness for fifty years. But now that we are old and sick, we suffer more and more from cold and hunger; more and more we find that doors are shut to us; and our shame weighs down upon us like a mountain. There seems to be no way for our children to escape the cold and starvation. How could there be any joy or love between husband and wife in such extremity! Handsome looks and soft smiles are but a drop of dew on a blade of grass; promises of lifelong friendship and love are but cherry blossoms before a gale! You suffer more because of me just as I'm more worried because of you. As I look back carefully on our happiness of long ago, I see that it was the cause of our grief and distress today. However we may have come to this predicament, isn't it better for a solitary phoenix to gaze into the mirror calling for its mate than for the whole flock to perish together! To separate in adversity only to come together again in prosperity is not the human thing to do. But I ask that we part now, since to be separated or to be reunited is all part of our fate."

Choshin was very pleased with her words. As they were about to part, each with two of their children, she said to Choshin, "Since I'll be going toward my home village, will you please go south?"

Just as he and his wife were about to go their separate ways, Choshin awoke from his dream. In the flickering lamplight he could see that night had fallen. In the morning Choshin found that his hair and beard had turned white and that the affairs of the world had become meaningless to him. He had no wish to go on living in this world of suffering; all his worldly desires had melted away like ice. He went and dug in the spot where he had buried his son [in his dream], and found a stone Maitreya [the Buddha of the Future]. He washed it in water and placed it in a nearby temple. Thereafter he relinquished his position, donated all his possessions to the construction of a monastery, and devoted the rest of his life to doing good deeds. Nothing is known about what happened to him after that or where he lived out his life.[32]

There is, of course, much more to the *Samguk sagi* and *Samguk yusa* than what I have offered here. And in addition to these two great books of early Korean history and literature, many other volumes of hanmun prose survive from the Koryŏ period. These were composed by such distinguished Koryŏ scholar-statesmen of the twelfth and thirteenth centuries as Yi Kyu-bo (1168–1241), Yi Il–lo (1152–1220), Ch'ae Cha (1188–1260), and Yi Che-hyŏn. Especially noteworthy are the "personified" stories (*i-inch'e* or *kajŏnch'e sosŏl*), generally didactic, satirical tales in which inanimate objects such as liquor, paper, and coins are given human attributes and become the main characters. The setting for all of these stories is ancient China. All the characters are Chinese and much of the material is drawn from the early Chinese chronicles.

Notes

1. Cho Tong-il, *Hanguk munhak t'ongsa* (A Comprehensive History of Korean Literature), 2nd ed. (Seoul: Chishik sanŏp sa, 1989), I:373.
2. There were eleven compilers altogether, with Kim Pu-shik in charge of the entire project. See Shin Hyŏng-shik, *Samguk sagi yŏngu* (A Study of the *Samguk sagi*) (Seoul: Ilchogak, 1981), 356.
3. Cho Tong-il, *Hanguk munhak t'ongsa,* II:92.
4. Ibid., 94.
5. Iryŏn, *Samguk yusa,* ed. and tr., Yi Pyŏng-do, rev. ed. (Seoul: Kwangjo ch'ulp'ansa, 1979), 179.
6. Ibid., 180. Additionally, in referring to the death of the kings of the Three Kingdoms Iryŏn uses the same Chinese character used for the death of the Chinese emperors. See *Samguk yusa yŏngu nonsŏnjip* (Selected Essays on the *Samguk yusa*) (Seoul: Paeksan charyowŏn, 1986), I:503–4.
7. Kim Pu-shik, *Samguk sagi* (*History of the Three Kingdoms*), ed. and tr., Yi Pyŏng-do (Seoul: Ŭryu munhwa sa, 1977), 619.
8. See Yi Ki-baek's essay in *Samguk yusa yŏngu nonsŏnjip* (Selected Essays on the *Samguk yusa*), I:121–37, esp. 125–26.
9. Shim Ch'ang-sŏp, "Samguk sagi yŏlchŏn ŭi munhakchŏk koch'al" (A Literary Examination of the *Yŏlchŏn* Section of the *Samguk sagi*), *Munhak kwa chisŏng* (Literature and Intellect), 10, no. 1 (Spring 1979): 191.
10. Kim Pu-shik, *Samguk sagi,* 233–34.
11. Ibid., 233.
12. Cho Tong-il, *Samguk shidae sŏlhwa ŭi ttŭtp'uri* (Explications of Stories of the Three Kingdoms Period) (Seoul: Chimmundang, 1990), 206.
13. Kim Pu-shik, *Samguk sagi,* 696.
14. Ibid..
15. Cho Tong-il, *Hanguk munhak t'ongsa,* I:375.
16. *Samguk yusa yŏngu nonsŏnjip,* I:167.
17. Ibid., 168.

18. Ibid., 168–69.

19. The Chinese characters for the name Tangun mean either "sandalwood king" or "altar king," depending on which of two characters is used for *tan*. The name, however, may not be Chinese at all but rather a transliteration of an Altaic word meaning "shaman-king." See Richard Rutt, *A Biography of James Scarth Gale and a New Edition of His History of the Korean People* (Seoul: Royal Asiatic Society, Korea Branch, 1972), 323, n. 1.

Hwanung is supposed to have been given three treasures by his heavenly father when he descended to earth. It is thought that these were probably such things as the mirror, bell, and sword that shaman-kings used in seasonal rites to propitiate the various gods of nature and insure an abundant harvest and the safety of the people. Hwanung was also accompanied by three masters of rain, wind, and clouds. This probably refers to the agricultural superiority of recent immigrants to Ko Chosŏn, since rain, wind, and clouds have a special importance for agriculture.

20. For a succinct discussion of the Tangun myth, see Cho Tong-il, *Hanguk munhak t'ongsa,* 1:67–71.

21. Detailed in Yi Kyu-bo's poem "Tongmyŏng wang p'yŏn" (The Lay of King Tongmyŏng), which its author says is based on the lost *Ku Samguk sa.*

22. Rutt, *Biography of James Scarth Gale,* 329, n. 7. According to Rutt, the birth of a hero from an egg may indicate "miraculous birth, or hint at a bird totem . . . or be a folk memory of choosing leaders by casting votes (or lots) in a receptacle."

23. See Cho Tong-il, *Hanguk munhak t'ongsa,* 1:67–69, and 72–85.

24. Trans. Peter H. Lee, in *Anthology of Korean Literature: From Early Times to the Nneteenth Century,* rev. ed. comp. and ed. Peter H. Lee (Honolulu: University of Hawaii Press, 1990), 5.

25. Cho Tong-il, *Hanguk munhak t'ongsa,* 1:80.

26. Cho Tong-il, *Samguk shidae sŏlhwa ŭi ttŭtp'uri,* 240–43.

27. Iryŏn, *Samguk yusa,* 432–33.

28. Ibid. 395. Also see Cho Tong-il, *Samguk shidae sŏlhwa ŭi ttŭtp'uri,* 246–51.

29. Iryŏn, *Samguk yusa,* 437.

30. Ibid., 438–39.

31. Ibid., 447–48.

32. Ibid., 356–58.

5

Notes on Shijo

The shijo is the most popular and most Korean of all traditional Korean poetic forms. It flourishes today as it has for nearly six hundred years, not only in Korea but wherever there is a Korean community. Throughout its long history it has been the poetic form best loved and most accessible to amateurs, and it has so remained. Today, when literacy in hangŭl is nearly universal in Korea, it is the one classical poetic form accessible to everyone, reader or writer. Thus its popularity and central importance. Although we don't know exactly when shijo originated, we know it was sometime during the latter part of the Koryŏ dynasty (918–1392). The earliest shijo date from the late fourteenth century.

A new poetic form is not born out of a vacuum; it develops from a real need. What real need of *yangban* men—for the early shijo were composed almost exclusively by these men of the gentry—did shijo fill? For one thing, hyangga, which had served as lyric poetry for aristocratic men from the time of Shilla to early Koryŏ, had gone out of use by mid-Koryŏ times. This meant that the new wave of scholar-officials who had come into their own after the seizure of power by the military in the last decades of the twelfth century had no vernacular lyric form in which they could properly express their thoughts and feelings. There was, of course, hanshi—poetry written in hanmun—and also kyŏnggich'e ka. But kyŏnggich'e ka were more didactic and expository than lyrical, and their diction was more Sino-Korean than Korean, with only a few Korean words and phrases sprinkled among the formulaic verse lines.

Learned Korean men (and a few women) of the times wrote lyric poetry in hanshi, usually five or seven Chinese characters per line, but how could this have been the same as writing lyric poetry in their own language? Besides, although hanshi and kyŏnggich'e ka could be read or recited, they could not be sung; vernacular poetry was better suited for singing.[1] Wellborn men of learning and power thus needed lyric poetry that was Korean in syntax, diction, and vocabulary, though copiously sprinkled with Sino-Korean words and phrases. It is believed that the shijo, an offshoot of several earlier vernacular poetic forms, developed out of this need.[2]

From the beginning the best shijo appear to have been those that expressed intense feelings: regrets about aging; sorrow over spurned love or loss of power and honor; reaffirmations of loyalty to a lost cause. Consider, for example, two of the earliest extant shijo:

> Sticks in one hand,
> Branches in another:
> I try to block old age with bushes,
> And frosty hair with sticks.
> But white hair came by a shortcut,
> Having seen through my devices.
> (U T'ak: 1262–1342)[3]

> The white snow has left the valleys
>   where the clouds are lowering
> Is it true that somewhere
>   the plum trees have happily blossomed?
> I stand here alone in the dusk
>   and do not know where to go.
> (Yi Saek: 1328–1396)[4]

Even in these fourteenth-century shijo the form appears well established, probably suggesting a much earlier origin for the shijo. Its three-line format probably owes to both the hyangga and Koryŏ kayo. The three-line opening verse of the Koryŏ kayo "Man-junch'on pyŏlsa," for example, is close in form to a standard shijo (*p'yŏng shijo*). Additionally, there is the influence of the folk song, probably the main source of all vernacular poetry. It is the music and vernacular diction of the folk song, filtered through the hyangga and Koryŏ kayo, that make up the heart of the shijo's lyricism.[5] Korean poetry, unlike English or Chinese poetry, uses no rhyme; the shijo relies primarily on syllabic cadence along with alliteration and assonance for auditory effects. The basic poetic phrase of the shijo—and most forms of classical Korean poetry—consists of alternating phrases of three and four, four and four, or two and three syllables.

For much of their long history shijo were called *tanga,* literally "short song." The term *shijo* is thought to be relatively recent, adopted sometime during the 1920s.[6] The clearest and most succinct description of shijo available in English is that of Richard Rutt in his excellent book *The Bamboo Grove.* I will quote only a portion of it here:

> The form of sijo is extremely elastic. There are three lines. Each line has a major pause in the middle and a subsidiary pause in the middle of each half-line. The number of syllables in each of the four subsections of a line varies from two to five or more, but the variation which occurs in each part of the poem is different.[7]

With each of its three lines normally having fifteen syllables, the shijo typically consists of forty-five syllables. But because the form is elastic, a shijo can have as few as forty-one or as many as fifty syllables.[8]

While the first and second lines are nearly identical in form and syllable count, there is considerable variation in the last line. The similarity between the first and second lines is one of function and content. In most shijo, the first line declares the theme; the second reinforces it either through a vigorous restatement or a more concrete illustration. But both in function and in content the last line is quite different, and thus its different form. For the third line not only brings the poem to a close, but frequently it also sharpens the theme developed in the first two lines by introducing a jolting twist or countertheme. While its first phrase is fixed at three syllables, its second phrase is invariable "syllable-heavy," as Bishop Rutt has so aptly characterized it, ranging generally from five to nine syllables. Thus, not only can the first half of the final line vary the most but it can also be the longest of any half-line of the poem.[9]

That this three-part structure of the shijo develops out of its three-line format is illustrated by one of the earliest and most famous of all shijo, attributed to Chŏng Mong-ju (1337–1392), one of the last scholar-statesmen of the Koryŏ dynasty. Legend has it that Chŏng composed this shijo in response to an ultimatum in the form of another shijo from his political foe, Yi Pang-wŏn (1367–1422), General Yi Sŏng-gye's fifth son and later the third king of the new Chosŏn dynasty. In translating the shijo one typically divides each line into two half-lines so as to emphasize the pause in the middle of each line. For this reason a shijo in English translation looks like a verse of six lines (actually six half-lines). The following translation is by Bishop Rutt:

> Though this frame should die and die,
>> though I die a hundred times,
> My bleached bones all turn to dust,
>> my very soul exist or not—
> What can change the undivided heart
>> that glows with faith toward my lord?[10]

The first line, consisting of two half-lines with a pause between them, intimates that the theme of the poem is constancy, a recurring theme of early shijo. The theme is elaborated in the second line. By illustrating not only what could happen to the body in death— "bleached bones [turning] to dust"—but also the possibility of the soul's extinction ("my very soul exist or not"), the second line suggests greater calamity overtaking the poet. It is in the context of this great calamity that the third line must shape and resolve the poem's message. The final line, accordingly, clinches the theme of the poem in the strongest possible terms: "What can change the undivided heart / that glows with faith toward my lord?"

In the original the emphasis falls especially heavy in the first half of the final line, which sounds loud and staccato with its well-known Sino-Korean phrase *ilp'yŏn tanshim*, "the undivided heart." Bishop Rutt's translation comes very close to re-creating these sound effects, not only by reproducing the six syllables of the "syllable-heavy" second phrase but also by stressing each of the three preceding syllables ("What can change"), and thereby making the message of the line both emphatic and unmistakable.

In some shijo, the first half of the last line gives an even stronger jolt both in sound and in sense, redefining or twisting the theme introduced in the first two lines. In this way the final line of a shijo sometimes resembles the couplet that closes a Shakespearean sonnet. Compare, for example, Shakespeare's Sonnet 130:

> My mistress' eyes are nothing like the sun,
> Coral is far more red than her lips' red.
> If snow be white, why then her breasts are dun,
> If hairs be wires, black wires grow on her head.
> I have seen roses damasked, red and white,
> But no such roses see I in her cheeks.
> And in some perfumes is there more delight
> Than in the breath that from my mistress reeks.
> I love to hear her speak, yet well I know
> That music hath a far more pleasing sound.
> I grant I never saw a goddess go,
> My mistress, when she walks, treads on the ground.
> > And yet, by Heaven, I think my love as rare
> > as any she belied with false compare.

The first twelve lines of the sonnet, its three quatrains, are comparable to the first two lines of the shijo, for the second and third quatrains essentially restate or develop the theme stated in the first quatrain. The crux of the poem occurs in its concluding couplet and is signaled by the words "And yet, by Heaven," which in both sense and feeling turn the poem around.

Similarly, some shijo introduce a countertheme in the last line, as we can see in the following shijo by Yang Sa-ŏn:

> Men may say the mountain's high,
>   but all of it's beneath the sky;
> There really is no reason why
>   we may not climb if we climb and climb,
> But usually we never try.
>   We only say: "The mountain's high."[11]

The first two lines build tension by only hinting at the theme. The implied, unanswered question is: What is the reason for the failure to climb the mountain (Mount Tai in Shandong, China)? Is the mountain too high, or is it that men don't try hard enough? It is only in the first half of the final line that the answer is given: It's *man himself*. In the original the first half of the final line reads "*sarami che ani orŭgo*" (man himself not climbing). Because the first word of the syllable-heavy second phrase, *che* ("himself") is set apart both in sound and in sense, almost like an exclamation, the emphasis on it is doubled. The poem's real theme is thus declared vigorously and unequivocally: It is *man himself* who is responsible for failing to climb the mountain.[12]

I suggested at the outset that the shijo is the most Korean of the various forms of traditional Korean poetry. It is certainly the most enduring of the traditional poetic forms, as shown by its continuing popularity and vitality among Koreans of all classes both in Korea and abroad. What, then, are the qualities of the shijo that make it so enduring, enabling Koreans everywhere to identify themselves with the sound, sense, and form of its poetry? In attempting to answer this question let us begin by comparing a shijo with a haiku, the traditional poetic form so beloved of the Japanese and thought to be quintessentially Japanese. Both the shijo and the haiku are short three-line poems, the shijo normally having forty-five syllables and the haiku seventeen. Everything else about them, however, seems very different. Let us consider an example of each, both on similar topics, and while conceding the arbitrariness of such a comparison let us try nonetheless to detect some of the distinct qualities of each form. The shijo is by Im Che and the haiku a well-known piece by Basho.

> Green grass covers the valley.
>> Do you sleep? Are you at rest?
> O where is that lovely face?
>> Can mere bones lie buried here?
> I have wine, but no chance to share it.
>> Alone, I pour it sadly. (Im Che: 1549–1587)[13]

> The summer grasses—
> Of brave soldiers' dreams
> The aftermath. (Basho: 1644–1694)[14]

Both Im Che and Basho are looking over a field of green grass that shows no sign of lives once filled with loveliness, sorrow, and tumult. How flickeringly transient human life seems in comparison with the eternal rhythm of nature. In both poems we experience keen regret as well as acceptance of life's temporality amid nature's permanence. And yet how different the two poems are. As Donald Keene has observed, the haiku demands that we join in and complete the poem.[15] For unless we can evoke for ourselves a vivid picture of the grass-covered field that was once the scene of a pitched battle, the poem will probably mean little to us. The haiku does not come alive until completed by our own imagination and attendant emotions.

The shijo by Im Che, on the other hand, is more straightforward. More is explained by the narrative voice, both scene and feelings explicitly evoked by the poet. It is as if the poet asks us to accompany him as he surveys the grass-covered valley, as he remembers the loveliness of the person now gone, indulging in bittersweet memory as well as in the present moment. The poem is slower paced, almost relaxed in its unfolding. Instead of the haiko's flashes of suggestiveness and fragmentary, semiveiled glimpses of reality, the shijo offers openness, plain clarity even. It is this unassuming, unselfconscious lyricism that seems to give the shijo a kind of constancy that wears well, for it speaks in the same clear voice each time we encounter it. We might almost compare it to the flavor of rice, which in part because of its relative blandness we can eat every day and still like.

It is this seeming artlessness of the shijo that many see as one of the main characteristics of Korean literature, in contrast with the perceived indirectness and suggestiveness of Japanese literature. Of course, I am not suggesting that all shijo are like the one by Im Che or that all haiku are like the one by Basho. Perhaps the most we could say is that there is probably no shijo that is quite like the haiku by Basho, and that most shijo are more like those by Im Che and Yang Sa-ŏn.

Having originated before the invention of hangŭl, the earliest extant shijo were transmitted orally or in hanmun translation until they were written down in hangŭl after the middle of the fifteenth century. Some of those early shijo, therefore, come down to us in both hanmun and hangŭl. An example, mentioned earlier, is the ultimatum supposedly delivered to Chŏng Mong-ju by Yi Pang-wŏn. It is known by its hanmun title, "Hayŏ ka," which is simply a hanmun version of the poem's first line, which goes something like "What if you should live this or that way?"

The shijo is not limited to topics of high seriousness. Its subjects are as various as its tone. There are shijo on loyalty, love, love of nature, mortality, the joys of drinking, and the pleasures of idleness. There are also slightly longer shijo called *sasŏl shijo*, which, as I shall discuss later, are often decidedly satiric. Because the shijo was written in hangŭl, which as we saw in chapter 1 was considered suitable primarily for women, a few of its most accomplished practitioners were women. Their shijo contain some of the finest love lyrics ever written in Korean. Here are two examples:

I will break the back
    of this long, midwinter night,
folding it double,
    cold beneath my spring quilt,
that I may draw out
    the night, should my love return.
        (Hwang Chin-i: early sixteenth century)[16]

Night covers the mountain village;
    a dog barks in the distance.
I open the brushwood gate
    and see only the moon in a cold sky.
That dog! What is he doing, barking
    at the sleeping moon in the silent hills?
        (Ch'ŏn Kŭm)[17]

The first shijo is the most celebrated poem by Hwang Chin-i, rendered in English by one of the best translators of Korean poetry. Excellent as it is, however, the translation cannot fully re-create the exquisite lyricism of the original, especially the music of the alliteration and assonance. Listen to the interplay of alliteration and assonance in the first line of the original Korean: "*Tongjit tal   kiinakiin pam ŭl   han hŏri rŭl   pŏhyŏ naeyŏ.*" The *t*'s, *k*'s, *p*'s (all unaspirated) and *h*'s for alliteration, the drawn-out *i*'s, and the *a*'s and *ŏ*'s recurring throughout this line orchestrate a music almost as lovely as Keats's "unheard" melodies. There is probably no way to reproduce this music in translation. In particular such phrases as "*kiinakiin*" in the first line, "*sŏri sŏri*" in the second, and "*kubi kubi*" in the final line defy translation into English, simply because there are no English words with precisely the same meaning, feel, and sound quality.

The shijo by Ch'ŏn Kŭm is equally superb, though in a different way. It is the interplay of visual images that makes the poem so memorable. In the first line a dog barking in a remote mountain village strikes a note of stark lonesomeness, though the bark itself is truly "unheard." The image is then juxtaposed with the pale white moon in the cold sky. The juxtaposition brings home not only the luminous chill of the night sky but also the starkness of solitude. Through these two images we feel the utter futility of the dog barking at the silent moon and the empty hills. Isn't this a poem about loneliness?

Sasŏl shijo

Besides the standard shijo (*p'yŏng shijo*), which we have been discussing, there are two other forms, *ŏt shijo* and *sasŏl shijo*. "*Ŏt shijo*" means "slightly altered shijo"[18] and it is so called because the middle line is expanded to six phrases instead of the normal four. There are only a few of them. It is a different matter, however, with the sasŏl shijo. Not only have a great many of them been composed since the eighteenth century; they also represent a significant departure from the traditional shijo both in form and in content, as well as in audience, readership, and social status of those who composed them.

When a standard shijo is sung, not only its words but the individual syllables are drawn out, frequently to a considerable extent. In a sasŏl shijo, the space where a word or syllable is normally drawn out is filled with a narrative of chatty words. The insertion of this narrative expands mostly the middle line of the shijo many times its normal length. But because the first and final lines usually have the same format as those of the standard shijo, though greatly lengthened, the sasŏl shijo retains the overall Shijo form.

The appearance and popularity of the sasŏl shijo at the beginning of the eighteenth century reflect important social and economic changes in Korean society at the time. These changes were brought about by the decline of the yangban (aristocratic) classes and the concurrent rise in importance of the *chungin* (middle) and merchant classes. Shijo were no longer the sole property of the upper classes. They were now composed and sung by and for the middle and merchant classes as well, and both their form and content had to be adapted to better serve the different tastes and needs of these newcomers.[19]

To draw a parallel from American literature, in language and subject matter the sasŏl shijo is a little like the poetry of Walt Whitman compared with that of Longfellow and Bryant. Just as the language of Whitman's poetry burst out of the formal constraints of his predecessors, so did the language of the sasŏl shijo burst out of the form and decorum of the traditional shijo. Sasŏl shijo are often earthy, comic, even coarse and indecent. These mostly anonymous poems describe life as it actually was rather than as it should ideally be. In subject matter, too, they breached traditional boundaries, singing of lust as well as love, commerce as well as politics, and abuses of power more than statesmanship. The sasŏl shijo is thus an important expression of the popular vernacular voice. By reaching down into the middle and merchant classes it not only broadened the shijo's appeal but also adapted the form to the changing conditions of later Chosŏn society.

The poem that follows is one of the most striking sasŏl shijo. Tension is built from the first line through the long middle section through a series of vivid natural images. In the first line, which is only three syllables longer than a standard shijo line, we are told about a mountain pass so high that even the wind and clouds must rest before blowing over it. Then in the very long middle section the great height of the pass is conveyed by a series of images of high-flying falcons and hawks that also must rest before flying over it. These vivid images build up to the climatic final line, where, in a totally unexpected reversal, we find that the poem is actually about the all-consuming love between a man and a woman rather than about clouds and birds. In Bishop Rutt's superb translation we gain a sense of how different a sasŏl shijo can be from a standard shijo:

> Pass where the winds pause before going over,
>> pass where the clouds pause before going over,

High peak of the pass of Changsong,
>   where hand-reared falcons and
>   wild-born falcons,
>   peregrine falcons and yearling hawks,
>   all pause before they cross.
If I knew that my love were over the pass,
>   I should not pause a moment before I
>   crossed.

>   (Anonymous)[20]

From the language and subject matter of the next example we can gain an even clearer idea of how much sasŏl shijo differed from traditional shijo:

Death-in-life girl, for heaven's sake
>   stop frittering my innards!
Shall I give you money? Shall I give you silver?
>   How many things shall I give you?
>   A Chinese silk skirt, a Korean court dress,
>   silk gauze petticoats and white satin belt,
>   a gossamer twist of hair from the North.
>   a jade hairpin, a bamboo hairpin,
>   an amber-handled silver spatula,
>   a golden spatula with a milky amber handle,
>   a coral brooch from the southern seas,
>   pure gold chopsticks engraved
>   with heavenly peaches
>   and hung with blue enamelled bells,
>   a hairpin made of yellow pearls
>   and embroidered shoes should I give you?
Silly one! That's a millionaire's dream:
>   just give me one chance at that
>   dimpling wrinkling cheek,
>   lovely as a flower, but cheap at
>   a thousand gold pieces!

>   (Anonymous)[21]

Shijo in English

In the fall of 1993 I offered a course in classical Korean literature in translation through the English department of the university where I have taught since the 1960s. I was quite apprehensive about the new course and wondered if anyone would sign up, since such a class had never been offered before at our university. To my surprise and delight about thirty students enrolled, and the course turned into a memorable experience for both the students and myself.

One of our most fruitful activities was to write some Shijo in English. Initially there was much hesitation, for many in the class feared they knew too little about shijo to try their hand at writing one. But once the initial apprehension was overcome, half of the class succeeded in writing at least one shijo in English. The students took heart in part from their discovery that there was some flexibility in the number of syllables in each of the three lines of a shijo. Much of the credit, however, goes to Katrina Gee, a senior English major. Having lived some years in Japan, she had become interested in the haiku and in haiku writing. After we spent a couple of weeks studying shijo she volunteered to write a shijo and explain to the class how she went about doing it. Her presentation was very effective and did much to banish any lingering doubts among the students.

The following is Katrina's summary of how she went about writing her haiku and shijo:

> For a better understanding of shijo poetry, I decided to try my hand at writing some. As a warm-up exercise I started with a form of poetry which I am more familiar with and that is similar to shijo—haiku. Haiku is a three-line poem with a syllable count of 5, 7, 5. There are three other rules: it must refer to nature, it must refer to a particular event which is taking place *now* and it must suggest to the reader what the poet is feeling during the observation. The best way to get started is to go out in nature and observe! Here's what I came up with:

> Leaf falling from tree
> Swirling, spinning gently down
> Softly leaving home.

The discipline of this kind of poem can be applied to shijo. In haiku and shijo, word choice is very important. Writing these kinds of poems helps the poet to see what is (and isn't) important in an experience. It also helps the poet to understand that simplicity and brevity are valuable in writing. Shijo carries this one step further by offering a contrast in the third line which sharpens the theme of the first and second lines. I decided to continue with my leaf theme, and find that I am more satisfied with my shijo poem:

> A leaf is falling from home
>   because he wants to be alone.
> Where he travels is unknown
>   because his fall is yet unshown.
> His clinging brother does not roam.
>   He only watches freedom's poem.

In Katrina's shijo we can see not only how it developed from her haiku almost line by line, but also how closely she observed the break, both in form and in content, that is supposed to occur between the first two lines and the final line. Not only does she give eight syllables to the first half-line of the final line, she also makes it a complete sentence, unlike all the preceding half-lines. In doing so she brings the poem to a complete stop at the end of the first half of the final line, thereby making this half-line seem more syllable-heavy than it actually is, which in turn serves to emphasize the point of the poem. That is how she achieves the twist or countertheme in the final line, which, as she explains, "by offering a contrast . . . sharpens the theme of the first and second lines."

In breaking each line of the shijo into two half-lines she follows a practice widely used in translating shijo into English because it clearly marks the pause in the middle of each line. Most of the other students also followed this format. And as they became more interested in the shijo and began writing their own, a few of them started looking for books in their local libraries that might have something to do with Korean literature, and specifically with shijo. One of their finds was a book written for young adults that had some shijo translations. Though they did not especially care for the translations, they found the translation format both helpful and to their liking. To underscore the formal and rhetorical break between the first two lines and the last line of the shijo, the editor-translator had physically separated the last line from the first two lines. The result was a shijo that resembled a two-stanza poem, a stanza of four half-lines followed by a stanza of two half-lines. In this format Katrina's shijo, for example, would look like this:

> A leaf is falling from home
> > because he wants to be alone.
> Where he travels is unknown
> > because his fall is yet unshown.
>
> His clinging brother does not roam.
> > He only watches freedom's poem.

Two of my students adopted this format for their shijo, because they felt it helped them deal more effectively with the countertheme they introduced in the last line.

Another notable event during the semester was Mrs. L's term project. She wanted to teach a segment on shijo in her son's eighth-grade English honors class in order "to give them a basic background and history of shijo poetry, and enough understanding of the subject to enable them to write their own shijo poetry." Using the shijo and haiku poems presented by Katrina, one of Shakespeare's sonnets for comparison, and a great deal of material from our class, Mrs. L successfully completed her project. Many of her eighth-grade students ended up writing their own shijo, two of which are given at the end of this chapter.

The shijo is bound to be the centerpiece of a general introductory course on classical Korean literature, not only because of its importance as poetry and its place in classical Korean literature but equally because of its accessibility to English-only students. I found shijo accessible to these students as readers and also writers of shijo in English. Writing great shijo is not the goal, for great poetry is produced rarely in any language. Rather, experience has taught me that having students try their hand at writing the shijo, adhering to its most basic rules, not only helped them better appreciate the classical shijo but also gave them an opportunity to turn the experience of their daily lives into poetry. I found it to be an excellent way to help them become more alert to their surroundings and inner selves and the uses of language.

The rules for shijo in English should be kept basic:

1. The shijo is a poem of three lines.
2. Each line has a pause in the middle; thus it is broken into two half-lines of seven or eight syllables each.
3. The final line should attempt a reversal or reemphasis, preferably in the first half-line.
4. The syllable count for the whole poem is flexible, ranging from forty-one to fifty. It might be added that shijo can be written on any topic.

The following are some of the shijo written by the students in my 1993 course:

> O lotus—how do you
>   thrive and survive in the mud?
> Living in but not of
>   the enveloping darkness.
> Mind, be like the lotus and live in
>   but not of the world. (Ferzin)

> The bird pecking at the ground
>   does not hear the smallest sound.
> He's busy is his battle
>   for his life and survival.

Are we who don't need to depend
    upon small crumbs more fortunate? (Pamela)

A bouncing ball, an orb,
    spins over the world blazing.
Kicked in northern snow,
    and by naked southern feet,
Arriving on artificial turf.
    Will the fire catch or die? (Lawrence)

Walking toward the cold, salty foam,
Squishing in the soft, wet sand,
My eyes behold the vast blue water.
My ears hear the roar of waves.

God's wonder is here for all—
My heart sings with great thanksgiving! (Katie)

You vowed to always love me.
    Rather, I believed you would.
I remember the first touch
    and the promises you made.
Didn't they mean anything?
    Or was I just your piece of clay? (Charlene)

The winter's fierce flooding
    Strips dirt from hollow banks.
The snow drifts rise and plummet,
    White cover for a darkened Earth.
My eyes close to the image of the seasons new,
    Will not my love warm my soul? (David)

Youth pushes and pulls its body
    While will is distracted by fleeting lust.
And we race, unmoving, for success
    Like jelly-fish listlessly stabbing for prey.

Oh how I yearn for older age,
     For roots and self-sufficiency. (JW)

Last night the moon shone brightly
Caressing lightly a pond's skin,
And dreams of her love for me
Were cast in the silvery stillness
     Until cruel clouds hid the moon away
     And rain drops dispersed my reverie. (Jason)

The tree stand alone and silent,
     For all the world to see.
It hears a thousand stories,
     And secrets kept untold.
If only it could speak to me,
     And share all that it knows. (Elizabeth)

I offer you a last red rose
     as flame-burnished leaves drop to our laps.
You lift the rose, longing for spring
     and red, leafy rains pelt our legs.
We have chosen the wrong time of the year
     to speak our true hearts in the shade. (Andrew)

Here are two poems written by the students in Mrs. L's son's eighth-grade English honors class:

The great motionless egret,
     calmly waiting for its prey.
Just a quick jab of its bill,
     and he'll have a meal this day.
Ah—an unexpecting victim,
     one less fish in this massive bay.

A mother is your place of birth,
     She is the love of your life.

There may possibly come a day,
When she won't be there to hold you.
So do yourself a favor,
Give your mother a great big hug today!

Notes

1. Hwang P'ae-gang, Cho Tong-il et al., ed., *Hanguk munhak yŏngu immun.* (An Introduction to the Study of Korean Literature) (Seoul: Chishik sanŏp sa, 1982), 401.

2. Cho Tong-il, *Hanguk munhak t'ongsa* (A Comprehensive History of Korean Literature), 2nd ed. (Seoul: Chishik sanŏp sa, 1989), II:177–83.

3. Trans. Peter H. Lee in *Anthology of Korean Literature,* rev. ed., comp. and ed. Peter H. Lee (Honolulu: University of Hawaii Press, 1992), 93.

4. Richard Rutt, *The Bamboo Grove* (Berkeley: University of California Press, 1971), #1. Unless otherwise indicated, translations from this book cited in the text are those of Bishop Rutt.

5. Cho Tong-il, *Hanguk munhak t'ongsa,* II:177–98. I am much indebted to Professor Cho's discussion of early shijo, kyŏnggich'e ka, and hanshi.

6. Rutt, *The Bamboo Grove,* 9. There is still some controversy over this question.

7. Ibid., 9–10. Bishop Rutt's book is not only the best introduction to shijo; it also gives the finest translations of many of the best shijo.

8. Chang Tŏk-sun, *Hanguk munhak sa* (A History of Korean Literature) (Seoul: Tonghwa munhwa sa, 1987), 315.

9. Rutt, *The Bamboo Grove,* 11.

10. Ibid., #56.

11. Translator unknown; quoted in ibid., 20.

12. See Rutt's fine discussion of this shijo in ibid., 20–22.

13. Ibid., #106.

14. Trans. Donald Keene, in *Anthology of Japanese Literature,* ed. Donald Keene (New York: Grove Press: 1955), 369.

15. Donald Keene, *Japanese Literature* (New York: Grove Press, 1955), 28.

16. Trans. David R. McCann in *Anthology of Korean Literature,* ed. and comp. Lee, 97.

17. Rutt, *The Bamboo Grove,* #166.

18. Ibid., headnote to "Sasŏl shijo."

19. Cho Tong-il, *Hanguk munhak t'ongsa,* III: 291–95.

20. Rutt, *The Bamboo Grove,* #228.

21. Ibid., #236.

6

The Literature of
Chosŏn Dynasty Women

Palace Literature

Until the invention of hangŭl in 1446, wellborn and learned men
enjoyed a near monopoly on the written word in Korea, because
they alone were adequately educated in hanmun. Most women
and ordinary people had neither the training nor the leisure to
become proficient in hanmun, a difficult and alien written language. Even the women of yangban families were discouraged
from any systematic training in reading and writing, since book
learning was considered both unnecessary and improper for
women, their sphere being strictly domestic. In fact, an absence
of learning was thought to promote virtue in a woman, and if
educated, she was expected *not* to exhibit her learning. If she
wrote, her writing was not to go beyond her family, and for this
reason her writings, including letters, were frequently destroyed
by actually having the writing washed off the paper. The daughters of even the best yangban families were taught only hangŭl, so
they might read those few works of Confucian moral instruction and
manuals of exemplary womanly behavior that were translated into
hangŭl.[1] One of the real achievements of hangŭl, therefore, was that
it conferred upon women and ordinary people a writing system that
was not only native and phonetic but also easy to learn. Hanmun
continued to be the written language of the yangban men; hangŭl
thus became the written language mainly of upper- and middle-class
Korean women who had some education as well as leisure. For this
reason hangŭl has been called *amgŭl*, "female letters."[2]

Even though Chosŏn women were discouraged from reading and writing, there were exceptional women who were proficient in both hangŭl and hanmun. For example, Lady Yun, mother of Kim Manjung, author of *Kuun mong* (A Nine Cloud Dream), is said through her home tutoring to have enabled her two sons to pass the civil service examination. Other women writers of note were Lady Shin Saimdang, mother of the great Confucian scholar Yi I (Yulgok); Hŏ Nansŏrhŏn; and Hwang Chin-i. Several of these women left works both in hanmun and in hangŭl.[3]

Among the hangŭl prose works written by women there are several that concern people and events inside the palace. The best known of these works of "palace literature" are *Kyech'uk ilgi* (Diary of the Year of the Black Ox, 1613), *Inhyŏn Wanghu chŏn* (Life of Queen Inhyŏn), and *Hanjungnok* (Records Made in Distress). These three works are distinguished not only because they are written in hangŭl but also because each appears to be written by a court lady who seems to have been an eyewitness to events within the royal palace.[4] Each in its own way provides us with invaluable glimpses of the tragic underside of life inside the palace, something rarely revealed to the outside world.

Inhyŏn Wanghu chŏn appears to be the most deliberately composed of the three. Clearly it is historical fiction with a pointed moral: virtue is eventually vindicated while evil is punished. Because it is the most deliberately composed, it also seems less factual than the others. *Kyech'uk ilgi* and *Hanjungnok,* on the other hand, seem more rough-edged, more factual, and less deliberately shaped. *Hanjungnok* consists of four partially overlapping memoirs composed at different times by Lady Hong (Princess Hyegyŏng) when she was in her sixties and seventies. And *Kyech'uk ilgi* is a diary supposedly composed by an unnamed court lady intimate with and devoted to Queen Inmok, second queen to King Sŏnjo (1567–1608). Neither, therefore, has any claim to be the artistic creation that *Inhyŏn Wanghu chŏn* is, for both are clearly partisan accounts of actual historical events. As literature, they are uneven though moving works. While vivid and dramatic, they also tend to be cluttered with overlapping

recitals of family and factional intrigues, some of which are difficult to unravel except for the specialist.

Kyech'uk ilgi is a relatively short work in two volumes. Its
story begins during the last years of King Sŏnjo. When the first
pregnancy of Queen Inmok, Sŏnjo's twenty-year-old second
queen, becomes known, both Kwanghaegun, the crown prince,
and his in-laws are greatly agitated because they believe
Kwanghaegun's position as heir to the throne is threatened. For,
despite having been designated heir to his father, Kwanghaegun
was after all a son born to one of King Sŏnjo's secondary consorts. A male child born of Queen Inmok, therefore, would have
a greater claim to the succession. And so after Kwanghaegun
succeeds to the throne, his two rivals are eliminated: first his own
elder brother and then Prince Yŏngch'ang, his thirteen-year-old
stepbrother, son of King Sŏnjo by Queen Inmok.

Most of the diary reads like an eyewitness account of what
Queen Inmok and Prince Yŏngch'ang suffer at the hands of
Kwanghaegun. Fearing his half-brother's claim to the throne,
Kwanghaegun persecutes mother and son relentlessly. He shuts
them up in one of the palaces, cutting them off entirely from the
outside world, and he tries year after year to take the prince away
from his mother.

The most poignant moments of the diary occur early in the
first volume when Queen Inmok tries desperately to protect her
young son from Kwanghaegun. For as long as she can, using one
pretext or another, Queen Inmok resists the king's insistent demands that she turn over the prince to him. But eventually she
has to give him up. And even though the prince is too young to
fully grasp the situation, when he is about to be wrenched from
his mother's protection and care he is frightened because he
senses that something terrible is about to happen to him. Here is a
brief excerpt from this part of *Kyech'uk ilgi:*

> Unable to give up her son, the queen wept in great sorrow. The two
> children [her son and daughter] also wept by her side. Weeping, the
> queen cried out: "God in heaven, what sin have I committed that you

make me suffer such grief! . . . All of you, being court ladies, you don't understand a mother's love for her son. How could I give him up!"

In the meantime, the court ladies waiting on the prince said to him, trying to calm his fears: "Since you, sir, will be gone only for three or four days for the sake of your health and will soon be back, please put on your socks and coat, and come out with us." To which the prince replied: "Since I'm to be taken out through the gate used for criminals, what good is it for a criminal to put on socks and coat?" "Who told you such a thing?" asked the court ladies. "No one has told me, but I know. Isn't the smaller, west gate used for criminals? They must think I'm a criminal since they are going to confine me just outside that gate." And he added, "I'll come out only if I'm to come out with my sister. I won't come out alone." Further saddened by these words, the queen wept. . . .

"Since the prince cries and complains so much about having to come out of the gate used for criminals, no matter how hard we try to talk him into coming out, there isn't much anyone can do even though he's only a child. Let everyone withdraw a little, and I'll come out with him," said the lady-in-waiting in answer to threats made by the king's servants. As it was getting very late in the day, finally they made preparations to come out: the queen, the princess, and the prince each borne on the backs of ladies-in-waiting Chŏng, Chu, and Kim.

"Let the queen and my elder sister come out before me, and I'll follow," the prince said. "Why in that order, sir?" "Because if I should come out first, I'll be out alone, and the others won't be coming out," said the prince.[5]

The little prince's premonition turns out to be accurate, for as soon as he appears the queen and princess are thrust back into the palace by the king's servants and mother and son never see each other again. Exiled to Kanghwa Island, the prince is later put to death. Most of the critical events of this tragedy occurred during the year of the Black Ox, the fifth year of Kwanghaegun's reign, which explains the title of the diary.

The second volume of *Kyech'uk ilgi* describes the further ordeals of Queen Inmok during the ten years following the year of the Black Ox. Sealed up in her palace, she suffers from the inexorable decay of her human and nonhuman support systems: every part of the neglected palace falls into ruin, while her attendants diminish year by year through betrayal, desertion, and death. Her imprisonment ends only when Kwanghaegun is overthrown by a coup in the fifteenth year of his reign. Here too ends this anonymous account of Queen Inmok's ordeal. The last page of the diary recounts how the gates of her palace are flung open and the queen is restored to freedom and her former status.

Kyech'uk ilgi is written from Queen Inmok's perspective, though its diary format accords it the appearance of documentary objectivity. But because it is such an obviously partisan account, many questions come to mind. Above all, how much of it is history and how much fiction? According to Yi Ki-baek, one of the most respected Korean historians, Kwanghaegun was "a monarch who displayed uncommon capacities in directing both domestic and foreign affairs."[6] He was especially adroit in his dealings with the Ming and Manchu courts and managed to prevent his country from being drawn into the conflict between the Ming and the emerging Manchus.[7] According to *Kyech'uk ilgi,* however, Kwanghaegun was a cruel and evil king. Was he then an able king who was evil in his dealings with his brothers, stepmother, and palace attendants?

Kim Yong-suk, one of the best-informed scholars on premodern Korean women and women writers, after carefully sifting the pertinent historical records, concludes that the picture of Kwanghaegun given in *Kyech'uk ilgi* deviates markedly from the account of him in contemporary historical records. Kwanghaegun, writes Professor Kim, was in fact a "wise and good king." Despite his best efforts, he could not save his own elder brother or his half-brother or finally himself from the political factionalism that raged during his reign.[8] She suggests several reasons for the gross distortions in the diary. First, it was composed after Kwanghaegun was overthrown. Second, it was probably the work of a court lady loyal to Queen Inmok. Third, following the pattern of extreme opposition between good and evil already established in traditional fiction of the Chosŏn period, the work distorts, simplifies, and exaggerates more complex situations involving Kwanghaegun, his brother and half-brother, and Queen Inmok. She suggests further that the Kwanghaegun seen in contemporary historical records, far from being evil and cruel, was actually an overly gentle and sensitive monarch.[9]

Hanjungnok consists of a series of memoirs by Lady Hong, widow of a crown prince who was put to death in 1762 by his father, King Yŏngjo, by being locked and buried in a rice chest for nine days. The memoirs begin with Lady Hong's happy but brief childhood in the family fold. At age nine, suddenly and unexpectedly, her childhood comes to an end when she is chosen as consort to Crown Prince Sado. To her parents and the older members of the family her selection must have been a great honor, but to a nine-year-old girl it is nothing less than a calamity, leaving her baffled and grief-stricken. Too young to fully appreciate the significance to herself and her family of her selection, she is devastated by what has befallen her. Her confusion and sorrow seem palpable even half a century later as she looks back on her sorrowful homecoming after the fateful second selection:

> When we arrived home, I was carried through the gate reserved for male visitors. Father raised the screen covering the palanquin and lifted me out. He had on his ceremonial robe and seemed uneasy treating me with deference. I clung to my parents and could not hold back the tears. Mother too was attired in her ceremonial robes, and the table was decked with a scarlet cover. Mother appeared somewhat awe-stricken as she kowtowed four times before accepting the missive from the queen, and twice before accepting one from Lady Yi.
>
> From that day on my parents began to use honorific expressions with me, and the elders of the clan treated me with respect—all this made me feel uncomfortable and indescribably sad. Greatly apprehensive, Father gave me thousands of words of advice. I felt like a sinner who has no refuge. *I did not want to leave Father and Mother. My heart felt as though it would melt away—nothing seemed to interest me.* [italics added][10]

Here we are made to feel not only her dismay at her parents' sudden strange formality but also her sorrow at the prospect of separation from her family and friends at such an early age. "With the passing of each day my grief grew more unbearable and I slept each night in Mother's arms," writes Lady Hong more than half a century later.[11]

The first ten years of her life in the palace are relatively stable and happy. Much loved by King Yŏngjo, her royal father-in-law, the queen, and Lady Sŏnhŭi, mother of the crown prince, Lady Hong quickly adjusts to her new life, and when she gives birth to the royal grandson-to-be her success as consort to the crown prince seems assured. In the meantime her own family prospers too. Her father, upon passing the Senior Civil Service Examination, is appointed to a succession of ever more important government posts. These first years thus appear to have been her happiest in the palace, for soon afterwards she is caught up in the tragedy that overtakes the crown prince.

Lady Hong locates the origin of the crown prince's growing difficulties with his father in the estrangement that developed between father and son soon after the son's birth. She traces the estrangement to the king's decision to house the infant prince in a palace mansion quite removed from the king's own. According to her, the physical distance inadvertently led to an emotional distance between father and son as well:

> His [the infant crown prince's] physical appearance was magnificent; his disposition filial, friendly and clever. Therefore, he could have developed a most virtuous personality, *if only his parents had kept him near them and instructed him, loving and guiding him at the same time.* But instead, they lived far away from him. . . . [italics added].[12]

The crown prince, growing up with little parental guidance or affection and surrounded mostly by female attendants who allowed him to do as he pleased, acquired very little discipline, which displeased the king more and more. Subsequently, the prince . . . began to feel afraid of his father; while the father for his part came to suspect that his son might grow up in a way contrary to his hopes and expectations. Moreover, the character of father and son were utterly different. King Yŏngjo was clever and benevolent, well-informed on all about him, yet prompt in action; whereas the crown prince was reticent of speech and hesitant in action. Though he possessed a noble and virtuous mind, he could never find an immediate answer to even the most ordinary question. He was always slow to reply, and when it was the king who asked the question of him, he was even less capable of making a direct answer. . . . He used to wonder how he should answer, which disappointed the king.[13]

The absence of affection between the father and son obviously aggravated the matter. The father became increasingly more severe and unhappy with his son, and the son on his part grew more fearful and resentful of his father's harshness toward him. Inevitably, both the father and son "came to find less and less in common, and whenever they met, the king's resentment against his son predominated over his affection for him,"[14] recalls Lady Hong in anguish. The heart of the matter—what Lady Hong calls the prince's "sickness"—lay in the son's fear of his royal father and his repeated failure to gain the king's favor:

The king never understood his son and always showed displeasure at his words and manner, being unable to forgive him. This made the prince more and more terrified of his father, until eventually he fell sick. At these times he would relieve his feelings upon the eunuchs and court maids, or even, many times, upon myself.[15]

It appears to have been this sickness—a kind of madness overtaking the crown prince periodically—that drove him to a "clothes phobia" and the rape and murder of court attendants as well as brutalities against his own family and himself.

Midway through the memoirs there is a poignant illustration of this developing tragedy between the royal father and son. King

Yŏngjo, incensed with the crown prince for the numerous murders allegedly committed by him, visits unannounced to look into the matter personally. He asks his son if the reports of his misdeeds are true. The prince freely confesses his guilt and tries to explain his behavior:

> "It relieves my pent-up anger, Sire, to kill people or animals when I am feeling depressed or on edge."
> The king asked, "Why is that so?"
> "Because I am hurt," answered the prince.
> "Why are you hurt?" the king asked.
> "I am hurt because you do not love me and also, alas, I am terrified of you because you constantly rebuke me, Sire."
> The king seemed to experience a fleeting moment of fatherly compassion for his son. He calmed down somewhat and said, "I will act differently in the future."[16]

One of the most dramatic incidents in the memoirs, which also shows Lady Hong's exceptional intelligence, occurs soon after the crown prince is put to death. Although King Yŏngjo's anger towards his son appears to continue unabated even after the son's horrible death, his affection and concern for his royal grandson (and now the designated heir)—the future King Chŏngjo—seem not only unaffected but actually increased by the tragedy. Nevertheless, Lady Hong, fully aware of her son's precarious position, tries to do whatever she can to ensure the king's continuing affection for him. She therefore asks the king to keep his grandson with him and take charge of his education, even though this would mean her being separated from her beloved son, who is only ten years old. The critical moment occurs about half a year after the crown prince's death when Lady Hong arranges an audience for the purpose of entrusting the royal grandson to the king. As she is about to take leave of them her son cries inconsolably, unable to contain his grief at the prospect of being separated from his mother. Noticing his grandson's sorrow, King Yŏngjo, perhaps a little mortified as well as jealous, suggests to Lady Hong that the royal grandson remain with her. Immediately sensing the potential for royal displeasure and the resulting threat to her son's position, Lady Hong manages to do exactly the right thing, even if it should break her heart. Recalling the scene nearly half a century later, she writes:

> Thinking that the king might feel offended when, despite all his love for his grandson, the boy rejected the royal favour out of longing for his mother, I said, "If he should come to me, he will miss Your Highness; if he goes to Your Highness, he will miss me. So please take him with you, since he will feel just like this about being away from Your Highness."[17]

What breaks her heart is not so much her own grief but her son's unhappiness at being separated from her, and especially the sight of him "crying bitterly at his mother's apparent lack of feeling in forcing him to leave."[18] Camouflaging her own emotions, she manages to subtly flatter the aged monarch, thus ensuring her son's position. The king, understandably pleased with Lady Hong's reply, departs with his little grandson, feeling vindicated and soothed. Through her quick intelligence and her devotion to her son's welfare she not only avoids potential disaster but increases the king's affection for the royal grandson.

Although the main focus of *Hanjungnok* is on the tragedy of Crown Prince Sado and Lady Hong, the memoirs in their entirety present a much larger tragedy. In the second half of her memoirs, Lady Hong details the further tragedies that overtake her and her natal family after the death of Crown Prince Sado: the fall from power of her father and the unjust execution of her uncle and brother during the reigns of her own son and grandson, Kings Chŏngjo and Sunjo. For her brother's death especially, she blames herself, believing that her enemies at court, unable to strike at her, directed their venom at her brother. Throughout this part of her memoirs she takes great pains to clear her father of the charge that he conspired to bring about the death of Crown Prince Sado and supplied the rice chest in which he was entombed alive. She makes it clear that her father, on the contrary, did everything to protect the crown prince, herself, and the royal grandson. To protect the grandson he had risked looking as if he were ingratiating himself with the king soon after the death of Crown Prince Sado. His enemies seized upon this as evidence of his collaboration with the king in the execution of the crown prince.

In the latter part of her memoirs, written in her sixties and seventies, Lady Hong cries out to Heaven repeatedly, questioning why she and her family had to suffer so much and so undeservedly. In 1805, at age seventy-one, she returned to her memoirs one last time in order to give her own account of the events of 1762 so that King Sunjo, her grandson (then fifteen years old), could do justice to her natal family when he became older. She writes that her life was "one long series of disasters, and was like a well-frayed cotton thread," and that each word of the memoirs was soaked with her heart's blood and her tears.[19]

Hanjungnok is thus steeped in what Koreans call *han,* a distillation of long accumulated yet unredressed bitterness and sorrow. And that is probably why most scholars have construed the title to mean "Records Made in Distress" rather than "Records Made in Idleness." (The *han* in the title—which was not of Lady Hong's making—could be read as either distress or idleness. Both readings have been used in different editions of the memoirs.) In either case, its splendid though antique prose style, steeped in Lady Hong's passionate grief, lamentation, and rage, make *Hanjungnok* a work of unforgettable vividness, drama, and insight and one of the great memoirs composed in hangŭl.

Inhyon Wanghu chŏn is altogether different, more a carefully shaped work of historical fiction than history. It presents the exemplary life of Queen Inhyŏn, who was married to King Sukchong in 1681 when she was fourteen years old and deposed eight years later for childlessness and alleged jealousy,[20] only to be reinstated after five years by the remorseful king. Closely linked to this main story is that of the rise and fall of Lady Chang, who is portrayed not only as a rival to Queen Inhyŏn but also her exact opposite both in character and behavior: she is violently jealous, cunning, unscrupulous, and deceitful. Installed as queen in place of Queen Inhyŏn, Lady Chang produces an heir to the throne, thereby enjoying half a dozen years of royal favor and queenly powers. But when Queen

Inhyŏn is reinstated Lady Chang is dethroned. Subsequently she is also accused of causing Queen Inhyŏn's death through sorcery, which finally leads to her own death by poison. Thus both in form and in content *Inhyŏn Wanghu chŏn* is a carefully shaped moral tale in praise of virtue and castigation of evil.

The careful design of the novel is revealed not only in the contrasting characterization and fortunes of Queen Inhyŏn and Lady Chang but also in certain contrasting scenes that mark the key points in the ever-changing fortunes of the rival queens. There is an exact, though reverse, parallel between the fortunes of the two women: as Queen Inhyŏn's fortunes fall Lady Chang's rise, and as Queen Inhyŏn's rise, Lady Chang's fall. The vicissitudes of the two queens' fortunes are clearly shown in their formal enthronement, dethronment, and re-enthronment and by the exposure of Lady Chang's crimes and her death by poison. In addition, the novel provides two sets of contrasting scenes that further dramatize Queen Inhyŏn's fortunes.

One of these scenes centers in the observance of Queen Inhyŏn's birthday, the other in a series of processions that mark the three key stages of the queen's life: her arrival at the palace at age fourteen to marry King Sukchong; her expulsion from the palace in disgrace eight years later; and her triumphant return to the palace after five years of lonely confinement in her parents' mansion. Her first arrival at the palace was appropriately resplendent: "The royal colors with images of the dragon and phoenix, along with banners and golden halberds and battle-axes, all signifying sovereign power. . . ."[21] Eight years later, dethroned and at the nadir of her fortunes, she is driven from the palace on foot with nothing but the clothes on her back. So impatient is the king to see her gone. The description of this second procession scene is not only somber and precise but unusually realistic:

> Repeated orders for the queen to hasten her departure arrived from the angry king. The messenger who had been sent to the queen's family house for a palanquin returned without one, and reported that he had found only a few women servants there. The

ladies-in-waiting then managed to improvise a decent vehicle by covering the top of a city palanquin with a silk cloth. As they hastened into the palace with the hired palanquin, the queen was already passing by the Kyŏngmuk Hall on foot. Riding in the hastily-prepared palanquin, she left the palace by the Yogum Gate. Seven or eight maids and ladies-in-waiting followed the palanquin, wailing loudly. How miserable and shabby the procession was compared with the pomp and stateliness of the procession that had first brought her into the palace! Heaven seemed to sympathize with her misfortune, for dark clouds covered the sky as the palanquin left.[22]

Five years later when she returns to the palace and royal favor, the procession, we are told, is "magnificent and stately," even more so than when she first arrived at the palace. She is escorted this time by "several thousand soldiers of the royal guard, ministers and other high-ranking officials."[23]

The other set of contrasting scenes, focusing on the king's radically shifting attitudes towards Queen Inhyŏn as reflected in the observance of her birthday, is no less dramatic. It happens that her birthday falls on the twenty-third day of the fourth moon, just before her dethronement. The king forbids all celebrations or even any mention of the birthday. Instead, he announces to the assembled ministers and high officials his decision to dethrone the queen. But five years later, on the very same date, "the king, remembering this anniversary, sent delicacies with a letter of greeting, and issued an order to all the palaces in the capital to send tribute to her [Queen Inhyŏn]."[24] Soon afterwards she is welcomed back to the palace and reinstated as queen consort. The symmetry of these contrasting scenes tellingly illustrates Queen Inhyŏn's ever-turning wheel of fortune.

In *Inhyŏn Wanghu chŏn*, as in many traditional Chosŏn stories, the characterization of virtuous or evil characters seems to aim not at realism but rather at moral allegory. Each character appears more as a type of ideal virtue or utter depravity than as a believable human being. It is this exaggerated exemplariness or evilness that makes *Inhyŏn Wanghu chŏn* less believable than either *Hanjungnok* or *Kyech'uk ilgi*. For example, the virtue of Queen Inhyŏn and of

Pak T'ae-bo, the most exemplary and loyal of the scholar-officials in the story, seems so exaggerated that they seem hardly human.

This unreality is readily apparent if we compare the virtuous characters in *Inhyŏn Wanghu chŏn* with those in *Hanjungnok*. Let us examine two passages, one from each work, presenting carefully nurtured exemplary young girls from good yangban families. There is a marked difference in the way the two girls are portrayed. The first passage describes Queen Inhyŏn in her early teens, perhaps one or two years before she is chosen to become King Sukchong's second queen:

> In her retiring disposition, brilliant virtues, outstanding fidelity and modest nature, she was a model young lady. Sitting serenely in her chamber, she emanated the warmth of spring sunshine. Her graceful movements inspired such lofty and awesome feelings that those who saw her were reminded of a spray of plum-blossom in the snow and filled with the reverence experienced when suddenly finding oneself in a grove of evergreens under a bleak sky. Thus the love of her parents was redoubled, and the admiration of her kindred near and far grew till her fair name was gradually known to the world.[25]

Very little of this passage reminds us of a living, flesh-and-blood girl of twelve or thirteen. It is a set piece describing an imaginary, perfect young woman. The passage from *Hanjungnok,* on the other hand, presents a quite different picture. We see at once how much more realistically Lady Hong describes her first night in the palace after she was selected to be consort to the crown prince. She was nine years old at the time.

> Being surrounded by palace ladies, I was unable to sleep; I wanted Mother at my side. I was unhappy without her and could easily imagine how sadness must weigh heavily upon her heart. Lady-in-waiting Ch'oe, however, was strict and bereft of human feelings. She explained, "The laws of the kingdom do not allow you to stay on, My Lady," and with that, had sent Mother away,

so that I was unable to get any sleep. There was no human being as inconsiderate as she![26]

How vivid the voice of this distressed little girl who is suddenly thrust into a situation at once awesome and awfully uncomfortable. We can feel her sorrow and distress over her sudden separation from her mother and her having to sleep in a strange place sandwiched between two total strangers. It is an experience all too humanly felt.

In *Inhyŏn Wanghu chŏn,* even when virtuous characters suffer horribly, it is difficult for us to empathize with their suffering because they endure it so serenely. Perhaps this is why the evil characters in this story seem more human and believable than the virtuous ones. For example, Lady Chang, unlike the saintly Queen Inhyŏn, is unable to submerge herself entirely in the Confucian ideal of a virtuous and uncomplaining wife. Her rage, her jealousy, even her attempts to bring destruction upon her saintly rival are plausible, for she has traveled a long, hard road to her present position, and it seems quite natural that she should cling desperately to what she has attained. To a modern reader, therefore, the most believable and poignant passages in the story are likely to be those describing Lady Chang's bitter anguish, outrage, and misbehavior.

After enjoying the king's love and favor for half a dozen years and producing the long-awaited heir to the throne, she is dethroned by the king without a word of explanation. How could anyone blame her for being outraged by the king's inexplicable, irresponsible behavior? She vents her anger and frustration upon her little son, the crown prince, since the king himself is obviously untouchable. And when the king forbids the crown prince to visit her, the little boy objects tearfully to this cruelty: "Why am I not allowed to see my own mother?"[27] Her world crumbling all around her, deserted by the king and forcibly separated from her own son, Lady Chang is forced to watch with deadly jealousy Queen Inhyŏn's happy return to royal favor:

> When Lady Chang wandered at night around the inner palace where Queen Min [Inhyŏn] dwelt, she heard through the windows

the happy sounds of family life. As she stood outside listening to the queen, the king and the crown prince, she was obsessed with thoughts of vengeance.[28]

Even in her death agony, still defiant as she vomits blood, she is a more human figure than the saintly Queen Inhyŏn. Her fiery end seems to perfectly fit her tragic life.

The formal symmetry of the story insists on the stark moral contrast between Queen Inhyŏn and Lady Chang. We are meant to see the two women as exemplars of virtue and evil. But because Lady Chang is drawn with so much more realism, she seems not so much the source of evil as simply another victim of a greater source of evil. That source, though never explicitly stated, appears to be the total immunity, and hence total irresponsibility, of royal power. Because the king can do no wrong, he can and does become arbitrary and utterly irresponsible, with complete impunity. After eight years with Queen Inhyŏn he discards her in favor of Lady Chang, and after favoring Lady Chang for half a dozen years (during which she bears not only an heir but another son who dies in infancy), he discards her and reinstates Queen Inhyŏn. Thus Queen Inhyŏn, Pak T'ae-bo, Lady Chang, and the crown prince are all victims of King Sukchong's totally irresponsible behavior.

In all three works of palace literature examined here, the character of the monarch receives the most unflattering portrayal. Much of the tragedy in these works, so much of the suffering and the loss of so many innocent lives, appears to result from royal abuse of power. In all three works the king is portrayed as not only selfish, petty, lustful, and immature but also cruel, blind, arbitrary, and irresponsible. And these are works by palace women who had intimate knowledge of life within the palace.

Is there, then, a woman's point of view in these works? According to Kim Yong-suk, the underlying theme of Chosŏn women's writing is the representation of *han*, that quality mentioned earlier in conjunction with *Hanjungnok*. It is the han of being born a woman in Chosŏn dynasty Korea, where to be a woman was to be an inferior being.[29] Is not Professor Kim's suggestion borne out in these three works of palace literature? In fact, the title of Lady Hong's memoirs seems to characterize all three works, for each is essentially a record composed in distress or sorrow. And as we shall see, this theme of han is not limited to palace literature alone; it marks the works of Chosŏn women writers generally, regardless of their station in life.

Poetry

The shijo is the best-loved and most widely read and composed of classical Korean poetic forms. But of more than 4,000 surviving classical shijo poems, only 92 can be ascribed to women on the basis of diction and content, and of these only 59 are attributable to known women authors. Among these, no more than half a dozen are the poems of women of yangban families; the rest are the works of kisaeng, professional entertainers.[30] I cite these figures to show the overall paucity of published works by women during the Chosŏn dynasty.[31] For it is no exaggeration to say that besides the three works of palace literature previously discussed and the 92 classical shijo just mentioned, there are only a handful of published works by Chosŏn dynasty women either in hangŭl or in hanmun.

This extreme paucity of published works seems clearly tied to the status of Chosŏn women. During the Chosŏn dynasty a woman's sphere was thought to be entirely domestic. Except for kisaeng—who by law belonged to the lowest social class—women, and especially wellborn women, were to have no public life at all, for this was the sole preserve of wellborn men. Since the Confucian principle of namjon yŏbi (literally, "elevation of men and subjection of women") applied to all areas of public life during the Chosŏn period, all avenues of public participation were closed to women. At the same time women were expected to adhere strictly to such antifemale Confucian codes of conduct as the Three Tenets of Obedience and the Seven Evils for Expelling a Wife.[32]

Nowhere was this separation between men's and women's spheres so clearly drawn as in scholarship and writing. Since women were discouraged from pursuing either endeavor, it was a rare woman who wrote, and an even rarer woman who exhibited her learning or literary gifts in public. According to Yi Ik, a much-respected *Shirhak* (Practical Learning) scholar of the eighteenth century, "reading and learning are the domains of men. For a woman it is enough if she knows the Confucian virtues of diligence, frugality, and chastity. If a woman disobeys these virtues, she will bring disgrace to the family."[33] Furthermore, one of the seven rules of appropriate behavior for a married woman was that "she should not indulge in study or literature because they were considered improper for a woman."[34] Lack of learning was thought to be more conducive to virtuousness in a woman;[35] women of marked intelligence and artistic talent were thought to be "ill-fated."[36]

Despite all these obstacles, a number of women became learned, wrote, and even published, not only in hangŭl but in hanmun as well. As Chang Tŏk-sun has pointed out, these were extraordinary women, even odd or eccentric women, who clearly went against the grain of Chosŏn dynasty Korea, defying the antifemale mores and ideology of their society. Most of these women were extraordinary by birth, inclination, or circumstances: women who grew up in households of scholars where they could learn alongside their brothers; women with learned grandmothers or mothers who were willing to teach them; women who through their own innate gifts were driven to learn and write, often becoming "problem women," such as Hŏ Nansŏrhŏn; and finally talented kisaeng, who had to be accomplished in learning and literature because it was their job to entertain wellborn and learned men.[37] The most illuminating examples among these extraordinary women were probably Shin Saimdang (1504–1551), mother of the famous scholar-statesman Yi I (Yulgok); Hŏ Nansŏrhŏn (1563–1589), sister of Hŏ Kyun, author of *Hong Kiltong chŏn* (The Tale of Hong Kiltong); Hwang Chin-i (c. 1506–1544), the Songdo kisaeng famous for her beauty, wit, and poetic composition; and Hongnang, another sixteenth-century kisaeng of exceptional beauty and wit.

Lady Shin seems to have been an exemplary woman in every way: as daughter, daughter-in-law, wife, mistress of the household, and mother. She displayed her artistic gifts from an early age, and numerous episodes about her brilliant skill in painting have survived to this day. Although she seems to have been highly accomplished in both art and learning, extraordinary for a woman of her time, only two of her poems, both in hanmun, have survived. In this respect, too, she was perhaps in perfect conformity with the mores of her society, which discouraged wellborn women from public exhibition of their learning or literary accomplishments.

The two surviving poems both deal with her deeply felt homesickness, an emotion perhaps all the more intense because her elderly mother lived alone in Kangnŭng, quite a distance away. The first poem appears to have been composed as she journeyed toward the capital over the high mountain pass of Taegwallyŏng:

> Leaving behind my aged mother at home
> My heart aches on this lonely journey to Seoul.
> Looking back toward Pukch'on far away
> I see the white clouds drifting above a mountain in
> twilight.[38]

In the second poem Lady Shin, now living in the capital, recalls the familiar scenes of her natal home and experiences intense longing and anxiety for her mother:

> My home is one thousand li away
> over mountains one upon another.
> But I yearn to go back day and night,
> in sleep or awake.
> The solitary moon over Hansŏngjŏng pavilion,
> A streak of wind past Kyŏngp'odae beach,
> Seagulls scatter from the sand
> and again gather together.
> Fishing boats sail in and out on the sea.
> When could I ever again tread

the path to Kangnŭng
To sit beside my mother and sew with her?[39]

A fragment of another hanmun poem of hers has survived, a mere two lines of what must have been a longer poem. Here is a rough translation of this striking piece:

Every night I pray to the moon,
That I will see you again in this life.[40]

Because her poems are so vivid and moving we very much regret that more of Lady Shin's work has not survived, especially poems she might have written in hangŭl. Her surviving work, probably no more than a small part of all she wrote, shows that even her extraordinary successes did not exempt her from the intense grief Chosŏn women generally experienced upon marriage, because of the near permanent separation from their parents and other family members. In an age when the strict code of conduct for a married woman made it difficult to visit her parents' home no matter how close by, how much more difficult it must have been for Lady Shin to visit her family home in distant Kangnŭng! That she was a favorite daughter of her parents and was devoted to them probably made her suffering that much more intense. Kim Yong-suk mentions a telling episode, part of an account of Lady Shin given by her son, Yulgok, which adds to our mental picture of her: Lady Shin would sometimes ask one of the maids to play the *kayagŭm,* a traditional Korean string instrument, and while listening to the music she would sob quietly.[41]

No other Chosŏn woman's life more clearly underscores the tragic plight of a gifted woman than Hŏ Nansŏrhŏn's.[42] Throughout her short life she had to struggle against restrictions, not the least of which was the absolute subordination of women to men in Chosŏn dynasty Korea. Nansŏrhŏn was a spirited, beautiful daughter of a high-ranking scholar-official, a woman whose poetic gifts had been recognized from early childhood and who had been personally tutored by one of the notable poets of the age. Could such a woman become an utterly silent, acquiescent, obedient daughter-in-law and wife as prescribed by their society? Many gifted Chosŏn dynasty women were able to do so, extinguishing whatever individuality or creativity they possessed. But not Hŏ Nansŏrhŏn. Self-expression through poetry could not be denied her even after marriage, when, as a popular saying had it, a married woman was expected to be deaf for the first three years, dumb for the next three, and blind for another three.[43]

Into her poetry she seems to have poured out all her sorrows as well as her dreams. In "Kyuwŏn ka" (A Woman's Sorrow), her sole surviving hangŭl poem, a kasa of fifty lines, she vividly portrays her unhappiness. Because of the evil karma of past, present, and future and a chance connection made in this world, the poet is married to "a shallow, lightweight playboy of the capital."[44] (Nansŏrhŏn seems to have been married to an intellectually inferior man who failed to appreciate her as a woman, wife, or poet.) Her daily life is careworn and she feels she is treading on thin ice. What intensifies her pain and bitterness is her dawning awareness of the rapid and irretrievable passage of her youth. This is why the poem begins with the following lines:

> The day before yesterday I was young,
>> but today I am already aging.
> It is no use recalling
>> the joyful days of my youth.

It is this juxtaposition of the relentless passage of time with the futility and emptiness of her marriage that gives intensity and poignance to the poem. It is as if the passage of time mocks and accentuates her deepening sorrow over the loss of her youth and beauty. In vain she tries to hush her clamoring heart. Alone in an empty room, awaiting the return of her uncaring husband, she watches the relentless procession of the seasons: the plum blossoms outside her window bloom, fade, and fall, spring after spring. She keeps her vigil on a bitterly cold winter night, but when summer returns, the drizzle of a long summer day makes her heart ache just as much. In the absence of her beloved she unwraps and hugs a lute to play a tune. When she tries to sleep, the rustling of leaves and the chirping of insects keep her awake. Lamenting her unhappiness, she recalls the story of the Weaver and the Herdboy in the sky. Even though separated by the Milky Way, they never miss their yearly rendezvous. What unpassable river, then, has kept her husband apart from her without a word for all these years? As the poem ends, she wonders if anyone in the world could be as wretched as she: can she go on living with so much grief? "Kyuwŏn ka" is thus a poem of great intensity packed with vivid images of bitter disappointments and sorrow. The tone and substance of the poem are unified by this strong current of bitterness and grief, which is kept barely under control throughout.

Hŏ Nansŏrhŏn's miseries did not end with her unhappy marriage. The death of her children and the exile of her older brother, victimized by the vicious political factionalism of the time, added to her unhappiness. In "For My Brother Hagok," from the single volume of her hanmun poems that has survived, she writes movingly of her grief for her older brother living in exile far from the capital:

> The candlelight shines low
>   on the dark window,
> Fireflies flit across the housetops.
> As the night grows colder,
> I hear autumn leaves rustle to the ground.
> There's been no news for some time
>   from your place of exile.
> Because of you,
> My mind is never free from worry.
> Thinking of a distant temple,
> I see a deserted hillside
> Filled with the radiance of the moon.[45]

"Mourning My Children" is perhaps the most heartbreaking of her poems:

Last year I lost my beloved daughter,
This year I lost my son.
Alas, this woeful ground of Kangnŭng!
A pair of mounds stand face to face.
The wind blows through the white birch
And the ghostly lights flicker in the woods.
I call to your spirits by burning paper money,
By pouring wine on your mounds.
Do you, the spirits of brother and sister,
Play together fondly each night!
This child growing inside me
Dare I hope it will grow safely to full term?
In vain I chant a magic verse of propitiation,
Tears of blood and sorrow swallow up my voice.[46]

Rarely did Nansŏrhŏn write of a woman's happiness or good fortune. She seems to have identified most deeply with the pain and sorrow of suffering women, regardless of their social status. She wrote of a displaced court favorite, but she also wrote repeatedly, as in "A Poor Woman," of poor, solitary women:

She weaves through the night without rest.
The rattling of the loom sounds lonesome.
This roll of silk in the loom,
Whose dress will it make when it is finished?
Her hand clasps the metal scissors,
The chill of the night stiffens all her fingers.
For others she has made bridal clothes,
Year after year alone in her room.[47]

The more gifted and spirited a woman was in Chosŏn dynasty Korea, the more doomed she seems to have been. Hŏ Nansŏrhŏn died at age twenty-seven, preceded in death by all her children. Just before her death she is supposed to have burned a roomful of her poetry manuscripts. After her death Hŏ Kyun, her younger brother, compiled a volume of her hanmun poetry from what he and other family members had preserved and it is these poems that have come down to us.

No one in the history of classical Korean literature composed lovelier, more lyrical love poems than the kisaeng poets. Because of their peculiar status in Chosŏn society, they alone of all the women were free to sing of their love for men. Hwang Chin-i and Hongnang—the best among them—have left us love poems of incomparable loveliness and poignancy. Although their poetic legacy is scanty—six shijo by Hwang Chin-i, one by Hongnang, and a handful by others—how much poorer Korean classical poetry would be without them. As a whole their poetry is a passionate celebration of love, but their problematic relationships with their yangban client-lovers gives the celebration an unmistakable tinge of regret, sorrow, and bitterness. Even in the midst of their passionate trysts they seem obsessed with thoughts of the imminent parting, and even their joyful expectation of the next meeting seems colored by their realization of the temporariness and precariousness of their love. It is this double awareness that gives the poems their incomparable poignancy.

Another quality that sets the shijo by Hwang Chin-i and Hongnang apart from most other classical shijo is the purity of their Korean diction. The best of Hwang Chin-i's shijo are composed almost entirely in simple, easy, and delicate vernacular Korean words. So too is the one shijo by Hongnang. In fact, if we were to arrange Hwang Chin-i's six surviving shijo in the order of purity of their Korean diction, we would find that the two with the fewest Sino-Korean words are the two most lyrical and lovely. One of those includes just a single hanmun word—*chŏng,* meaning feeling—while the other has just two. Here is the first of those two shijo:

> Alas, what have I done?
> Didn't I know how I would yearn?
> Had I but bid him stay,
> how could he have gone? But stubborn

> I sent him away,
>   and now such longing learn![48]

In a fascinating discussion of this shijo David R. McCann points to an exceptional item of artistry in its contruction. Nearly all classical Korean poems have end-stopped lines. That is, the end of a verse line constitutes its conclusion both in sound and in sense. But this poem differs, because the end of the second line runs on to the beginning of the third, resulting in added emphasis to this particular portion of the poem:

> ... But stubborn
> I sent him away ...

Clearly these two half-lines form the pivot of the entire poem. The additional stress given to them by the poet's extraordinary deviation from traditional poetics adds to their significance both in sound and in sense, further intensifying the pain and chagrin the poet feels because of the separation she herself has brought on. Thus, what seems so artless is in fact the effect of a great deal of art.

The second of the two shijo is the most famous and best loved of Hwang Chin-i's poems.

> Tongittal kinakin pam ŭl
>   han hŏri rŭl pŏhyŏnaeyŏ
> Ch'unp'ung nipul are
>   sŏri sŏri nŏhŏttaga
> Ŏron nim oshin nal pam iŏttŭn
>   kubi kubi p'yŏrira.

(Recall David McCann's excellent translation of this shijo, reprinted in chapter 5.) Consider the lovely lilt and feel of its simple and exquisite Korean syllables and words, such as "*kinakin*" in the first line, "*sŏri sŏri*" in the second, and "*kubi kubi*" in the last. "*Sŏri sŏri*" and "*kubi kubi*" represent two diametrically opposed activities: *sŏri sŏri* describes the feeling as well as the action of carefully folding something over and over again, while *kubi kubi* describes the feeling and action of spreading something out to lengthen it. Together they convey the poet's passionate longing for her lover during the long, dark winter nights as well as the joyful expectancy with which she awaits her lover's return with the coming of spring.

The least lyrical of Hwang Chin-i's shijo has the most hanmun words and phrases, but even here we can see the poet's consummate artistry. For this shijo is less lyrical not because it is a poor work but because it is a different kind of poem, a satirical poem, and its hanmun words and phrases help give a keen edge to its satire. One of those phrases, *pyŏkkyesu,* meaning a jade-green mountain stream, is a pun on the name of the man whom the poet satirizes, a member of the royal family who is supposed to have boasted of his indifference to Hwang Chin-i's charm.

Another shijo just as purely Korean in diction and just as lyrical as Hwang Chin-i's best is the single surviving poem by Hongnang, a sixteenth-century kisaeng of Kyŏngsŏng, in the far northeastern corner of Korea. It is addressed to her lover, Ch'oe Kyŏng-ch'ang, a scholar-official who was returning to the capital after an extended tour of duty in Kyŏngsŏng. Here is Richard Rutt's superb translation:

> I chose a wild willow branch
> > and plucked it to send it to you.
> I want you to plant it
> > by the window where you sleep.
> When new leaves open in the night rains,
> > think it is I that have come to you.[49]

The only Sino-Korean word in the poem is *ch'ang,* meaning window, but it is a word that had practically become Korean through long usage. The diction of the poem can therefore be considered entirely Korean. What a lovely and boldly suggestive poem it is! Hongnang sends her beloved a wild willow branch, a living token of her love, and asks him to keep it by the window of his bed-chamber so that she will be close by him at night, if not in flesh then in love and spirit. And during the night, moistened by gentle rain—another very suggestive image—the wild willow, which is nothing less than her surrogate self, will revive so that when he looks on it in the morning it will seem as fresh and alive as when she first plucked it to send to him. That Hongnang should wish to send her beloved a *wild* willow branch seems especially fitting. For she is Ch'oe Kyŏng-ch'ang's wild, out-of-bounds, untamed love, just as his wife back in the capital is his legal, domesticated spouse, the mother of his children, and a daughter-in-law to his parents. So impressed was Ch'oe by the poem that he translated it into hanmun, one of the highest compliments a man of his position and education could have paid at the time to a kisaeng.[50]

Because kisaeng were *ch'ŏnmin*, the lowest class socially and legally, their relationship with yangban men was at once extraordinarily free and circumscribed. They could entertain them, drink or recite poetry with them, and even become their lovers, but they could seldom become members of their families. They were merely their playmates; they could seldom become their wives, their parents' daughters-in-law, or the mothers of their children. Because of their low social and legal status, their contact with yangban men had to be temporary and occasional. When the liaison was over they were abandoned or repudiated. They would find themselves at the mercy of their wellborn men both physically and emotionally if they should fall in love with them. They had to wait for them to visit, then try to hold them as long as they could, but they knew that sooner or later their lovers would return to their families, their wives, and their own social class. It was the fate of kisaeng to be abandoned by their yangban men sooner or later. And perhaps this explains why most *kisaeng* love poems, though the loveliest and most lyrical celebrations of love in all of classical Korean poetry, are so often tinged with the sadness of parting and the chagrin of fruitless and futile longing.

This insidious aspect of the kisaeng's relationship to the yangban is clearly illustrated by what happened to the lovers Hongnang and

Ch'oe Kyŏng-chang. Three years after their separation Hong-nang, hearing that Ch'oe was seriously ill, hastened to his bedside, traveling nonstop for seven days and nights. The news of this reunion shocked the court. It was considered especially deplorable because it occurred during a time of national mourning for the death of a member of the royal family. Ch'oe was therefore summarily dismissed from office and Hongnang sent packing to Kyŏngsŏng.[51]

There was another twist to this excruciating double bind the kisaeng suffered. While absolute fidelity was required of a well-born Chosŏn dynasty woman, it was the last thing expected of a kisaeng, since she was supposed to be ready to entertain whichever man commanded her services. A crucial part of the famous story of Ch'unhyang hinges on this availability. Ch'unhyang, daughter of a kisaeng, is automatically expected to be a kisaeng as well. Thus, when the new district magistrate demands her services, she has no socially or legally approved way of resisting. Ch'unhyang nearly loses her life by resisting his demands and remaining faithful to the man she loves. Her last-minute rescue and triumph by a sort of *deus ex machina* is just that, the wildest daydream come true. And perhaps that is why the story of Ch'unhyang is the most popular and enduring of classical Korean stories. A kisaeng's freedom was her privilege as well her bondage, as the Ch'unhyang story so painfully illustrates. Though free in her intercourse with men, she had to remain free of emotional entanglements as well, because these were precisely what was forbidden to her. It was as if Chosŏn women were not allowed to be whole but were merely a stunted half serving either as a wife who bore children and managed the family and household, or as an occasional lover and playmate.

Unpublished Poetry: Kyubang Kasa

Only a small number of poems by women were published during the Chosŏn dynasty. But as one of the most remarkable research findings in the field of Korean literature has shown, Chosŏn yangban women in fact wrote thousands of kasa in hangŭl.[52] Though these poems were unpublished, they circulated widely among family members, relatives, and close friends, especially in the southern and middle provinces of Korea. This mostly anonymous poetry, published only since 1948,[53] has come to be known as *kyubang* or *naebang* kasa (inner-room kasa), after the women's quarters in the traditional Korean home. The consensus among Korean scholars is that they originated in the first decades of the eighteenth century, during the early years of King Yŏngjo's reign, just when the kasa of literati men had reached its peak in development.

What seems so significant about this paucity of *published* works coupled with the abundance of *unpublished* poetry is how it so accurately reflects the social status of wellborn women during the Chosŏn dynasty. As we have seen, women were supposed to have no public life at all, the public realm being the sole preserve of men. They were expected to live out their lives entirely within the inner quarters of their household. And since it was only within that sphere that they could express themselves, it was there that their compositions were allowed to circulate and flourish. To the world outside the family circle it was as if their poetic compositions did not exist, and this is why I have called these kasa the unpublished poetry of Chosŏn dynasty women. Most simply defined, the kasa is the freest of the traditional poetic forms. Its basic line is similar to the typical shijo line and consists of two half-lines, each comprising two words of either three and four syllables or four and four syllables. Having no set stanzaic division, a kasa can range from two dozen lines to over a thousand. Most kasa are narrative and descriptive.

According to Kwŏn Yŏng-ch'ŏl, the leading scholar on kyubang kasa, the largest number of these anonymous poems were admonitions addressed to daughters and granddaughters by mothers and grandmothers—and occasionally by fathers and grandfathers—on the occasion of the young women's marriage and departure from home. Young brides from good families would thus arrive at their husband's household with half a dozen or more of these kasa hand-copied on rolls of paper called *turumari*. These prized possessions would remind them of their beloved parents and their natal home.

And when it became their daughter's turn to be married and leave home, they would give her the turumari they had brought from their own home along with any additional poems they might have composed or copied in the meantime from other women of their extended families or village.[54] This tradition undoubtedly accounts for the preponderance among the kyubang kasa of the *kyenyŏ ka* (song of admonition), the parents' instructions on how their daughter must conduct herself in her new home.

The subject matter of kyubang kasa was not limited to parental admonitions. It ranged from joyous occasions such as a son's success in the state examination or seasonal get-togethers of women of related families, to women's complaints about their lives as neglected wives, teenage widows, or old maids. Many kyubang kasa have a single subject, but more have multiple themes, in which the poet touches on various matters that preoccupy her at the moment. For example, a kasa that begins with a parental admonition to a daughter on her proper conduct as bride might include not only celebrations of the family's good fortune but also bitter complaints about the poet's own life, or even descriptions of a seasonal get-together. Some poems thus stray quite far from the topic announced by the title.[55]

Altogether Professor Kwŏn sees more than twenty-one separate categories of kyubang kasa. Two of these are primary categories—the kyenyŏ ka (the earliest as well as numerically the largest) and the *chat'an ka* (song of lament), thematically the most significant. The rest are derivatives of these two. Next in importance is the *hwajŏn ka* (song of an outing for flower-viewing), celebrating the seasonal outings of women of related households or of the village.[56] In number of extant poems, the hwajŏn ka ranks second only to the kyenyŏ ka.

The kyenyŏ ka early became nearly formulaic in both form and content because the pattern of an exemplary bride had become fixed through a number of homiletic texts produced both in hanmun and in hangŭl for her edification. These texts were drawn from the various Confucian and neo-Confucian classic texts on the subject. Two of the most influential were Queen Sohye's

Naehun (Admonitory Words to Women), the first such work in hangŭl, published in 1475, and *Yŏgyesŏ* (Words of Admonition to Daughters; c. 1635), composed in hangŭl by the noted Confucian scholar-statesman Song Shi-yŏl. Others of similar content and purpose soon followed. *Sohak* (Book of Lesser Learning), *Yŏllyŏ chŏn* (Five Biographies of Faithful Women), *Yŏgye* (Moral Teaching for Women), and *Yŏch'ik* (Rules of Conduct for Women) were translated into hangŭl and published during the reign of King Chungjong (1506–1544).[57]

Most kyenyŏ ka were thus modeled on the framework established by these homiletic works. The main guidelines were rephrased in easier and more intimate idiomatic language, often reflecting the personal concerns of the mothers or grandmothers who composed them. They gave specific instructions on how the young bride should conduct herself as daughter-in-law, wife, and mistress of the household, on all occasions. As we shall see in the following example, some of these guidelines were specific and detailed.

The standard kyenyŏ ka begins with anxious words addressed to the daughter, words elicited by the nature of the occasion itself, the daughter's more or less permanent leave-taking from her family home. Take the following poem, for example:

> Listen, my dear child,
> Tomorrow is the day of your leave-taking.
> Leaving your parents' home,
> You will be entering your husband's.
> As your heart must be,
> So is mine, also uneasy.
> Your things loaded on a white horse
> And the gilt saddle firmly tied down,
> As I send you off out the gate,
> I have much advice to give you. . . .[58]

After these prefatory words the kasa counsels the young bride on eleven specific items, usually in the following order. The first nine consist of things she should remember: (1) how to fulfill her filial duties to her parents-in-law; (2) how to serve her husband faithfully; (3) how to deal with such close relatives as brothers- and sisters-in-law; (4) how to perform the annual ancestral rites; (5) how to deal with guests; (6) how to govern herself during pregnancy; (7) how to raise children; (8) how to deal with servants; and (9) how to manage the household and its economy. The last two items deal with what the bride ought not to do: (10) never leave the husband's house, especially at night, without permission except in an emergency; and (11) never relax her watchfulness over all the foregoing matters, because they represent the sum total of wisdom handed down through the ages. To these eleven items the parent might add a few last-minute words of advice gleaned from her own experiences.[59]

The kyenyŏ ka is thus a manual of exemplary behavior for a young bride. Its express purpose is to inculcate the womanly virtues of total obedience and submergence of the self in conformity with the male-centered Confucian ethos of the Chosŏn dynasty, as exemplified in such creeds as *samjong chido* (the three tenets of obedience for women) and *namjon yŏbi* (elevation of man and subjection of woman).[60] We see this aspect of the kyenyŏ ka in its many details. For example, in the section on serving her husband the poem counsels the bride to think of him as if he were "heaven." She should therefore never relax in his presence, whether in language, posture, or attitude; she should not eat at the same table with him or use the same closet for her clothes; and she should never show jealousy or resentment toward the secondary consorts.

According to Professor Kwŏn, approximately 480 out of 700 of these admonitory kasa that he has studied include the eleven prescriptive items along with the prefatory and closing verses.[61] The standard kyenyŏ ka, however, tells us little about the young bride's actual life in her husband's household. We learn almost nothing about the heartaches, hardships, and joys she must have experienced as a young woman—most likely she was still in her teens—in a totally unfamiliar household. There, at least during the first few years, she was expected to be little more than a servant, to be utterly obedient, and to please not only her parents-in-law and husband but also her brothers- and sisters-in-law.

As literature, therefore, the standard kyenyŏ ka are not as interesting as the nonstandard kyenyŏ ka, which deviate markedly both in form and content even though they too are finally admonitory in intent. Although the nonstandard kyenyŏ ka too were composed mostly by mothers for their newly married daughters, the most interesting of them do not adhere strictly to the eleven-item format described earlier. Instead, their admonitory verses are based largely on the mother's own experiences as a young bride: her own trials and the lessons gleaned from them. For this reason the verses seem to deal more with what is actual than with what is merely ideal.

One of the most interesting nonstandard kyenyŏ ka is a lengthy, widely known kasa called "Poksŏn hwaŭm ka" (Song of Blessing, Virtue, Calamity, and Indecency). What makes this poem by a Lady Yi so remarkable is that her admonition to her daughter is based on her own dramatic story of raising her husband's household from poverty to affluence mostly through her own intelligence and hard work. The dramatic power of the poem is enhanced by the insertion, just before the conclusion, of the life story of another woman, Kwoettong Ŏmi,[62] whose career forms a moral and dramatic contrast to Lady Yi's by tracing an exactly parallel but opposite course.

"Poksŏn hwaŭm ka" begins with the following lines:

> People of this world, listen to my story.
> Unhappy I am that I was born a woman.
> A great-granddaughter of Sir Yi Han and
> The granddaughter of the scholar Chŏng. . . .[63]

Brought up in a comfortable scholarly household, she not only masters by age fifteen all the classical texts deemed appropriate to the education of a wellborn woman, but is also much praised for her beauty and virtue. At fifteen she is married off to the scion of another notable family. But when she arrives at her in-laws' home she discovers that the family has sunk into dismal poverty. The neighbors wonder out loud if such a well-brought-up bride will be able to survive the difficulties that await her. The following day her older brother, who has accompanied her, grows concerned over the abject poverty of the groom's family and suggests to his sister:

> Since the family's situation is as it is,
> It is no use. Let us return home.
> I cannot leave you here alone.
> How can I let my dear sister endure such hardships!
> So let us return home. Don't say another word.

To which our heroine replies that she is determined to submit to the life assigned her by heaven. But she asks him not to tell their parents about the poverty of her husband's family.

The poet sustains the drama of her poem by using vivid and dramatic details. On the third day, when the new bride ventures into the kitchen for the first time, she finds it "utterly empty except for a kettle," and when in desperation she sends a maid-servant to a neighbor to borrow some rice, the servant is unceremoniously sent back with a curt message that the previously loaned rice should be paid back first. Now begins the bride's trials and hardships. She sells or pawns her own valuables to buy food for the household, but even then she has to go without food for a day or two, because "after serving the parents-in-law and her husband / And dividing [the rice] among the servants there is nothing left for her."

Prosperity comes slowly. Neglected fields are brought back into cultivation; silk threads produced from silkworms are woven into colorful silk garments. Savings grow slowly but steadily, thrift leading to affluence. The family house is repaired and reroofed in tile, and to cap off the family's rising fortune, her husband takes the top place in the state examination.

The poem concludes right after the interpolated story of Kwoettong Ŏmi. The closing verses, as befits a kyenyŏ ka, are the mother's admonitions. She counsels her daughter to take to heart the lessons from her own life story and from the contrasting life story of Kwoettong Ŏmi.[64]

"Poksŏn hwaŭm ka," though very different from the standard kyenyŏ ka, nevertheless belongs to the same genre, for both in form and in content it is basically admonitory. What distinguishes it from the standard kyenyŏ ka as well as making it so much more interesting as literature is that it achieves its moral by an artfully constructed real-life story. In the process, while upholding the ideal of prescribed duties and responsibilities of the bride, it also gives us glimpses of what the actual life of a newly married woman of even a very good family must have been like: a life of hardships and burdensome obligations laid upon a young woman suddenly thrust into the unfamiliar and often unsympathetic environment of her husband's family.

In the extremely restricted lives of yangban women there seems to have been one day a year when they were permitted to have an outing together to view the spring flowers, share a picnic lunch, and generally enjoy themselves. On such occasions the more literary among them would compose a kasa celebrating the outing. These were the hwajŏn ka and hundreds of them have been collected. According to Kwŏn, the form and content of hwajŏn ka, like kyenyŏ ka, became standardized over the years, incorporating several set items framed by prefatory and concluding stanzas.

Beginning with a call to join the outing, the standard hwajŏn ka proceeded through a series of appeals to women, including complaints about their hard lot and the need to make the best of their restricted lives:

> . . . in this life as evanescent as clouds in the sky,
> Why should we labor all our lives,
> Denying ourselves any games or entertainments?
> Had we been born talented and handsome men,
> We would have dressed fashionably and
> Traveled to the southern or northern capital,
> To this or that celebrated place.[65]

How pitiful their lot, the kasa goes on to say. As women, they cannot enjoy a single one of the numerous games men can enjoy freely. Denied the freedom to travel even a few miles outside the family compound, they hold precious their once-a-year outing. Of all the seasons, spring is best, neither too hot nor too cold. So an auspicious spring day is chosen, invitations are sent to women of other yangban families in the village, and after the permission of the parents-in-law is obtained, each woman anxiously awaits the day of the outing.

The poem next describes the careful preparation for the outing. The site cannot be too distant, since the outing has to be a one-day event, and it must be a place of natural beauty, with azaleas and other spring flowers in bloom. Each woman prepares a separate dish, and also the material for the flower-cakes that will be the centerpiece of their picnic feast.

Who would come to the outing?

> Mrs. Kim from the village down below,
> Mrs. Pak from the village up above,
> The eldest daughter-in-law from the family in back,
> The new daughter-in-law from the family out front,
> An old maid from the north village,
> A young lady from the south village.
> They all came, their servants walking in front of them. . . .

Some of the women pilfer a few cakes to carry back to their husbands while others devour large cakes one after another. These hints of comedy are quite rare in standard kyubang kasa. After the women have picked flowers, feasted on the flower-cakes, and composed celebratory kasa the outing draws to a close and each woman bids fond farewell to the others. Unless there is a village wedding or some similar event, they will not meet again until the following spring.[66]

Again it is the nonstandard hwajŏn ka that is more interesting than the standard variety. Let's consider a popular hwajŏn ka that turns out to be nothing at all like a standard hwajŏn ka. Although it begins in a typical fashion, summoning village women to a spring outing, it then diverges markedly from the standard format. While several women begin reciting, singing, dancing, and generally enjoying themselves, a young widow breaks into a tearful account of her sad life. Married at thirteen, widowed at sixteen, she is unable to forget her deceased husband, constantly seeing his face in her mind's eye. Sleeplessness torments her; though she wishes to sleep, hoping she might glimpse him in her dreams, she cannot. "I wish so much to die, for how can I go on like this?" she concludes. These words are like a cue for the entrance of a woman nicknamed Tendong Ŏmi. And now the poem slips into a lengthy, detailed account of this woman's tragicomic, calamity-filled life. Since this takes up nearly two thirds of the poem, the tone and character are no longer those of a typical hwajŏn ka.

Tendong Ŏmi is a long-suffering woman, four times widowed. Every time she marries and starts to get ahead financially, a calamity strikes, leaving her forlorn, bereaved, and impoverished. There is something at once tragic and comic about the way she is pursued so relentlessly and inexplicably by calamities. Her first husband dies in a fall from a high-rising swing; the second is taken by a raging epidemic; the third is buried in a landslide; and the fourth perishes in a fire, which also badly burns her only son, a son more precious because he is born so late in her life. This last calamity accounts for her nickname *Tendong* (a burned child) *Ŏmi* (ma).

After this final calamity she returns to her native village, and there on a spring outing of the wellborn women of the village she gets to tell about her life. Tendong Ŏmi's story effects a catharsis not only for the young widow—whose weeping had triggered the account—but also for the rest of the women. The young widow forgets her own grief in her pity for Tendong Ŏmi, and so does everyone else. The cheerful mood of their outing is restored, the women's grief and troubles purged by the pity they feel for the overwhelming tragedy of Tendong Ŏmi's life. As if to underscore the renewed cheerfulness of the occasion, the poem concludes with an oddly repetitive, formulaic, and lengthy enumeration of the various felicities of spring.[67]

While the kyenyŏ ka and hwajŏn ka make up the most numerous groups of the kyubang kasa, the most powerful variety is the chat'an ka, the kasa born of Chosŏn women's bitter rage against their own condition in life. Whereas the kyenyŏ ka generally affirms and upholds the mores of Chosŏn society, the chat'an ka rails against the moral and legal injustices of that society toward its women.[68] In instance after instance the nameless poet pours out her unhappiness at being born a woman. The following chat'an ka, for example, speaks in bitter self-mockery:

> The life of a woman is nothing less than
> A record of hardships. . . .
> Upon the birth of a daughter,
> Even a beggar frowns;
> Upon the birth of a daughter,
> Even a passer-by commiserates . . . .[69]

In another chat'an ka the poet laments:

> For what wrongs committed in our previous life,
> Are we born a woman in this?
> To be parted from our beloved parents
> When we're barely fifteen,
> To be forever parted from our beloved father and mother
> It is sad, unutterably sad.[70]

In these unattributed poems we hear, perhaps more directly than in any other works of classical Korean literature, the heart-felt complaints of Chosŏn women. We hear of married women who are allowed no freedom of movement, unable to visit their natal family a few miles away; young women having no say as to whom or when to marry; and young widows condemned to self-immolation or to lifelong loneliness by the laws and mores of the times. One poet, for example, likens her married life to the fate of "an innocent prisoner confined deep in a dungeon, / Shedding tears day and night like a condemned person."[71] Forbidden to step out of the family compound, she is not allowed to visit her natal home until ten years have passed, unless one of her parents dies in the meantime. Another poet vents rage and bitterness over her total lack of freedom:

> Not allowed to play, as I please,
> Even one game out of ten;
> Not permitted to visit a place
> Even a few miles distant. . . .

Awaiting in vain her in-laws' permission to visit "her natal home less than a few miles away, / Hoping to make the visit this year or next," she mocks her impotence, fearing she might never make the visit in her parents' lifetime.[72]

Some of the saddest and yet funniest of these poems deal with the plight of women who, through no fault of their own, were left unmarried until age forty or fifty, and this at a time when most women were married off before they were twenty, and frequently during their early teens. But since the responsibility for a daughter's marriage rested entirely with the parents, a failure to marry is seen to be the parents' fault. Either they lack initiative on behalf of their daughter or they entertain unrealistic expectations concerning the prospective groom's family background or career prospects. "Nochŏ'nyŏ ka" (Song of an Old Maid), a chat'an ka widely disseminated in the North Kyŏngsang area, describes the tragicomedy of a forty-year-old spinster:

> My parents, so close-minded, genteel in their poverty,
> Care only about appearances.
> Because they are foolish and impractical in everyday
>   matters,
> Their only daughter grows old unmarried.
> Listen to my complaint, as I sit alone in a bleak empty
>   room,
> Turning this way and that, unable to sleep. . . .
> My parents do not talk of marriage at all, only of
>   poverty.

> A guest comes—might he be a go-between?
> I call the servant boy over to ask.
> But he's only a dun from the medicine shop.
> A letter arrives—might it be a proposal?
> I call the boy over to ask.
> But it's only the notice of an uncle's death.

Toward the end of the poem the narrator looks at herself in the mirror. Though she finds herself still youthful and attractive from this angle or that, she tells herself it's futile; it's simply her stupid fate to live and die an old maid. The poem ends with the following lines:

> Without a mate on a long night
> And without a friend on a long day,
> Sitting or lying down,
> I return to my melancholy thoughts,
> Regretting I cannot put an end
> To this wretched life.[73]

The most poignant chat'an ka have to do with the sad plight of young widows condemned to a kind of living death by the moral, legal, and social constraints placed upon them by society. It was their duty to maintain outwardly their lifelong fidelity to their deceased husband, however much they might suffer inwardly from their heartache and solitude. One such chat'an ka, "Ch'ŏng-ch'un kwabu ka" (Song of a Youthful Widow), begins as follows:

> Though all things between heaven and earth undergo
>   changes,
> Unchangeable is my fate,
> The life of loneliness in an empty room.[74]

As the poem proceeds so does the intensity of the widow's unhappiness:

Why did my lord—affectionate, kind, loving,
   well-spoken,
Handsome, forthright, and tall—
Why still young, did he have to become a ghost of the
   nether world? . . .
I still see his every gesture and movement before my
   eyes,
And his deathbed words still ring in my ears. . . .
I've become ill from crying, and day follows upon
   day.
Even now, 604 days later, my tears have not
   ceased. . . .
The more I think of my life, the sicker I become.
Shall I cut off my hair and become a nun,
And study devotion to the Buddha?
Shall I become a bodhisattva with prayer beads around
   my neck?
If I can't do either, *I shall get drunk and go mad.*
   [emphasis added]

Wrung out of a wellborn Chosŏn woman, these are indeed desperate words. We can feel the depth of her grief. Widowed at sixteen, she is condemned to spend her youth in tears. At times, "imagining she hears her lord's voice, / Happily she goes outdoors, only to find / It's the call of a lone gull that's lost its mate / In the moonlit autumn night."

In "Kwabu ch'ŏngsang ka" (Song of a Young Widow), another young widow, alone in her room, grieves while watching the buds on the fruit trees swell and bloom, moist with the misty spring rain. Her cry of sorrow deepens as the poem proceeds, and at the end her plea to the spirit of her deceased husband becomes a shriek of self-abandonment: "Take me, take me, I beg you, take me where you are, / For I cannot, I cannot, I cannot keep to my empty room."[75]

What is the literary significance of all these kyubang kasa, and what is their place in classical Korean literature? Taken as a whole, these poems' historical and literary significance are unquestioned, for they represent the single most significant voice of wellborn Chosŏn women speaking of their lives. Here as in no other genre of classical Korean literature we hear women speaking to us directly and intimately of their heartaches, frustrations, and sorrows as well as of their felicities and joys. But because so many of these poems have been unearthed and published and because so many are not only lengthy but also lacking in the vividness, freshness, and individuality of good poetry, it is essential that the thousands of surviving kyubang kasa be subjected to careful sifting. The truly exceptional kyubang kasa need to be identified, annotated, and thoroughly discussed so that they may take their rightful place in the canon of classical Korean literature.

Notes

1. Kim Yong-suk, *Hanguk yŏsok sa* (A History of the Customs and Manners of Korean Women) (Seoul: Minŭm sa, 1989), 86–89.
2. Chang Tŏk-sun, *Hanguk munhak ŭi yŏnwŏn kwa hyŏnjang* (Korean Literature from Early Times to the Present) (Seoul: Chimmundang, 1986), 409. According to Professor Chang, Korean women kept hangŭl literature alive both as writers and readers, for even the hangŭl stories written by anonymous men were written mostly for women.
3. Ibid., 408–12.
4. In the case of *Inhyŏn Wanghu chŏn,* the question of authorship has not yet been definitively settled. See *Virtuous Women: Three Classic Korean Novels,* trans. Richard Rutt and Kim Chong-un (Seoul: Royal Asiatic Society, Korea Branch, 1974), 182–4.
5. Kang Han-yŏng, ed., *Kyech'uk ilgi* (Diary of the Year of the Black Ox, 1613) (Seoul: Ŭryu munhwa sa, 1974), 63, 64–66.
6. Ki-baik Lee [Yi Ki-baek], *A New History of Korea,* trans. Edward W. Wagner with Edward J. Shultz (Cambridge: Harvard University Press, 1984), 215.
7. Ibid.
8. Kim Yong-suk, *Chosŏn yŏryu munhak ŭi yŏngu* (A Study of Chosŏn Dynasty Women's Literature) (Seoul: Sungmyŏng yŏja taehakkyo ch'ulp'ansa, 1979), 353.
9. Ibid., 266–71, 310–53.
10. Trans. Peter H. Lee, in *Anthology of Korean Literature,* rev. ed., comp. and ed. Peter H. Lee (Honolulu: University of Hawaii Press, 1992), 239–40.
11. Ibid., 240.
12. *Memoirs of a Korean Queen,* ed. and trans. Yang-hi Choe-Wall (London and New York: Kegan Paul International, 1985), 34.
13. Ibid., 38.

14. Ibid., 39.

15. Ibid., 46.

16. Ibid., 70.

17. Ibid., 104.

18. Ibid.

19. Ibid., 32, 33.

20. During the Chosŏn dynasty jealousy was one of seven failings for which a wife could be divorced by her husband. In addition to Queen Inhyŏn's childlessness and supposed jealousy, the intense and often violent political struggle between the Westerner and Southerner factions that flared up whenever a new queen or crown prince was to be installed probably played a part in her deposition, but *Inhyŏn Wanghu chŏn* makes little mention of this.

21. *Virtuous Women,* trans. Rutt and Kim, 187.

22. Ibid., 205.

23. Ibid., 212.

24. Ibid., 211.

25. Ibid., 185.

26. Trans. Lee, in *Anthology of Korean Literature,* comp. and ed. Lee, 242.

27. *Virtuous Women,* trans. Rutt and Kim, 216.

28. Ibid., 217.

29. Kim Yong-suk, *Chosŏn yŏryu munhak ŭi yŏngu,* 19–42.

30. Hwang Chaegun, *Hanguk kojŏn yŏryu shi yŏngu* (A Study of Classical Korean Poetry by Women) (Seoul: Chimmundang), 1985, 55–59.

31. By *published* I mean those works that were circulated fairly widely outside the circle of immediate family, relations, and close friends in either manuscript or printed form.

32. The Three Tenets of Obedience were obedience to one's father before marriage, to one's husband after marriage, and to one's son after the death of the husband. The Seven Evils for Expelling a Wife were disobedience to parents-in-law; failure to bear a son; adultery; jealousy (of concubines or other women); hereditary or incurable illness; garrulousness; and theft. See Yung-Chung Kim, ed. and trans. *Women of Korea: A History from Ancient Times to 1945* (Seoul: Ewha University Press, 1979), 52–3.

33. Cited in ibid., 154.

34. Ibid., 157.

35. Kim Yong-suk, *Hanguk yŏsok sa,* 86.

36. *Women of Korea,* 162.

37. Chang Tŏk-sun, *Hanguk munhak ŭi yŏnwŏn kwa hyŏnjang,* 408.

38. Kim Huran, "Shin Saimdang: Perfect Woman and Artist," *Koreana* 4, no. 2 (1990):48. Translator not cited.

39. Ibid.

40. Kim Tal-chin, trans and ed., *Hanguk hanshi* (Korean Poetry in Chinese) (Seoul: Minŭmsa, 1989), III:54. This volume contains both the hanmun original and Kim's hangŭl translation.

41. Kim Yong-suk, *Chosŏn yŏryu munhak ŭi yŏngu,* 37.

42. Her real given name was Ch'o-hŭi; Nansŏrhŏn was her pen name.

43. Kim Yong-suk, *Chosŏn yŏryu munhak ŭi yŏngu*, 14.

44. This and the following excerpt from the poem are from Im Ki-chung, ed., *Chosŏnjo ŭi kasa* (The Kasa of the Chosŏn Dynasty) (Seoul: Sŏngmungak, 1979), 119–23.

45. Kim Tal-chin, trans. and ed., *Hanguk hanshi,* III: 74.

46. Ibid., III, 72.

47. Quoted in Kim Yong-suk, *Chosŏn yŏryu munhak ŭi yŏngu,* 369.

48. David R. McCann, *Form and Freedom in Korean Poetry* (Leiden: E.J. Brill, 1988), 22.

49. Richard Rutt, *The Bamboo Grove* (Berkeley: University of California Press, 1971), 76

50. Chang Tŏk-sun, *Hanguk munhak sa* (A History of Korean Literature) (Seoul: Tonghwa munhwa sa, 1987), 337.

51. Ibid.

52. The latest estimate by Kwŏn Yŏng-ch'ŏl is in the tens of thousands; he himself has collected over six thousand. See Kwŏn Yŏng-ch'ŏl, *Kyubang kasa kangnon* (The Forms of Kyubang Kasa) (Seoul: Hyŏngsŏl ch'ulp'ansa, 1986), 3. This number may have to be reduced because it probably includes many variants of the same poems. See Kim Tong-yŏng, *Kasa munhak nongo* (Essays on Kasa Literature) (Seoul: Hyŏngsŏl ch'ulp'ansa, 1977), 101–2.

53. McCann, *Form and Freedom in Korean Poetry,* 49.

54. Kwŏn Yŏng-ch'ŏl, *Kyubang kasa yŏngu* (A Study of Kyubang Kasa), (Seoul: Iu ch'ulp'ansa, 1980), 23–24.

55. Ibid., 30–31.

56. Kwŏn Yŏng-ch'ŏl, *Kyubang kasa kangnon,* 9.

57. See Chang Tŏk-sun, *Hanguk munhak sa,* 284–85; *Women of Korea,* ed. and trans. Yung-Chung Kim, 156; Cho Tong-il, *Hanguk munhak t'ongsa* (A Comprehensive History of Korean Literature), 2nd ed. (Seoul: Chishik sanŏp sa, 1989), III:334; and Kwŏn Yŏng-ch'ŏl, *Kyubang kasa yŏngu,* 183–84. Professor Kwŏn traces the general framework of the kyenyŏ ka specifically to Chu Hsi's "Rules to Abide By for Women" in *Chuja kahun* (Family Precepts of Chu Hsi).

58. Kwŏn Yŏng-ch'ŏl, *Kyubang kasa yŏngu,* 175. The poem cited here is actually a model constructed by Professor Kwŏn from hundreds of standard kyenyŏ ka in his collection.

59. Ibid., 73–181.

60. Kwŏn Yŏng-ch'ŏl, *Kyubang kasa kangnon,* 9–10.

61. Kwŏn Yŏng-ch'ŏl, *Kyubang kasa yŏngu,* 173.

62. This name is nearly impossible to translate accurately. Literally "Dog-Turd Mother," it probably means a worthless or no-good mother. Its colloquial and comic tone suggests that the interpolated story is a different kind of kasa, most likely a *sŏmin kasa* (kasa of the common people).

63. This and the following quotations from the poem are my translations of the version in Kwŏn Yŏng-ch'ŏl, *Kyubang kasa yŏngu,* 303–11.

64. Ibid.

65. As with the kyenyŏ ka quoted on p. 125, here Professor Kwŏn makes up a standard hwajŏn ka out of the common items he found in 525 actual hwajŏn ka.

Kwŏn Yŏng-ch'ŏl, ed., *Kasa munhak taegye* (An Encyclopedia of Kasa) vol. I, *Kyubang kasa* (Sŏngnam: Hanguk chŏngshin munhwa yŏnguwŏn, 1979), 259.

66. Ibid., 259–70. The hwajŏn ka must have been popular, for they elicited a few mock hwajŏn ka, mildly satirical poems usually composed by men who were near relations of the women whose kasa they were making fun of.

67. Kim Mun-gi, *Sŏmin kasa yŏngu* (A Study of the Kasa of Common People) (Seoul: Hyŏngsŏl ch'ulp'ansa, 1983), 310–39.

68. Kwŏn Yŏng-ch'ŏl, *Kyubang kasa kangnon*, 9–10.

69. Ibid., 19.

70. Ibid.

71. Ibid., 40.

72. Ibid., 43.

73. Kwŏn Yŏng-ch'ŏl, ed., *Kasa munhak taegye, vol. I, Kyubang kasa,* 127. See also Kwŏn Yŏng-ch'ŏl, *Kyubang kasa kangnon,* 25–26. The popularity and wide dissemination of this particular kasa probably owe to its appeal to a popular audience as an oral narrative, for it was part of the repertoire of itinerant popular singers called *kwangdae,* who could adapt their performance to the occasion and audience. And this probably explains its survival in many variant forms. Kim Mun-gi argues in his *Sŏmin kasa yŏngu* that kasa such as "Noch'ŏnyŏ ka" blur the distinction between kyubang kasa and sŏmin kasa because they were composed and recited for women of both yangban and ordinary households. This development occurred in part because poor yangban in the eighteenth and nineteenth centuries became more and more like ordinary people. It seems to have been this contact with popular culture that gave the kyubang kasa its comic quality, which is absent in most standard kyubang kasa.

74. This and the following excerpts from the poem are translations of the Korean original in Kwŏn Yŏng-ch'ŏl, *Kyubang kasa kangnon,* 65–67.

75. Ibid., 70.

7

Hŏ Kyun: *Hong Kiltong chŏn* and the Hanmun Lives

Hŏ Kyun (1569–1618) is best known for *Hong Kiltong chŏn* (The Tale of Hong Kiltong), supposedly the first novel composed in hangŭl. But we must not think of *Hong Kiltong chŏn* as a novel in the modern sense of the word, for it is a fairly short tale with little believable development either in characterization or in plot. Rather, this work can best be appreciated in its historical context together with Hŏ Kyun's other works, particularly his hanmun essays and lives (*chŏn*).

Hong Kiltong chŏn has long been a popular favorite. For it is, first of all, an entertaining story full of wondrous and heroic adventures perfectly tailored to appeal to a mass audience. It was composed in hangŭl rather than hanmun, thereby making it accessible to ordinary men and women of Hŏ Kyun's times. But its enduring popularity is perhaps explained by the timelessness of its story more than by anything else: the mythic hero—here, Hong Kiltong, championing the cause of the illegitimate and the poor—who brings justice to an unjust world.

Hong Kiltong is the second son of a Minister Hong. Stigmatized from an early age by his illegitimacy (his mother was a maidservant) he suffers humiliating rebukes even from the household servants. All the normal paths to social and professional advancement are barred to him because of his illegitimacy, making him a social outcast even though he is the son of a minister. Frustrated and bitter, he sets himself to the study of martial arts.

One moonlit night his father scolds him for his late-night exer-
cises: "What's gotten into you—not asleep so late at night?"
Kiltong, answering respectfully, blurts out the cause of his rest-
lessness:

> "I have always enjoyed the moonlight, but there is something else
> tonight. While Heaven created all things with the idea that man-
> kind is the most precious, how can I be called a man when such
> value does not extend to me?"
>
> The minister knew what he meant, but scolded, "What are you
> talking about?"
>
> Kiltong bowed twice and explained. "Though I grow to man-
> hood by the vigor your excellency has passed to me, and realize
> the profound debt I owe for your gift of life and mother's up-
> bringing, my life still bears one great sorrow: how can I regard
> myself as a man when I can address neither my father as *father*
> nor my brother as *brother*?" He wiped off his flowing tears with
> the sleeve of his jacket.[1]

Throughout the story it is this grievance against the unjust treat-
ment of the illegitimate that motivates Hong Kiltong. For example, in a talk with his elder brother late in the story, Kiltong
suggests that had he been allowed to address his father as "Father" and his brother as "Brother," he might not have left home
and become the leader of bandits. Still later, explaining his behavior to the king, he says:

> "It would have been my wish respectfully to serve Your Majesty
> for eternity. But I was born the child of a lowly maid-servant and
> was denied the career a civil officer might enjoy in the Office of
> Special Counselors or that of a military officer in the Liaison
> Office. So it was that I took to roaming the country as I pleased,
> and it was only by raising havoc with government offices and
> offending the court itself that I finally succeeded in bringing my
> plight to the attention of the throne."[2]

Following an abortive attempt on his life by his father's jealous concubine, Kiltong leaves home and becomes the leader of a

gang of bandits. At this point in the story the grievances of Kiltong and other illegitimate sons appear to become joined with the grievances of other social outcasts, such as this group of bandits. Under Kiltong's leadership the bandits collectively adopt the name "Save-the-Poor" and commit themselves to social and economic justice.

Their first target is Haein Monastery, one of the principal Buddhist monasteries in the south, a wealthy landowning institution that exploits many tenant farmers despite its supposed devotion to otherworldly ideals. Next, going through every province in Korea, Kiltong and his band stop "in each township to confiscate the wealth unjustly gained by magistrates and to succor the poor and helpless. But they never preyed upon the common people nor ever once touched the rightful property of the state. So it was that the bandits submitted to Kiltong's will."[3] Later Kiltong states that he never once "abused the common people but confiscated only the wealth of magistrates amassed through exploitation of the people."[4]

The story thus appeals not only to our natural sympathy for those unjustly relegated to the bottom of the social ladder, but also to our dream of seeing justice reign in the world. Kiltong's marvelous exploits, incredible as they are, thus represent the fictional fulfillment of our fondest hopes and daydreams. Hence the story's enduring popularity.

But there is more to *Hong Kiltong chŏn* than wish fulfillment. For the work was produced in the aftermath of the devastations brought on the people and the country by the Japanese invasions of 1592 and 1597. This watershed event in the history of the Chosŏn dynasty (1392–1910) exposed the impotence, ineptitude, and corruption of the ruling classes. The country's rulers were found to be utterly incompetent and also indifferent to the suffering of the people. We get a glimpse of the explosiveness of popular resentment against the rulers in such incidents as the torching of the palace complex in the capital by the slave population, especially those buildings housing the slave registers, even before the Japanese forces entered the capital.[5]

"Suffering through the invasions of the Japanese and Manchus," writes So Jae-yŏng, "internally people came more and more to distrust the court officials and yangban who constituted the ruling classes, while externally, fired by concern for their nation and hatred of enemy nations, they came to yearn for the emergence of a national hero."[6] Throughout the long years of the Japanese and Manchu invasions (the latter in 1627 and 1636), people saw only too clearly that their rulers could not and would not protect them. This led inevitably to the deepening of popular disaffection with the ruling classes and to widespread hopes for the emergence of a national leadership that would defend the people as well as right the wrongs they suffered. Such was part of the historical and ideological background of *Hong Kiltong chŏn.*

In fact, Hŏ Kyun had written about just such a leader as Hong Kiltong in one of his hanmun essays, "Homin ron" (On Heroic Leaders). In this essay Hŏ divides the masses into three categories: *wŏnmin,* the embittered; *hangmin,* the blind followers; and *homin*, the heroic leaders. Wŏnmin and hangmin, though bitterly oppressed by their rulers, will not rise up until led by the homin. When the most opportune moment arrives, the homin come to the fore, drawing to them the wŏnmin and hangmin, who by themselves lack the energy, spirit, and organizational power to challenge the regime. Led by the homin, "people are to be feared the most in the world," more than "tigers and floods," writes Hŏ.[7]

Kiltong is thus a fictional version of a homin, and the bandits he comes to lead are the wŏnmin and hangmin awaiting such a leader. Kiltong also seems to embody the frustrations and unhappiness Hŏ Kyun himself had been suffering for some time. Although Hŏ was wellborn, the brilliant, successful, and legitimate son of a high-ranking scholar-official, he felt deeply the injustice of the legal exclusion of illegitimate sons from government posts. He was convinced that such discrimination was wrong and injurious not just to the illegitimate sons but to the whole nation. For as he argues in an essay called "Yujae ron" (On Innate Gifts), Heaven hands out innate gifts without any regard to a person's social or family background. To exclude a gifted person from public service just because he is illegitimate is, therefore, nothing less than to spurn the gift of Heaven.[8] Such a national policy was not only foolish but harmful, Hŏ argued, especially to a small country such as Korea whose talent pool was limited in comparison with that of a country like China.

All Hŏ Kyun had to do was dramatize and develop these themes with details drawn from life, and he would have had a powerful story of enduring significance. Curiously, however, in *Hong Kiltong chŏn* Hŏ does little more than state these themes. Could he have been unacquainted with the necessary details and examples from real life with which to flesh out these themes? This doesn't seem likely. For in *Hong Kiltong chŏn* he does provide a few such examples—Kiltong's not being allowed to call his father "Father" or his brother "Brother" and his being scorned by his father's servants. And it was probably because he had befriended gifted illegitimate sons like Yi Tal, who taught poetry to both his elder sister, Hŏ Nansŏrhŏn, and himself, that he was able to identify with their misfortunes and give such a telling representation of their grievances as he does in the story of Kiltong.

But *Hong Kiltong chŏn* cries out for more such details from real life as well as for plot developments based on them. This is especially true of the plight of the wŏnmin and hangmin, who make up most of the bandits in *Hong Kiltong chŏn*. Originally these characters were probably landless peasants and slaves. Why had they become bandits? What natural or man-made calamities had driven them to their desperate way of life? What unspeakable abuses or hardships had their families suffered? Instead of Kiltong's wondrous vanishing acts and magical fabrication of eight Kiltong look-alikes the author could have told us about the former lives of those bandits. And when Kiltong transforms his company of bandits into the Save-the-Poor band, Hŏ could have given us some of the reasons for the change and for its ready acceptance by the bandits. Even a few such real-life details could have made the story much more vivid, powerful, and believable.

So why did Hŏ Kyun withhold them from his story? Surely it couldn't have been because he was unacquainted with them. During the first Japanese invasion, that of 1592, while fleeing to Kangwŏn Province, where he lost both his wife and first son,[9] Hŏ had witnessed the terrible sufferings of ordinary people preyed upon not only by enemy soldiers but also by local officials. One of his poems gives a wrenching description of what he witnessed as he and his family fled farther north toward Hamgyŏng Province:

> As the sun is about to set,
> An old woman is wailing in the ruins of a village.
> Her disheveled hair looks as if blighted by frost,
> And her eyes are shadowed as if by dusk.
> Her husband is in a cold jail cell,
> Because he cannot pay off the money he owes,
> And her son has gone off with the royal army.
> Her house has been burned down to the base of the
>   pillars;
> Hiding out in the woods she has lost even her hemp
>   petticoat.
> She has no work, she has no wish even to go on
>   living,
> Why is the petty clerk of the district
>   calling for her at the gate?[10]

Hŏ must have witnessed many other instances of suffering by those he calls wŏnmin and hangmin. Why didn't he make use of them in *Hong Kiltong chŏn*? Instead, because the hero uses magic to transcend the limitations on ordinary humans, the story becomes less believable. Kiltong's incredible, ever triumphant exploits have the effect of trivializing the story and undercutting its potential worth as a work of social criticism.

Why didn't Hŏ Kyun make Kiltong and his followers struggle realistically against their difficulties? After all, the illegitimate sons and the poor suffered failures and defeats in their attempts to improve their economic and social status. Wouldn't a story of such failures and their deadly consequences have been truer to the life of the times and more believable than what the author actually gives us? And wouldn't such a story, though grim and tragic, have more powerfully dramatized Hŏ's theme of protest against the wrongs suffered by the illegitimate and poor?

It may be that we are asking Hŏ Kyun to do what he never intended. Not having been brought up in the tradition of fictional realism, as we have been, he may never have considered the idea of developing his characters and plot realistically. Perhaps he intended simply to present his main concerns—the grievances of the illegitimate and the poor under the misrule of a bankrupt officialdom—to a mass audience as entertainingly as possible. Hence his use of hangŭl and reliance on Kiltong's magical powers. As for real-life details, Hŏ may have believed that they were already too well known to have to be spelled out. Besides, he probably felt that the proper place to spell out these issues for the court and his fellow yangban scholar-officials was in his hanmun essays and poems.

Instead of judging *Hong Kiltong chŏn* by today's literary standards we must try to appreciate what the work actually accomplished. This is why it is essential that we understand the historical, social, and political context of the work. In that context, didn't Hŏ Kyun accomplish what he set out to accomplish? That is, in Hong Kiltong he created a mythic hero who achieves impossible tasks such as unsettling the whole country so much as to compel the king to appoint an illegitimate son as minister of war; righting the wrongs suffered by the common people by confiscating the ill-gotten wealth of local officials, landowners, and Buddhist monasteries; and founding a new kingdom outside Korea, empowering those formerly despised as social outcasts and outlaws. This last item seems especially bold, since the founding of a new kingdom would have been treason had it been attempted within Korea. Since these goals could be achieved in Hŏ Kyun's lifetime only in the realm of imagination, Hŏ chose to give them fictional realization. And even though the story was only a vision to those who had no hope of ever achieving these goals—the illegitimate sons and poor peasants of Hŏ's day—wouldn't such wish fulfillment have provided more comfort and meaning than an account of grim failures and tragedies?

It has been suggested that because Hŏ Kyun wanted his story to appeal to the masses he needed to make it interesting, especially to those who read hangŭl or who needed the story read to them. And his tale of fantastic heroic adventures turned out to be immensely popular for hundreds of years. Had he produced instead a realistic tale of failures and tragedies, it would have been rejected out of hand by his intended audience, even if composed in hangŭl. For the common people would not have wanted to be exposed to more pain than they were already suffering. A story of failures and tragedies therefore, would never have gotten a hearing.

We must also consider the question of official censorship. Hŏ Kyun was undoubtedly limited severely by what the authorities of his time would have tolerated. The limits of that tolerance might have been Hŏ's use of the name of an actual rebel-bandit for the hero of *Hong Kiltong chŏn*. For by doing so Hŏ could have been seen as elevating to the status of a popular hero a historical figure who was condemned and executed. Had he expressed himself more directly with a realistic delineation of the most basic ills of his society, wouldn't he have been found treasonous by the authorities, especially since he chose to write the story in the language of the common people? Kiltong's fantastic exploits, made possible by his magical powers, might therefore have been the mask Hŏ needed to pass off his subversive ideas as harmless fantasies.

Because *Hong Kiltong chŏn* is supposedly the first hangŭl novel, it has been seen as an especially significant work deserving to be examined by itself. But I believe we can better appreciate its significance if we examine it as part of Hŏ Kyun's total surviving work, and especially if we consider it together with his five hanmun lives. These five pieces complement *Hong Kiltong chŏn* in that while the latter has more unreality in its detail, the lives perhaps have more reality. For example, in *Hong Kiltong chŏn* the hero overcomes all adversities, each triumph lifting him higher until he becomes king of an island nation outside Korea. In contrast, the central figure of each of the lives has to resign himself to bitter defeat, frustration, or silent withdrawal from the world. But there are also similarities in theme and detail between *Hong Kiltong chŏn* and the lives. The most striking similarity is that both *Hong Kiltong chŏn* and the lives offer protagonists, each of whom is somewhat of a misfit and nonconformist, an outcast who is given little recognition by the world despite his innate gifts.

The five hanmun lives are "The Life of Master Namgung Tu"; "The Life of Mr. Ŏm, a Recluse"; "The Life of Master Songok, a Recluse"; "The Life of Mr. Chang, a Hermit"; and "The Life of Chang, a Young Man."[11] All of them appear to be based on actual persons the author met at one time or another.

The longest of the five lives is that of Namgung Tu. Namgung is a gifted man of *chungin* origin (the chungin were a hereditary class of functionaries) who early passes his state examination with distinction. As he is about to start his professional career, however, he is struck down by a personal misfortune. Returning without notice to his home in the country, he finds his concubine in an adulterous relationship with a cousin's son, and he kills them both. The local officials, who resent Namgung's nonconformity and unbending pride, quickly arrest and imprison him. But he escapes with the help of his wife, who is then arrested and imprisoned herself and perishes in prison with their daughter.

Now a fugitive, Namgung trains for several years in the mountains under an elderly Taoist master who teaches him the vital powers that ensure long life. But because Namgung lacks one necessary virtue, that of endurance, he fails to qualify as a successor to his master. After seven years in the mountains he returns to society, remarries, and has children. At age eighty-three Namgung pays a visit to Hŏ Kyun and tells his life story. Hŏ tells us that he himself was living then in a place called Puan, having just been dismissed from office in Kongju. Of what Namkung Tu tells him, the most interesting and significant thing seems to be that Hŏ, too, must cultivate the virtue of endurance, because he has all the other qualities necessary for attaining illumination. The story concludes with Hŏ's comments on Namgung's story: impressed with the health and vitality the aged Namgung displays, Hŏ wonders why Koreans have not devoted themselves as much to the study of Taoism as they have to the study of Buddhism.

What are we to make of this story? Was Hŏ Kyun telling his own story in the guise of the mysterious Namkung Tu? For Hŏ, too, though a gifted man who had passed the state examinations with distinction, suffered political and social setbacks throughout his life. These included personal tragedies, official reprimands, dismissals from office, and political reversals, brought on by forces outside his control as well as by the personal failings he was most often accused of, impetuosity and nonconformity. Both Namkung and Hŏ were gifted men who were foiled in their careers by a combination of their own personality traits and misfortunes beyond their control.

The most personal of the lives is perhaps that of Yi Tal, Hŏ's own much-admired teacher of poetry, who suffered from the stigma of illegitimacy throughout his life. According to "The Life of Master Songok, a Recluse" (Songok was Yi's pen name), Yi was a brilliant poet and teacher who could not advance socially or professionally because of his illegitimacy. Despite his outstanding gifts, he was despised and persecuted by many. Ultimately he was reduced to wandering from place to place nearly like a beggar, unable to find a position he deserved. His unbending independence aggravated his difficult situation, because he stooped neither to his social superiors nor to petty officials, thereby earning their enmity. "Although people valued his poetry, they had no use for him. . . . Out of their ignorant jealousy and hatred they ended up killing him, but they could never take away his honored name," writes Hŏ.[12]

According to Hŏ, "in the core of his mind Yi Tal possessed an utter emptiness that allowed his mind to be boundless, and he paid no attention to his livelihood."[13] This is an especially intriguing comment. Is Hŏ suggesting that Yi had attained a kind of

Taoist enlightenment that made possible this disregard for the vicissitudes of his life? And was that perhaps what Hŏ most admired in his mentor and what he himself tried to achieve? Hŏ tells us in conclusion that nearly all of Yi's writings were lost except for four volumes Hŏ himself put together from what he had earlier managed to save.[14]

"The Life of Chang San-in" is perhaps the least interesting though the most puzzling of the lives. Chang is a physician from a family of physicians, both his father and his grandfather having been physicians before him. And what an extraordinary physician he is! He performs all sorts of wondrous feats, reviving dead fish and dead birds, and it seems he could even bring himself back to life. Having foreseen the Japanese invasion of 1592, he withdraws into the mountains just before the calamity strikes but is cut down by the Japanese anyway. That autumn, however, he appears at a friend's place on Kanghwa Island. Four days later he departs, telling his friend he is bound for the Diamond Mountains. Along with "The Life of Namgung Tu" and *Hong Kiltong chŏn,* this strange story seems to show how interested Hŏ Kyun was in the Taoist cult of mysteries and occult powers.

The most intriguing of the five lives is perhaps "The Life of Chang, a Young Man." It is not easy to describe Chang Saeng, the subject of this piece, because mystery envelopes him from the outset. The author himself begins his account with the following words: "I have never been able to find out what manner of man Chang Saeng was."[15] We are told that Chang was a man of exceptional handsomeness and singing ability who lived mostly by begging, and that he lodged for some time with Yi Han, a musician. Clearly Chang was no ordinary beggar, for on his begging rounds he was followed by a crowd of beggars, to whom he gave away most of the abundance of food he obtained.

In addition he is a man of many artistic gifts. After a few drinks he becomes a fabulously talented mimic of all kinds of persons, animals, and birds. He has other talents and mysterious connections in the city as well, which enable him to aid helpless persons in need. One spring day in 1592, the year of the first

Japanese invasion, he drinks a great deal, sings, and dances till nighttime at a crossroads, then falls asleep on a bridge. The following morning he is found dead. And yet later he appears at an important battle against the Japanese at a pass called Choryŏng. In his own words, he is merely gone "to discover an island nation in the heart of the Eastern Sea."[16] After telling a warrior friend how to keep himself safe during the year of the second Japanese invasion (1597), Chang vanishes for good.

From other details given, it appears that Chang was an extraordinarily free-spirited man of great artistic gifts who was sympathetic to the poor and helpless. But the gifts he possessed were obviously not those appreciated by the rigidly Confucian society of Hŏ Kyun's times, all the more so since Chang was a nameless man of uncertain birth. His story is infused with a sense of great loss. Just because Chang was not born into the right social class and therefore has no proper education, he has no way of making use of his extraordinary gifts. A few small favors here and there are all he can do. Living out his life as a sort of beggar and errand boy, he ends it in a feast of drinking, singing, and dancing, dying perhaps out of frustration and discontent, unappreciated by society.

If there is a common thread that runs through the five lives, it appears to be Hŏ Kyun's attempt to explore the meaning of life's so-called successes and failures. All five protagonists are social misfits, and it is this aspect of their lives that Hŏ focuses on because that is what he seems to find admirable in each. He seems to suggest that how we judge a life depends on the set of assumptions and standards we use. A life judged *publicly*, by conventional standards, might appear very different if judged by a different set of assumptions.

Take, for example, Mr. Ŏm, the only one of Hŏ Kyun's five subjects who comes from a yangban family. Even though he is so impoverished that he must cook, gather firewood, and do all the other household chores by himself, he decides not to follow the normal career path of a yangban, which is to pass the provincial and state examinations and become a scholar-official. He is utterly unambitious and devoted solely to caring for his aged mother, and it is for her sake alone that he passes the provincial examination. Once his mother passes away, he has nothing more to do with examinations and lives the exemplary life of a scholar in retirement, declining all job offers by the court. Ŏm's life, therefore, judged by the conventional standards of the time, is far from successful. Yet judged by the standards of Hŏ Kyun and Ŏm himself, it would not necessarily be a failure.

Similarly, Yi Tal—the talented poet and Hŏ Kyun's former mentor—was an utter failure publicly. Scorned for his illegitimacy, unable to secure any appropriate position in society, he became a wanderer. But wasn't his life an extraordinary success judged by a different set of standards? For few people have attained the expansiveness Yi achieved, a freedom of mind that undoubtedly helped make him the great poet he was.

In the life of Chang San-in we can discern a similar dichotomy between public failure and private success. Given his extraordinary medical skills, Chang could have achieved public success, perhaps becoming the royal physician or at least a physician of great fame and wealth. Instead he chose to go into the mountains in preparation for the impending Japanese invasion, and upon returning to life he decides to retire to the Diamond Mountains.

Namkung Tu's life reveals even more clearly the dichotomy between the failure of his public life and the success of his private life. Publicly he is a convicted murderer and a fugitive. Privately, however, his life looks very different. He was provoked to murder by the affair between his mistress and his cousin's son. And if not for his lack of endurance he would have succeeded his Taoist master. Retaining vigor of mind and body until age eighty-three, he attained considerable wisdom. It is this wisdom he imparted to Hŏ Kyun in Puan after Hŏ's dismissal from office in Kongju: "Don't be guilty of secret evil deeds; don't deny the existence of spirits; continue doing good deeds; rid yourself of greed; continue cultivating your mind, and you'll achieve enlightenment."[17]

Chang Saeng's is perhaps the most intriguing case. Publicly

his life is nearly invisible, especially to Hŏ Kyun's own ruling class. To the members of that class he was simply one of the toiling mass of slaves, beggars, bandits, servants, entertainers, and tradesmen who constituted the bottom of Chosŏn society. Publicly, therefore, Chang's life had no significance. But what a difference his life made privately. For he was an unusually free-spirited, generous, and talented man, a man who *made a difference* to those among whom he lived. He made a difference to people from so many walks of life: beggars who followed him around; a maidservant who took music lessons from him and whom he helped in a crisis; a warrior; and a host of unnamed underground characters. He kept his free spirit to the very end, dying unbowed, still dreaming, still dancing, still singing, and perhaps welcoming death in a kind of Taoist embrace of the end of this life. His largeness of spirit enabled him to transcend death: we are told that worms rising from his corpse metamorphosed into winged creatures.[18] His ability to make light of death seems reflected in his remark to his warrior friend: "I'm not really dead. I'm merely going to discover an island nation in the heart of the Eastern Sea."

These lives seem to tell us directly what *Hong Kiltong chŏn* tells us indirectly—that however gifted and virtuous you might be, you got nowhere in Chosŏn society without the right lineage. The five lives thus represent Hŏ Kyun's more sober and realistic appraisal of his society. In them we see Hŏ challenging the mistaken institutional values of the yangban class, his own class, by demanding an end to its collective blindness and a commitment to value a man for his abilities and accomplishments rather than his lineage and social status. For the tragedy of the nation, as Hŏ saw, lay not only in the wasted lives of gifted men but also in the life of the nation itself, for Korea, "a poor and weak nation sandwiched between two barbarian nations," could ill-afford the loss of such men.[19]

Both *Hong Kiltong chŏn* and the hanmun lives show Hŏ Kyun's keen interest in Taoist mysteries and occult powers. Hŏ was also deeply interested in Buddhism throughout his adult years. Though repeatedly censured for it, he never gave up these interests. Why was he so drawn to Buddhism and Taoism, considering he was born and bred in a Confucian household and rose to prominence as a Confucian scholar- official?

The answer seems to be that in Taoism and Buddhism he found a more imaginative, more intuitive, and less worldly alternative to the Confucian world view. He appears to have found in Taoism and especially Sŏn (Zen) Buddhism an escape from the shallowness, narrowness, and excessive worldliness of the Confucian orthodoxy of his time. More a poet than a scholar, interested in all branches of learning, including the Western learning then trickling into Korea from China—he was supposedly the first to import a Catholic hymnal into Korea—Hŏ seems to have sought systems of learning, ethics, and beliefs that opened a path not only to common sense, reason, and logic but also to the world of emotional, subconscious, and instinctual truth and selfhood and even to a kind of otherworldliness. In other words, he seems not to have been content to remain merely a Confucian; he needed to see more, feel more, experience more, and understand more.

In his public life Hŏ pushed for institutional reforms concerning illegitimacy, remarriage for widows, improved security of the northern borders, better training of soldiers, and other measures he thought essential for the health of the nation. In his personal life he seems to have pursued a carefree lifestyle—not only dabbling in Buddhism and Taoism but cultivating the friendship of illegitimate sons and *ch'ŏnmin* (persons of the lowest class), and drinking and womanizing during prescribed periods of mourning. He must have known such behavior would harm his career, and indeed it is remarkable how many times he was dismissed from a post soon after he was appointed. Because of his family connections and recognized brilliance, he continued to be appointed to office. But his appointments were criticized by those at court and he would soon be dismissed for one alleged misdeed or another. After one such dismissal he wrote a poem that appears to express a mixture of relief and ruefulness:

I have long studied many religions
For my mind had nowhere to stop.
I had not yet sent away my wife,
It is harder to stay away from meat.
My youthful dreams have already vanished,
Why should I be troubled by this accusation!
All live in accordance with what they are born to,
My dream is to return to Sangido Monastery. [20]

Hŏ Kyun's tragedy appears to have been that he was a man far ahead of his time. A high-ranking member of a rigidly hierarchical, male-dominated, myopic, and morally bankrupt society, he wanted to live by the light of his own vision and experience, to enjoy inner as well as outer freedom. This perhaps explains his friendships with the marginal and outcast, his interest in Sŏn Buddhism and Taoism—officially frowned upon at the time— and his publication of his beloved sister's poetry after her death. His free and generous mind could not endure the stifling orthodoxy of his own ruling class. He must have felt compelled now and then to transgress the rigid boundaries imposed by officialdom and its Confucian ideology, and this may explain his frequent dismissal from official posts.

Even though he was himself wellborn and rose rapidly to prominence as a scholar-statesman, Hŏ Kyun was deeply distressed by the plight of gifted illegitimate sons. He befriended a number of them and tried in various ways to assist them in their futile effort to gain social and professional acceptance. It is therefore not surprising that he should have composed tales championing the cause of the illegitimate, misfit, nonconformist, and poor, exposing the self-destructive blindness of his own class and society. Perhaps it was his recognition of this narrowness that ultimately led him to turn against his class. Accused of treason in a fierce factional struggle at the court, he was executed in 1618 along with many of his followers. He was fifty years old.

Notes

1. Trans. Marshall R. Pihl in *Anthology of Korean Literature,* rev. ed., comp. and ed. Peter H. Lee (Honolulu: University of Hawaii Press, 1992), 121.

2. Ibid., 141.

3. Ibid., 129–30.

4. Ibid., 137–38.

5. Ki-baik Lee, *A New History of Korea,* trans. Edward W. Wagner with Edward J. Shultz (Cambridge: Harvard University Press, 1984), 210.

6. So Jae-yŏng, "Imbyŏngnan ŭi ch'ungkyŏk kwa munhakchŏk taeŭng" (Literary Response to the Shock of the Japanese and Manchu Invasions), in *Hanguk munhak yŏngu immun* (An Introduction to the Study of Korean Literature), ed. Hwang P'ae-gang, Cho Tong-il, et al., (Seoul: Chishik sanŏp sa, 1982), 419.

7. Yi Yi-hwa, *Hŏ Kyun ŭi saenggak* (Hŏ Kyun's Thought) (Seoul: Yŏgang ch'ulp'ansa, 1991), 87–91.

8. Ibid., 138–39.

9. Ibid., 42.

10. Hŏ Kyŏng-jin, *Hŏ Kyun* (Seoul: P'yŏngmin sa, 1984), 75.

11. My discussion of these five lives is based on the versions in Yi Ka-wŏn, trans. and ed., *Yijo hanmun sosŏlsŏn* (Yi Dynasty Novels in Chinese: Selections) (Seoul: Minjung sŏgwan, 1961).

12. Ibid., 65. Hŏ is speaking figuratively here. Though Yi suffered much persecution, he was never actually killed.

13. Ibid.

14. Ibid.

15. Ibid., 74.

16. Ibid., 77.

17. Ibid., 51

18. Ibid., 77.

19. Quoted from Hŏ's essay "Yujae ron" in Yi Mun-gyu, *Hŏ Kyun sanmunhak yŏngu* (A Study of Hŏ Kyun's Prose Works) (Seoul: Samichwŏn, 1986), 103.

20. Yi Yi-hwa, *Hŏ Kyun ŭi saenggak,* 44.

8

Kuun mong and "Unyong chŏn"

Kuun mong (A Nine Cloud Dream) by Kim Man-jung (1637–1692) is considered by many to be a classic of Chosŏn dynasty prose fiction. Chŏng Pyŏng-uk, for example, has called it "the exemplary work of classical Korean fiction."[1] It has also been described as "the oldest major novel" written in hangŭl, although many scholars now believe that it was composed in hanmun and that the surviving hangŭl versions might therefore be translations.[2] If by a novel we mean prose fiction that gives a faithful and detailed rendering of everyday reality, *Kuun mong* certainly does not qualify. For its story is related neither to T'ang China—the time and locale of the story—nor to seventeenth-century Korea, the supposed time and place of its composition. Instead, *Kuun mong* may best be described as a blend of romance and fairy tale, for it is filled with supernatural occurrences and features the improbable realization of a young man's fondest daydreams of sexual conquests and career successes.

The main story takes place within a dream. (*Kuun mong* is one of a large number of Korean stories with the Chinese character *mong*, "dream," in the title.) In fact, the dream takes up all of the work except for the beginning and end. The hero, Hsing-chen (Sŏng-jin in Korean), is a young Buddhist monk who dreams he is reborn as another person. In form, at least, the story thus resembles one of the earliest Korean stories on record, the Buddhist story of Choshin in *Samguk yusa*. Hsing-chen is the most favored disciple of Master Liu-kuan, and in his dream he is expelled from idyllic Lotus Peak Monastery for flirting with the eight fairy maidens of Lady Wei. He is then reborn as Yang Shao-yu (Yang

So-yu in Korean) in the household of the hermit Yang and his wife Liu in Tang China. The eight fairy maidens of Lady Wei are also expelled. Reborn as beautiful women, they eventually become Shao-yu's two wives and six concubines.

Raised by his mother (the hermit Yang returns to the world of the immortals soon after Shao-yu's birth), Shao-yu grows up to be a handsome youth exceptionally gifted in both literary and martial arts. At sixteen he takes top place in the imperial examination, and soon he is engaged to Jewel, the beautiful and gifted daughter of Minister Cheng. Within a few years, after a succession of extraordinary literary, diplomatic, and military triumphs, Shao-yu is the most successful and favored of the scholar-statesmen at the imperial court. The only incident even resembling a setback occurs when he declines a proposed marriage with Princess Orchid, the daughter of the empress-dowager and the emperor's own sister, because he is engaged to Jewel. (Their nuptial rites have been postponed until Shao-yu can find time to bring his mother to the capital.) When he persists in his refusal he is imprisoned. But a rebellion in Tibet saves him, since the emperor needs him to lead an expeditionary force against the Tibetan rebels. Before his triumphal return from the Tibetan campaign, the impasse arising from Shao-yu's refusal is resolved by Princess Orchid, who persuades her mother to adopt Jewel into the royal family, thereby making it possible for both Jewel and the princess to marry Shao-yu.

When Shao-yu retires after a long, successful career at the imperial court he is granted a palace not far from the capital, which was once a retreat for Hsuan-tsung, the sixth emperor of T'ang. There, surrounded by his two wives, six concubines, and numerous offspring, Shao-yu lives in happiness and splendor. And then one day, as he looks over the former pleasure grounds of Emperor Hsuan-tsung, he is suddenly struck by the realization that "man's life is no more than a moment of time."[3] At just this moment an old monk appears and shocks Shao-yu/Hsing-chen out of his dream and back to his real life as a novice monk in his dingy cell at Lotus Peak Monastery:

The mist disappeared. The old monk had gone. Shao-yu looked round, but the eight women had vanished. The whole terrace and its pavilions had gone too. He was sitting in a little cell on a prayer mat. The fire in the incense burner had died out. The setting moon was shining through the window. He looked down at himself, saw a rosary of a hundred and eight beads around his wrist. He felt his head; it was freshly shaven. He was no longer Yang the Grand Preceptor, he was once more a young monk. His mind was confused, until at last he realized that he was Hsing-chen, the novice at the Lotus Peak Monastery. He remembered: "I was reprimanded by my teacher and was sent to hell. Then I transmigrated and became a son of the Yang family. I came [in] top in the national examination, and became Vice-chancellor of the Imperial Academy. I rose through various offices and finally retired. I married two princesses and was happy with them and six concubines, but it was all a dream. My teacher knew of my wrong thoughts, and made me dream this dream so that I should understand the emptiness of riches and honor and the love between the sexes.[4]

For a supposed classic of Korean prose fiction, *Kuun mong* is a curious work. Not so much because the story is located entirely in Tang China, for it was the fashion of the yangban writers of Kim Man-jung's time to place their stories in early China. Rather, the story seems to have so little to do with the reality of human life as it is lived at any place or time. But it is not difficult to understand why the work has been popular. It is a narrative made lively by high, though unbelievable, adventure and numerous amorous encounters, and the many poems interspersed throughout add to the romance and seeming sophistication of the main characters. The key to the work's popularity, I believe, is that it caters to two contradictory daydreams: great worldly success on the one hand, and total withdrawal from the trials and tribulations of this world on the other. In depicting Shao-yu's great successes, the story offers what must have been the fondest dream of every Confucian scholar-official: high office, exceptional poetic gifts, the love of many beautiful women, and a dozen successful children. But in Shao-yu's ultimate rejection of all these tokens of worldly success, the story also pays lip service to the Buddhist ideal of total withdrawal from this life and its momentary illusions.

Novelistically, however, the central problem with the story of Shao-yu is that it has no development; it begins in adolescence and ends in adolescent daydreams. It is symptomatic of this lack of development that Shao-yu reaches the pinnacle of his knowledge, ability, and wisdom at sixteen. At that age he is already superior to almost every other mortal in manly charms, poetic gifts, musical accomplishments, military strategy, diplomacy, even statesmanship. He has nothing more to learn intellectually, emotionally, or socially about himself or the world. What development there is in his life after age sixteen consists merely of changes in time, place, office, and consorts. Despite his scholarly, military, diplomatic, and romantic achievements, his story is essentially the same experience repeated over and over with only superficial variation. Even in his amorous adventures there is little meaningful growth after his very first encounter, with Chin Ch'ae-bong (for both it is their first brush with love). Although he becomes involved with seven other women, all ideally beautiful and accomplished both in body and in mind, there is something mechanical, abstract, almost unreal about these encounters. The story of Shao-yu's life thus advances essentially through repetition, not through development. For this reason, there is no sense of our hero undergoing a process of discovery or self-discovery, and therefore no sense of the hero's inner growth or maturation.

As for Hsing-chen, the novice whose story frames the dream-life of Shao-yu, his life is nearly as dreamlike. As Yun Chang Sik has pointed out, Hsing-chen lives in a state of innocence like Adam and Eve in the Garden of Eden before their fall, and it is for this reason that through his dream of Shao-yu he must *fall* into the world.[5] For without that dream he has very little knowledge or experience of the joys and pains of life in this world. But the problem is that even after his fall into the secular world Hsing-chen experiences very little of real life, for Shao-yu's life consists entirely of wish fulfillment.

Ostensibly, the theme of *Kuun mong* is the spiritual enlightenment Hsing-chen achieves when he awakens from his dream life as Shao-yu. He finally comes to understand the Buddhist teaching that life, however splendid and delightful, is a mere dream. But I am not sure that either the frame of the story or the enclosed dream life supports this message. For Buddhism is based on the belief that human life is filled with misery and grief resulting from the constant, inevitable frustration of our desires, and that we must therefore rid ourselves of those desires. Buddhism is thus filled with a profound sense of the tragedy of human life: from birth to death human life is steeped in pain and sorrow. Buddhism appealed to many people in that its view of the world closely mirrored the reality of their own lives. Hence the appeal of the Buddhist ideal of total withdrawal from the world.

But if our life should be without pain or sorrow, and if our desires, even the most fantastic ones, are never frustrated, why should we try to withdraw from the world? Shouldn't we instead try to continue in it as long as we could? Since Shao-yu's every desire is fulfilled and he hardly ever experiences pain or sorrow, how can Hsing-chen's memory of his dream life support the Buddhist claim that in this world our desires lead only to suffering? As Yun Chang Sik has pointed out, Shao-yu's "abrupt" negation of his worldly success is therefore totally unconvincing.[6]

The point of Shao-yu's life would seem to be that the world is yours if only you possess good looks, brains, and luck. For then even the supernatural powers will come to your aid when you need them. And even if this pleasure-filled life should be a mere dream, it is the only thing worth pursuing, for what life, however long, could possibly compare with such a delightful life as Shao-yu's? Thus, like an addict who longs to return to his drug-induced visions, Hsing-chen should want to return to his dream life as Shao-yu. That life is nothing less than the never-never world of adolescent daydreams wholly and deliciously fulfilled, and therefore immensely more satisfying to a young man than even the fairyland of Lotus Peak Monastery.

What is most curious as well as most disappointing about

Kuun mong is that it reflects so little of seventeenth-century Korea in the tragic aftermath of two calamitous foreign invasions. Nor does it reflect the author's own troubled personal life resulting from the deadly factionalism at the court. Kim Man-jung himself suffered numerous political setbacks and long banishments, eventually dying in exile. If *Kuun mong* is related at all to the author's life or to seventeenth-century Korea, it seems only by way of a total escape from it. For Shao-yu's life takes place in a fairyland where there seems to be no sickness, pain, misery, sorrow, or untimely death, a place where humans neither exhibit nor experience negative emotions such as jealousy, grief, or hatred. In *Kuun mong* Kim Man-jung created a world of pure fantasy that is utterly different from the world of seventeenth-century Korea. It is a work of pure escapism.

The unreality of *Kuun mong* is even more striking when it is contrasted with "Unyŏng chŏn" (The Life of Unyŏng). One of hundreds of Chosŏn dynasty stories that have been discovered in both hangŭl and hanmun versions, "Unyŏng chŏn" is another dream story, of unknown authorship, supposedly written in hanmun. It is the tragic story of Unyŏng, a woman in the palace of Prince Anp'yŏng, (a historical person). Although it is the story of one particular palace woman, it could also be seen as a story of palace women collectively. Their lives, it turns out, were more like those of servants and slaves than those of privileged women.

According to one source, at any one time during the Chosŏn period there were five to six hundred women serving in royal palaces.[7] Coming to the palace in their early teens or even younger, these hundreds of women grew to maturity in service. But only a handful could ever hope to be noticed and chosen by the king or prince as secondary consorts or favorite concubine. The rest were doomed to live out their lives as little more than human furnishings. Shut up inside the palace walls, cut off from their own families and the outside world, they despaired of ever having their own men or families. Most of them thus led lonely, rigidly regulated, and even tragic lives against their will. In "Un-yŏng chŏn," for example, they are prevented on pain of death from having any contact with the outside world.

The story is also called "Susŏnggung mongyurok" (A Dream at Susŏng Palace), and as the title suggests, it takes place mainly in a dream. One spring day the narrator, one Yu Yŏng, makes an excursion to Susŏng Palace, once the residence of Prince Anp'yŏng, the third son of King Sejong. The palace, situated at the foot of Mt. Inwang, has been in ruins since the Japanese invasions of 1592 and 1597. There Yu enjoys a bottle of wine. Drunk and sleepy, he dozes off. He dreams he is awakened by a chill in the air to find all other visitors gone and a bright moon shining overhead. But then he notices a young man and a most beautiful young woman sitting together nearby. They turn out to be Unyŏng and Master Kim, and it is their story told to Yu that forms the heart of "Unyong chŏn."

Unyŏng is the most favored of the ten ladies-in-waiting in the palace of Prince Anp'yŏng, all of them hand-picked by the prince himself. The prince has distinguished himself by his calligraphy and his patronage of artists and writers, and as a mark of special favor he encourages his ladies-in-waiting to study the classics and compose poetry. As a result, these beautiful young palace women come to excel in their appreciation and composition of poetry. As a patron of art and poetry, the prince often entertains the brightest young artists and poet-scholars of the kingdom. On these occasions he shows off the compositions of his waiting women, but without attribution. The poet-scholars are struck by the polish and sentiments revealed in these poems and compare them favorably to the best works of the Tang poets.

One day an especially gifted young poet-scholar, Master Kim,[8] visits the prince. Because of Master Kim's youth, the prince al-lows Unyŏng and the other ladies-in-waiting to remain in atten-dance and prepare ink and brush for him and his guest. This is unusual because the prince has never before allowed his guests—all male artists or poet-scholars—even a glimpse of his favored palace women. And thus comes about the tragic meeting of Unyŏng and Master Kim, who fall helplessly in love without exchanging even a word.

It was utterly forbidden for a palace woman to have anything to do with a man other than her lord. Likewise, no man from outside the palace was ever allowed contact with any of the palace women. Prince Anp'yŏng repeatedly states that it would be a capital crime if any of his ladies-in-waiting came to know even the name of a man outside. It would have been impossible therefore for Unyŏng and Master Kim to become openly intimate; they could meet only in absolute secrecy, and at the risk of their lives. Nevertheless, Unyŏng takes the first step by slipping a letter to Master Kim in which she openly declares her love for him. Finding her love reciprocated, she then arranges a series of trysts with Master Kim, first outside the palace and then almost nightly within. All are made possible with the help of her sister ladies-in-waiting, who are also risking their lives.

Twice Prince Anp'yŏng, detecting expressions of loneliness and longing in Unyŏng's poems, questions her. The second time he asks specifically if she is thinking of Master Kim. Each time Unyŏng stoutly protests her innocence. Of the four other ladies-in-waiting housed in the palace's west wing, Charan is the most sympathetic to Unyŏng, and it is she who helps to arrange Unyŏng's first meeting with Master Kim outside the palace and subsequent meetings inside. Later it is also Charan who dissuades Unyŏng and Master Kim from eloping by pointing out to them the grave consequences. Unyŏng cannot steal away, Charan tells her, because

> the calamity will surely extend to your parents as well as us in the west wing; and since the world is like the inside of a fishnet, unless you can rise to the heavens or enter into the bowels of the earth, where will you flee even if you run away? And if you are caught, calamity will surely fall not only on you alone. . . . [9]

On the other hand, Charan adds, should Unyŏng's beauty fade a little, the prince's regard for her would decrease, and if she were to take to her bed pretending illness, he would be sure to give her permission to return home. Such would be the best hope of escape for Unyŏng and Master Kim, Charan advises.

Before long, however, the lovers' trysts in the palace are exposed through the careless words of Master Kim's disgruntled servant. Unyŏng along with the other ladies-in-waiting are summoned before the furious Prince Anp'yŏng, who orders that the women be flogged to death. At this point all the women speak out passionately and eloquently in defense not only of Unyŏng but of their own conduct. One after another they stress a theme repeated throughout the story: Shut up in the palace while still young and beautiful, they have been wasting away their lives, for they are barred from ever achieving what is most natural and fulfilling in life—love, marriage, and a family of their own. Unsŏm, one of the other ladies-in-waiting, is the first to speak:

> Since love and desire between man and woman spring from the yin and yang principle of Nature, every human being, whether high- or lowborn, is possessed by it. But imprisoned deep in the palace, we feel so lonesome that our eyes fill up with tears just looking at the flowers, and we go out of our minds merely looking at the moon. It is like keeping the nightingales on a plum tree from pairing up or the swallows flying in the fields from building their nests. . . . Even though we understand that once outside the palace walls we can taste the pleasures of life. . . because we've been shut up so long deep inside the palace, we have neither the physical strength to do anything for ourselves, nor the power to control our mind's desires completely. Sir, it is only our fear of your displeasure that keeps our feelings and desires tightly wrapped up within ourselves, thus withering away till death.[10]

In this crisis, too, it is Charan who is most outspoken in defense of Unyŏng and the help given her by herself and the others:

> Since our guilt is beyond measure, how can I keep my thoughts to myself and not disclose them? Since we are simple women who come from ordinary families . . . how could we alone not feel the

love and desires that naturally exist between man and woman? Even the greatest kings and heroes of antiquity . . . were subject to these feelings. How then could your lordship expect Unyŏng alone not to have the same feelings of love and desire? As for Master Kim, not only is he an outstanding scholar of our time, but you yourself brought him into the palace, and it was you yourself who commanded Unyŏng to prepare the ink for his writing brush. Shut up deep inside the palace for a long time, she was sorrowful whenever the moon was bright or whenever it was a spring day with flowers blooming. Like the paulownia leaves that fall with the rain she felt her heart ache whenever it rained at night. Meeting a bold and handsome youth she lost her soul to him instantly, and sick with love she wasted away daily. . . . In my foolish mind it seemed nothing would add more to your lordship's accumulated good deeds than allowing Master Kim and Unyŏng to meet once to satisfy their heart's longing. As for Unyŏng's infidelity of the previous day, I am to blame for it, not Unyŏng. . . . Prostrate I beg you, sir, to take my life and spare Unyŏng's.[11]

Finally Unyŏng speaks. She admits her guilt and she asks that she alone be punished, holding her companion ladies-in-waiting blameless. Moved by the passionate and selfless pleas of each of the five women, the prince releases all but Unyŏng, whom he confines alone in another part of the palace. During the night Unyŏng hangs herself with her silk handkerchief.

It is inevitable that Unyŏng, awakened in body and mind, should fall in love with someone like Master Kim. But as Charan suggests in her eloquent plea, the prince himself is responsible for Unyŏng's passionate love for Master Kim. For the prince promoted Unyŏng's intellectual awakening by educating her in the study of the classics and poetic composition, and in this sense he trained her to appreciate Master Kim's poetic and scholarly gifts. He also brought the two of them together, though unwittingly. Unyŏng's only fault, if it is a fault at all, is her failure to restrict the expression of her nature to the socially approved channel of total submission in body and soul to the service of

Prince Anp'yŏng alone. In her passionate love for Master Kim and her resulting defiance of the imperative of her social position, do we not see something like the spirit of individualism emerging in the form of her attempt to fulfill her own desires? Unyŏng is of course destroyed by the reigning power structure and unyielding mores of her feudal society. But in her death she exemplifies the fate of women of her class as well as of other Korean women of her time who dared to defy the mores and morality of that society.

The heart of the story is finished with Unyŏng's suicide. What follows is a brief, trivialized account of the prayers for Unyŏng's soul offered by Master Kim at a Buddhist temple. Master Kim soon follows her by starving himself to death. At this point the narrative returns to Yu Yŏng, who awakens from his dream.

"Unyong chŏn" has much that makes it superior to *Kuun mong*. First of all, its setting is Korea and Korean history. More important, it succeeds where *Kuun mong* fails. Unlike *Kuun mong,* "Unyŏng chŏn" presents a believable physical setting and realistic characterization and plot development and effectively fuses these basic elements of fiction into a powerful story of historical and social significance and reality. Finally, the story is allowed to play out to its inevitable tragic conclusion, unlike so many other Chosŏn period stories, to which a contrived happy ending is routinely tacked on. When a powerless woman or man dares defy the ideology of a monolithic power structure, how could anything but tragedy result from it? According to So Jae-yŏng and Chang Hong-jae, "Unyŏng chŏn" is the only tragic love story so far discovered among the hundreds of Chosŏn stories.[12]

A few questions concerning the setting and time of the story remain problematic. For example, why does the story take place in the household of Prince Anp'yŏng and why is the frame of the story—the narrator's dream—set at the ruins of Prince Anp'yŏng's palace after the Japanese invasions of 1592 and 1597? How is the tragedy of Unyŏng and Master Kim related to the national tragedy of the Japanese invasion? We know that the Japanese invasions, by exposing the incompetence, indifference, and corruption of the ruling class, alienated the people from their rulers and fostered a radical skepticism toward the traditional conception of class relationships. Does the story signal this shift in attitude, especially the growing self-awareness of individual men and women among the oppressed classes? Women of all classes were among the most oppressed people of Chosŏn society, and many of them suffered horribly from the Japanese and Manchu depredations. As for the setting of the story at the ruins of Prince Anp'yŏng's palace, are the remains of the palace meant to symbolize the devastations suffered by the class to which the prince belonged? These are just a few of the questions that require further study as we continue to examine this important story and its variant texts.

Notes

1. Kim Man-jung, *Kuun mong,* ed. Chŏng Pyŏng-uk (Seoul: Minjung Sŏgwan, 1972), 3.
2. Richard Rutt and Kim Chong-un, trans. *Virtuous Women: Three Classic Korean Novels* (Seoul: Royal Asiatic Society, Korea Branch, 1974), 3.
3. Ibid., 173.
4. Ibid., 175.
5. Yun Chang Sik, "The Structure of the *Kuun mong* (A Dream of Nine Clouds)," *Korean Studies,* 5 (1981): 32.
6. Ibid., 39.
7. Kim Tong-uk and Hwang P'ae-gang, *Hanguk kososŏl immun* (An Introduction to the Classical Korean Novel) (Seoul: Kaemunsa, 1985), 535.
8. In the original, he is called Kim Chinsa, *Chinsa* being the title given to those who have passed the first of the state examinations. My discussion of "Unyŏng chon" is based on the text in *Hanguk kojŏn munhak taejŏnjip* (Collected Works of Classical Korean Literature), (Seoul: Sejong ch'ulp'an konghoe, 1970) 5:188–222.
9. Ibid., 214.
10. Ibid., 217.
11. Ibid., 218.
12. So Jae-yŏng and Chang Hong-jae, ed. *Unyŏng chŏn* (Seoul: Shiinsa, 1984), 6.

9

The Literature of Shirhak:
Yŏnam, Pak Chi-wŏn

Intense self-examination and self-criticism inevitably follow in
the wake of national calamities, for nothing else so clearly ex-
poses the roots of a society's ills. Long accepted abuses of power
and privileges, gross inequities, and the obsolescence of established institutions may all be papered over during normal times,
but in a catastrophe they are exposed for everyone to see.
Voices of discontent and criticism formerly silenced or muted
gain loud expression.

During its more than two thousand years of recorded history,
Korea has suffered few national calamities more devastating than
the Japanese invasions of 1592 and 1597 and the Manchu invasions of 1627 and 1636. The entire country was repeatedly laid
waste, exposing the bankruptcy of yangban rule, both civil and
military. Preoccupied with factional power struggles, the yangban
were capable neither of protecting the country from invasion nor
of restoring it to any degree of normalcy afterwards by promoting
domestic justice and economic recovery. As a result, the country
suffered and deteriorated in every respect.

To many observers the root problems exposed by the Japanese
and Manchu invasions seemed to require nothing short of a fundamental overhaul of Chosŏn institutions. It was in this context that
the Shirhak (Practical Learning) movement arose. Although a few
government officials endeavored to bring about badly needed reforms, the main criticism and impetus for change came from those
outside the government, "those who were not permitted to participate in the political process."[1] Most Shirhak scholars were thus

from the Namin (Southerner) faction, whose adherents had long been excluded from important government posts.

The proponents of Shirhak believed that until the inner workings of their diseased society were uncovered, they could not remedy its various ills. They therefore undertook an exhaustive study of Korean society: its political and economic institutions, agricultural technology, commodity exchange system, geography, history, language, and so forth. Though most Shirhak scholars accepted the Chinese philosopher Zhu Xi's interpretation of Confucianism, in their investigations into the country's ills they insisted on *seeing things as they actually were* rather than as they were supposed to be according to traditional Confucian prescriptions. They sought truths that could be verified factually or through their own study and experience—thus the name Practical Learning.

Since the Shirhak scholars were interested first and foremost in remedying the actual ills of their society, and since the national economy was largely based on agriculture, it was natural that they should focus first on agricultural reforms. Their aim was to improve the living and working conditions of the peasantry by introducing fundamental changes to land ownership, tax collection, corvee labor, military obligations, and many other aspects of Chosŏn society that affected the life of the peasant.

Pangye (Yu Hyŏng-wŏn, 1622–1673), was the first Shirhak scholar to devote his life to reforming the many abuses of land ownership. In the opening section of his life's work, *Pangye surok* (Pangye's Occasional Notes), which took nineteen years to complete, he wrote:

> Nothing can be achieved unless the system of land ownership is right. . . . Unless the laws governing land ownership are right, the economic life of the people cannot be sound. Neither the system of taxation, nor the annual tributes of local produce, nor the corvee obligations can be sound. The number of households cannot be accurately known, nor the military ranks be properly filled, nor will there be an end to litigation, nor will criminal punishment be reduced, nor will bribery be stopped. . . . What is the reason? It is that land is the basis of all things in this world.[2]

Thus for Pangye, the reform of Chosŏn society began with creating the right system of land ownership, which in turn would increase the wealth of the Korean people and their nation.

According to the reforms in land ownership instituted at the beginning of the Chosŏn dynasty, land apportioned to merit subjects and officeholders was to be retained only during their lifetime or their tenure in office. But this principle was never put into practice, and soon much land had reverted to private and hereditary ownership by a privileged few. Describing the worsening condition of his time, Pangye writes:

> While the fields of the rich stretch on and on without end, the poor have not even land enough to insert a gimlet. The rich become richer; the poor poorer. In no time, the unscrupulous speculators come to own all the land, while the [displaced] peasants and their families roam the land, ending up finally as hired hands.[3]

Because Pangye believed that the wealth and power of the nation ultimately depended on an independent, self-sufficient peasantry, he was most interested in improving their living conditions. Since the yangban were exempt from taxation as well as military and corvee obligations, and since slaves were obligated mainly to their masters, the peasantry made up most of the state's basic economic and military resources. The state, therefore, could not flourish unless the peasants were strong and content. The problem was how to improve their lot.

Pangye's solution, a "public land system," was perhaps the most notable feature of his land reform proposal. Under this system land would belong to the state, which would apportion it to every able-bodied adult peasant male. Although the amount of land to be given was the minimum necessary for the peasant's livelihood and taxes, still it was a revolutionary idea, for never in the Chosŏn dynasty had those who actually cultivated the soil been apportioned land for their own use.[4] What Pangye and later Shirhak scholars advocated was thus, as Ki-baik Lee has put it, the creation of "independent, self-employed farmers who themselves held and tilled their own lands," for Shirhak scholars believed that "the interests of the official class and of those who tilled the land were in fundamental harmony. . . ."[5]

While Shirhak scholars such as Pangye were focusing on agriculture, a second group of Shirhak thinkers concentrated on manufacturing and commerce. The scholars of this second school believed that an expansion of manufacturing and commerce was essential to the prosperity of Korean society. These scholars were greatly influenced by what they learned on their official trips north to Peking, the capital of Qing dynasty China.[6] Hence the name of their school: Northern Learning. In China they saw many things that made them reflect on their own society, and out of their experiences and reflections came proposals for its reform. It wasn't so much that they slavishly admired Chinese society; rather, they wanted to correct the defects of their own society by applying what they learned in China. What they wrote therefore constituted "a severe indictment of the *yangban* society of that age."[7]

Yŏnam (Pak Chi-wŏn, 1737–1805), one of the founders of Northern Learning, was among the most innovative writers of his time. Although he wrote in hanmun rather than hangŭl, his satirical novels and tales—perhaps the most searing criticism of contemporary yangban society—make him not only the premier Shirhak writer but also one of the major figures of Korean literature.

His best-known work, *Yŏrha ilgi (Jehol Diary,* 1780), is a record of his journey to the Qing emperor's summer retreat north of Beijing. His observations of Qing society constantly led him to reflect on his own society. For example, he closely observed the many brickmaking facilities he saw throughout northern China and came to believe that brick construction would greatly improve both public works and private housing. His journal includes lengthy discussions of the superiority of bricks over stones in large- and small-scale construction. Bricks, for instance, being uniform in shape and size, are not only easier to transport but do not require a stonemason to select and shape them. Even in the traditional Korean *ondol* floor (warmed by heating ducts underneath) bricks would be superior: they would form a smoother, flatter surface and heat would be transmitted more quickly and uniformly through them. More than such closely observed details, however, what has made *Yŏrha ilgi* a classic of Korean literature is its inclusion of such wonderful satiric tales as "Hŏ saeng chŏn" (The Story of Master Hŏ) and "Hojil" (A Tiger's Reprimand).

"Hŏ saeng chŏn" is a utopian work of sorts, presenting one of Yŏnam's visionary schemes for Korean society. A utopian vision is by its very nature implicitly critical, for by dreaming of a perfect society elsewhere the writer indirectly expresses a profound disaffection with the current society. The depiction of an ideal society is thus a foil by which the imperfections of the existing society can be exposed.

Our first impression of Hŏ saeng is not very encouraging, for he seems oblivious to his physical surroundings and to the practical necessities of daily life. While his wife ekes out a living for them by taking in sewing, he does nothing but read. He has never taken the state civil service examination and seems to possess no practical skills by which to earn a living. Thus, at the outset of the story Hŏ saeng appears to be yet another useless yangban who lives off the industry of others, very much the parasite satirized in Yŏnam's other tales.

Pushed into moneymaking by the nagging of his wife, however, Hŏ saeng proves to be a man of vision and business acumen. With 10,000 yang borrowed from the richest man in town, he proceeds to make a huge profit by cornering the market on fruit and then horsehair (which was used in making hats and other products). Most significantly, unlike those of his class who did not wish their hands soiled by money, Hŏ saeng not only knows how to make money but can use it effectively. In the disposition of his profit he shows himself to be a visionary. Meeting with a band of thieves who have been disturbing the countryside, he asks whether they would give up thievery if given the chance to settle down with a wife and an ox to become honest farmers. Of course they would, they answer. Hŏ saeng thereupon hires a fleet of ships, takes the thieves to an uninhabited island, and helps them establish a thriving agricultural community. After culling all those who can read and write—lest their presence poison this new utopia by introducing a parasitic class like the yangban to prey on the industry of others—Hŏ saeng returns to the mainland.

Back in Korea, Hŏ saeng finds that the yangban rulers are unwilling to undertake even the easiest of the reforms he proposes to save the country. Reality dashes his dreams. And since eighteenth-century Korea has no use for a visionary like Hŏ saeng, he soon vanishes without a trace. The utopian vision that forms the heart of "Hŏ saeng chŏn" thus appears like a fleeting dream amid contemporary Chosŏn society.

Though meager in detail, "Hŏ saeng chŏn" reveals the depth of Yŏnam's unhappiness with Korean society. In the story, the country's economy is so moribund that a single man with 10,000 yang can corner the market on several vital commodities, paralyzing key segments of the nation's commerce. Worse, ordinary men are driven to thievery not by an evil nature but by necessity. Given an opportunity to work for a living, they become honest and productive members of society. But Yŏnam sees little prospect for genuine improvement in the condition of the country. As we see at the end of the story, so fixed are the yangban in their traditional ways that they oppose even such minor reforms as changing their hair and dress styles. This is a criticism Yŏnam repeats toward the end of *Yŏrha ilgi,* where he lashes out against the blind adherence of his own yangban class to the outward forms prescribed by ancient tradition. Such preoccupation with form, as in hair style or dress, Yŏnam saw as both trivial and foolish. Mere form had replaced substance in the yangban's observance of tradition.

Another feature of the story is Yŏnam's attitude toward money and commerce. Members of the yangban class were to concern themselves mainly with the study of ancient sages, the great poets of China, and statecraft. The business of money, trade, and manufacturing was beneath them; it was left to the lower classes. Yŏnam challenges this traditional attitude, seeing that commerce

and manufacturing are the very foundation of a nation's livelihood. Unless these matters are well managed, a nation and its people cannot prosper. Why, then, shouldn't the yangban, supposedly
the ablest members of society, take an active interest in them? Here,
of course, Yŏnam is expressing the main thrust of Shirhak thinking:
to see things as they really are, unfettered by tradition and prejudice,
and to bring about concrete improvements in the life of the people.
This goal accounts for the emphasis Yŏnam and Pak Che-ga, another leader of Northern Learning, placed on "wheeled transport
vehicles, money [and] bricks"[8]—in other words, those things that
would revitalize domestic trade and commerce of all kinds as well
as improve private housing and public works.

Yŏnam directs his sharpest barbs at his own class. He believes
the yangban scholar-officials have brought the country to its present
moral, political, and economic bankruptcy through their own hypocrisy, parasitic lifestyle, and head-in-the-sand attitude. In his satirical
sketch "Yangban chŏn" (The Story of a Yangban), Yŏnam charac-
terizes a yangban as a good-for-nothing who is incapable of earning
his own livelihood. He puts these jeering words into the mouth of a
yangban's wife, for who else would know a yangban through and
through! The woman's husband is about to be jailed for failing to
repay a loan of government grain on which he had been living. She
tells him: "You always love to study, but you're no good at returning the government grain. A yangban you say, but your kind isn't
worth a penny."[9]

In this sketch, a yangban is at best an empty shell with no real
substance; at worst he is a parasite or a thief who preys on others'
industry:

> They do not till the soil or engage in trade. With a smattering of
> classics and histories, the better ones will pass the final examination
> [becoming officials], lesser ones will become doctors. The red di-
> ploma of the final examination is no more than two feet long, but it
> provides everything one needs—indeed it is like a purse.... His
> stomach [will become] full with the "yes" of servants. In his rooms
> he can tease female entertainers with an ear pick, and his grains piled

in the courtyard are for the cranes to peck. Even a poor scholar in the country can decide matters as he wishes. He can have his neighbor's oxen plow his fields first, or use villagers for weeding. Who will dare behave rudely to him? Even if he fills your nostrils with ashes, catches you by the topknot, or pulls your hair at the temples, you cannot show resentment.[10]

"Hojil" provides a funnier and even more devastating indictment of the yangban.[11] It is a fable in which the main character is a famished man-eating tiger and the object of satire one Master Puk Kwak, a Confucian scholar. In this story the yangban's vaunted Confucian virtue and morality turn out to be nothing more than pretense, as we see in the following brief summary:

A famished tiger is looking for a man to eat. But he is not keen on a physician or shaman, fearing they might be poisoned to the marrow of their bones by the bitterness of the many patients and clients who have been killed off by their lies and mumbo-jumbo. So the tiger decides on Master Puk Kwak, a yangban scholar, since a scholar is supposed to be clean, with nothing hidden about him. In the meantime, Master Puk, reputedly a profoundly learned moral exemplar, is carrying on an affair with a young widow who has already had five children by five different men. One night the widow's five children hear whispers coming from her room; it sounds like their mother and Master Puk. But how could that be? Since Master Puk ought not to be alone with their mother, a widow, the children decide it must be a wily fox disguised as him. Armed with sticks and clubs, they rush into the room. Master Puk barely escapes, but in the darkness outside he falls into a pool of excrement and sinks up to his neck. When he finally manages to climb out he is confronted by the tiger, who has been stalking him. But the tiger blocks his nostrils and turns his head away. "How awful the scholar stinks!" the tiger exclaims, frowning. The terrified Master Puk prostrates himself before the tiger, kowtows three times, and begs for mercy: "Great is the virtue of the tiger, for you set an example for emperors, sons, generals. All look to you. . . ." "Don't come near me," the tiger warns. And then he continues:

Yes, I've heard that Confucian scholars are wily, and now I know it's true. Whereas you usually have nothing good to say about me, now just because you're in danger and in front of me, you act as if you've never vilified me. So instead you flatter me. How could anyone believe what you say?[12]

Most of Yŏnam's satirical tales contain an urgent call for radical reform of the yangban class. In "Hŏ saeng chŏn," as we have seen, Yŏnam suggests that the yangban promote commerce, both domestically and internationally. He also proposes fundamental social changes so that those at the bottom of society can make an honest living through their labor. And in "Yangban chŏn" and "Hojil" he calls for a fundamental reshaping of the yangban character and role in society: yangban must give up undeserved privileges, shed pretense and hypocrisy, and become productive members of society instead of living off the labors of others.

Ironically, but not surprisingly, Yŏnam draws his worst characters—idlers, hypocrites, and parasites—from the yangban class, and many of his exemplary characters from the lower classes. The latter provide a glimpse of the sorts of people he appears to have respected. Most are errand boys or manual laborers, such as night-soil collectors, and all have little formal education. Occupying the bottom of the social hierarchy, they are despised for their menial station in life, even though it is *their* labor and service that make possible the yangban's life of privilege and leisure.

In "Kwangmun cha chŏn" (The Story of Kwangmun), for example, the main character is a former leader of a group of teenage beggars living in a cave beside a creek flowing through the capital. Kwangmun is a good-hearted and honest fellow who helps others in whatever way he can. When a child beggar dies, he sees to it that the child is buried decently in a cemetery, and afterwards he prays for the peace of the child's spirit. As Kwangmun's virtuousness becomes known, he is recommended to a wealthy pharmacist who employs him as an errand boy. He proves trustworthy, and through his antics he also becomes the town peacemaker and comedian. Because he is so homely and funny, he can break up a fight just by making the combatants laugh. He is also the favorite manager of the city's most popular kisaeng as well as an arranger of loans, all because he is trusted by everyone. He is often urged to marry, to which he replies: "Generally everybody admires handsomeness, not only men but women as well. Since I'm so homely, how could I expect anybody to be attracted to me?"[13] And when his friends urge him to get a house of his own, he replies: "Since I have neither parents, siblings, nor children, what need do I have of a house? In the morning I go out into the city, and all day long I wander around singing, and when evening comes I just find a place to sleep in a rich man's house."[14] A person who occupies a very low place in society; a grown man who is a sort of all-purpose errand boy; a man without family, property, or money; but a man who has everyone's trust and, most significant, who brings peace and laughter to others—such is one of Yŏnam's exemplary characters.

Perhaps the most exemplary of Yŏnam's fictional characters is Ŏm Haeng-su of "Yedŏk sŏnsaeng chŏn" (The Story of Master Yedŏk). Ŏm Haeng-su is a night-soil man: he collects human excrement and sells it to small farmers outside the city who use it as fertilizer. The story is in the form of a dialogue between one Master Sŏngyul, a noted scholar, and Chamok, one of his disciples, who has decided to part with his master because of the latter's friendship with Ŏm. Chamok considers it a dishonor that his master should befriend a night-soil man. Master Sŏngyul proceeds to explain to Chamok why he respects the night-soil man:

> Since Ŏm Haeng-su makes his living by carrying away excrement, maybe we can say he's extremely filthy. But if you were to look into how he makes his living you would see that his life is actually quite fragrant. Although his body is much soiled, his adherence to virtue is utterly unbending. Even if all the bells in the world were to rust, his virtuousness would suffer no alteration. Thus there is cleanliness in filth, filth in cleanliness. How many people could look at Ŏm Haeng-su without becoming red in the face? That's why I call Ŏm Haeng-su my teacher. How dare I call him a friend! It's because I could not bring myself to call him by his name that I have given him the title of Master Yedŏk.[15]

The night-soil man, the lowliest of the low in society, helps feed all those who despise him. For the filth he carries to the farmers fertilizes the crops they sell to the city dwellers. Not only does Ŏm play a vital role in food production, but the excrement itself is valuable, as Yŏnam noted in *Yorha ilgi:* "Although dung is an extremely filthy thing, [the Chinese] value it like gold in order to use it in their fields. Thus not only is there no excrement on the road, but a man will follow closely behind horses picking up their dung."[16]

Of all Pak Chi-wŏn's works, I find "Yŏllyŏ Hamyang Paksshi chŏn pyŏngsŏ" (The Life of Mrs. Pak of Hamyang, a Faithful Wife, With Comments) the most powerful and intriguing.[17] (A complete translation of this story appears at the end of the chapter.) It is a work Yŏnam wrote fairly late in life and was based on an actual event that occurred in 1793 while he was district magistrate of Anŭi, now part of South Kyŏngsang Province. It consists of three sections— a personal reflection, the story itself, and a factual account of the event.

The first section begins with Yŏnam's reflections on the tradition of the faithful wife (*yŏllyŏ*) and concludes with an expression of regret about what seemed to him an excessive zeal for martyrdom shown especially by widows from families of ordinary people. In yangban families, he writes, there are compelling reasons for widows not to remarry. For one thing, the law bars sons of twice-married women from all but minor government posts. But why should ordinary people follow this tradition of never remarrying? For the remarriage law does not affect them at all. The answer seems to be, as Yŏnam points out, that during the 400 years of the Chosŏn dynasty the remarriage taboo has grown so strong and pervasive that women of all classes, regardless of social standing, now adhere to it. Indeed, for the young widows of ordinary families in the countryside, and even teenage widows, it is not enough to honor their deceased husbands by merely remaining unmarried throughout their lives. Instead they must follow their husbands in death by drowning themselves or drinking poison, even if there is no pressure from their parents to remarry. Yŏnam concludes this brief first section with a quiet but troubling question: "Though this is indeed fidelity, isn't it excessive?"

There follows the story itself, a poignant account of a yangban widow and her two grownup sons. One day the widow overhears her sons discussing a plan to block someone from obtaining a government post. Alarmed, she asks them why they want to do such a thing. They reply that they have heard of a scandal involving a widow in an earlier generation of the man's family. Shocked and pained, she asks how they could possibly know about what might have happened in the women's quarters of someone else's family. They reply that they are going on hearsay. She reprimands them for acting on something as uncertain as hearsay, especially when they are themselves sons of a widow. And then, taking a brass coin from her bosom, she asks if they can see the rim. No, they reply. She then asks if they can see inscriptions on the coin. No, they again reply. Tearfully she then tells them:

> This is the testament to your mother's struggle with death. The rim and inscriptions were worn away by my fingering it constantly for ten years. For most of us, life's vitality flows from the female–male principle of our life, which is concentrated in our passions and desires. Our thoughts, born of loneliness, lead to sorrow and heartaches. Because a widow is always lonely, she can never escape from her sorrows and heartaches. How could a vigorous and healthy woman be without feelings and desires, even if she is a widow?
>
> Some nights I would have nothing but the shadow of the dim, flickering light to commune with. On such nights I could hear only the sound of rain dripping from the eaves, or the leaves of the paulownia tree rustling to the ground, or the cry of a lone seagull as daybreak approached, for the crowing of the rooster would be too far away to hear. Unable to sleep, I would lie awake listening to the snoring of the young maidservant. To whom could I have confided my sorrow and sleeplessness then? It was at such times that I would spin this brass coin on the floor and then grope around for it. Sometimes I would find it resting against something

that had blocked its path. After finding it I would spin it again and again, and by the time I had spun it five or six times the night would have passed and it would be daybreak. During the first ten years I came to spin the coin fewer and fewer times each year, and after those ten years had passed I needed to do it only once every five days, and then just once every ten days. Now my vitality has declined so much that I no longer have to spin it. Still, I have kept it in my bosom the last twenty years, wrapped in many folds of cloth. I kept it all these years so that I wouldn't forget what it did for me, but also because I wanted to look at it now and then as a reminder to myself.

When the mother finished her story, Yŏnam tells us, she and her two sons embraced one another and wept.

The meaning of this fictional middle section—most likely Yŏnam's own creation—seems clear enough. It is the human cost of the institution of the faithful wife. Here we see a widow who survives only by killing herself bit by bit. She kills all that is vital and instinctual in herself until nothing is left but that image of the ideal widow required by the mores of Chosŏn society. Isn't this why she and her two grownup sons weep together at the conclusion of her story?

What is not entirely clear is what Yŏnam himself thought about the tradition of the faithful wife. Did he approve or disapprove of it? Based on his other writings he seems to have approved of the practice of yangban widows' remaining unmarried.[18] It thus appears that Yŏnam admired the heroism of the widow in the story and sympathized with her suffering. He probably thought that genuine heroism required self-denial and hardship and was to be expected of a society's elite.

The final section of the story is far more problematic, because it appears to include different voices representing different, even conflicting, views. One of the figures who come across clearly in this section is Yŏnam himself. Now in his late years, long after his eventful trip to China and the completion of his major work, *Yŏrha ilgi,* he appears before us as a thoughtful and compassionate government official. Called to government service late in life, he has been assigned to a small rural district where he might put into practice what he has learned in his years of study, reflection, and experience.

Yŏnam begins by giving the time and place of the actual incident: Anŭi in 1793, one year after he became district magistrate there.

One day, just before daybreak, he hears people whispering and sighing outside his chamber. He asks loudly if anything's the matter. They reply that the niece of Pak Sang-hyo (one of the petty clerks) has drunk poison upon finishing the obligatory three years of mourning for her deceased husband and is in critical condition. Because Pak is on duty, he has not been able to hasten to his niece. Yŏnam immediately orders him to go look after her.

Toward evening of the same day, Yŏnam asks if the widow has survived. He is told she died. Yŏnam proceeds to find out more about her. She lost both parents early in life and was raised by her grandparents. At nineteen she was engaged to a handsome but sickly youth from Hamyang named Im Sul-jŭng. A few months before the wedding, however, the groom-to-be was found to be so ill it was obvious to everyone that the marriage could not be consummated. Both families were therefore willing to cancel the engagement, but at the insistence of the bride-to-be the wedding took place. In less than half a year the young man died, leaving her a widow. She was devoted to her parents-in-law and filial in every way. She observed the first and second anniversaries of her husband's death with meticulous care, and exactly at the same hour on the same day she completed the rites and then killed herself.

Such is the summary of what happened to Mrs. Pak, a summary of her life as seen from the outside. She is presented as an exemplary widow, and family and elders on both sides have nothing but high praise for her. But at this point, halfway through this final section, an elderly clerk suddenly speaks out. His words obviously carry weight, for we hear them directly from the speaker himself. And for the first and only time we hear what seems to be the inside story of the young widow's tragedy.

According to the clerk, a few months before the wedding took place there had been talk of canceling it since the groom-to-be was obviously too sick to fulfill the role of a husband. And then just before the wedding, representatives of the Pak family visited the groom and found him grievously sick. He was coughing badly and looked like "a mushroom standing"—that is, frail, tender, vulnerable?—like "a mere shadow wandering about." Shocked, the grandparents proposed to arrange another marriage. But the bride-to-be was resolved to adhere to the engagement, and so the family had no choice but to consent. But, the clerk adds, "although the wedding ceremony was performed, it was really no more than a matter of keeping faith with a suit of empty clothes."

As if to emphasize the significance of this bit of the inside story given by the elderly clerk, immediately thereafter Yŏnam informs us that two magistrates and a scholar from the surrounding districts have composed official "lives" of Mrs. Pak as a *yŏllyŏ*, or faithful wife. Such official enshrining obviously has little connection with what the young widow must have actually gone through. What it does, it seems to me, is to heighten the significance of the elderly clerk's poignant words. The problem is how to read those words, and the glimpses they offer us into the reality of the widow's life, especially since they appear to present a view so troubling and so different from the officials' and villagers' views of the widow as a paragon of wifely virtue whose martyrdom should be celebrated.

A few phrases from the clerk's account stand out. Just before the scheduled wedding the bridegroom was found to be so sickly that he looked like "a mushroom standing," "a mere shadow wandering about." And "although the wedding ceremony was performed, it was really no more than a matter of keeping faith with a suit of empty clothes." These details seem to show beyond doubt that the wedding should not have taken place, that it was unnatural and against the interests of the young bride and the two families. Does the elderly clerk speak for Yŏnam himself? There is reason to think so. In a conversation carried on in writing with Wang Min-ho, a Chinese scholar Yŏnam met in China in 1780, he boasted of Korea's "400–year-old" tradition of a wife's lifelong fidelity to her husband even after his death. To which Wang replied:

In China the same custom has caused a great deal of harm. In some cases, just because a marriage proposal was received from the groom's side a woman was made a widow for life without the wedding ever taking place or without it ever being consummated, all owing to an unfortunate accident. And in fact these are not the worst cases. For between families with long-standing friendships, verbal promises have been made between parents even before the children's birth or during their infancy. And if some unfortunate accident should happen to the future groom, his betrothed would take poison or hang herself, asking to be buried in the same grave. Nothing could be more wrong than this. Therefore, men of virtue have denounced it as sinning with the corpse or sinning in the name of fidelity. Although laws have been made to prohibit such evil by punishing the parents, it has finally become established as a custom, especially in the southeastern area [of China].[19]

Yŏnam makes no rebuttal, even though Wang's words seem to undercut what he has celebrated as a praiseworthy Korean custom. Can we take his silence as his agreement with Wang? Since Yŏnam often expressed his sharpest social criticism indirectly through his fictional characters, the elderly clerk's words, which seem to echo Wang's criticism, may therefore perhaps be taken as Yŏnam's own.

What is most puzzling about the third section of the story is the attitude of the prospective bride, specifically her insistence on going through with the marriage despite unanimous opposition to it. Fully aware of the groom's poor health, knowing she is doomed to early widowhood and martyrdom, she still persists. Why would a nineteen-year-old-woman suppress all of her instinctual desires, all her hopes of love, children, and a long life and insist on marriage with "a suit of empty clothes"? Yŏnam is not of much help here, because he gives us very little of the prospective bride's inner thoughts, even though she is the title character of the story. Unlike the yangban widow in the fictional middle section, who speaks at length of her inner struggle, Mrs. Pak is silent except for a few words given to us indirectly through the elderly clerk. When her grandparents suggest canceling the marriage she objects strongly, "a drawn look on her face," saying "All the clothes I have sewn—who were they for and to whose measurements did I sew them? I am going to keep the initial promise I made." Even in the context of Confucian Korea, whose laws barred women of yangban families from remarriage—which did not apply to her anyway—her insistence on a doomed marriage is perplexing.[20]

Yŏnam's concluding words are full of sorrow and regret, but they also sound tentative because he appears to realize that all his thoughts concerning Mrs. Pak are little more than conjectures. Mrs. Pak was of one mind from start to finish, says Yŏnam, preferring to put an early end to her life rather than be pitied and talked about by her relatives and neighbors. He adds:

> Alas! I believe she did not follow her husband in death at once because the immediate duty confronting her was to take care of her husband's funeral; she did not die after the funeral because she had the rites of the first anniversary of his death to take care of; she did not commit suicide after the first anniversary probably because she had to take care of the second anniversary rites. By following her husband in death at the same hour on the same day, after taking care of the second anniversary rites and completing the prescribed period of mourning, she finally accomplished what she had resolved to do from the very beginning. Isn't she indeed a faithful wife!

But his very last words—"Isn't she indeed a faithful wife!"— seem at odds with the concluding words of the first section— "Though this is indeed fidelity, isn't it excessive?" It appears that the questions Yŏnam raised in the first section have not been resolved at the conclusion of the work.

Unquestionably, Yŏnam sees a good deal of moral strength in Mrs. Pak, but he also shows us her predilection toward martyrdom. Despite all the praise she receives from the local people and the magistrates, she comes across as rather pathetic, a mute, sad young woman with an impenetrable inner self. Isn't this what Yŏnam wanted us to see? Though he praises her fidelity, he calls it "excessive" and finds her life sad.

Ultimately, what might Yŏnam be saying about the tradition of the faithful wife? Most striking to me is his deep sorrow for the tragedy revealed in this young widow's death. The story suggests that something is terribly wrong with the high-sounding term *yŏllyŏ,* the faithful wife. It suggests that the tradition of the faithful wife drove many women to choose death over life. A tradition that sounds so virtuous thus turns out to be nothing less than a horrible oppression of women. In the end, "Yŏllyŏ Hamyang Paksshi chŏn pyŏngsŏ" is one of the most searing exposés by a Chosŏn man of his society's institutional inhumanity toward its women.

It is a great irony that Yŏnam, visionary though he was, never recognized the value of hangŭl. He wrote only in hanmun, and here he not only advocated but carried out bold stylistic innovations. Instead of rigidly adhering to classical hanmun he believed that the style of writing should fit the time and needs of the writer and his subject. His own innovative hanmun style was severely criticized by many, including King Chŏngjo, who ordered him to write something in a more classical style in exculpation of his "mistaken" ways. Of course, Yŏnam, a minor official at the time, had no choice but to obey. We can, however, sense his frustration in the words of one of his fictional characters, who protests against blind adherence to the style of the ancients:

> Even if a single passage or a single word seems a bit new or idiosyncratic, there is bound to be the question "Is there anything like this in the writing of the ancients?" Should the answer be no, "How dare you write like this!" is the angry rejoinder. But if such a passage were found in the writings of the ancients, what need is there for me to write another passage like it? [21]

Had Yŏnam carried his reforming zeal further by embracing the use of the Korean alphabet, how much more innovative and creative his work would have been! It took another scholar-official, Yu Kil-chun at the end of the nineteenth century, to recognize the importance of hangŭl. Despite Yŏnam's neglect of hangŭl, his link to the late-nineteenth-century movement for the reform and modernization (*kaehwa*) of the nation is significant both personally and intellectually. For Yŏnam's reformist spirit reappears in his grandson, Pak Kyu-su (1807–1876), an important minister under King Kojong and a nurturer of such early proponents of modernization as Kim Ok-kyun and Pak Yŏng-hyo.

The Life of Mrs. Pak of Hamyang, a Faithful Wife, With Comments[22]

According to a saying of the people of the Qi nation, "A faithful wife does not serve two husbands." That is also what *baizhou* in the *Shi jing* means.*. There is a stipulation in our legal code that "the sons of women married more than once are not to be appointed to important government posts." But how could this apply to ordinary people? During the 400 years since the beginning of the present dynasty, however, ordinary people have been so deeply indoctrinated that all widows, whether of yangban or ordinary family, have come to adhere to their widowhood and it has finally become a custom. Thus the title "faithful wife" of ancient times may now be applied to all widows of the present day. Even the child-wives of the provinces and the young widows of ordinary households believe that living alone in observance of their fidelity to the deceased husband is not enough. Although their parents make no effort to force them into remarriage and they need not fear blocking their sons' careers [since they are not of the yangban class], they frequently decide to withdraw from the light of day. Wishing to follow their husbands to the grave, they throw themselves into water or fire, take poison, or hang themselves, as though they were walking into paradise. Though this is indeed fidelity, isn't it excessive?

One day long ago two brothers, both well-known government officials of good name, were discussing in front of their mother

---

*The *baizhou,* or cypress boat, because of its context in the *Shi jing* (the Chinese *Book of Poetry*), came to stand for a wife's faithfulness to her husband even after his death.

their plans to block someone from obtaining a government post.

"For what fault of his are you planning to hinder another's official career?" the mother asked.

"There is talk of a scandal involving a widow in an earlier generation of the man's family."

"How could anyone from outside know about what might have happened in the inner quarters of another's household?" the mother asked again, alarmed.

"It's what is noised about in the wind [mere hearsay], ma'am."

"The nature of the wind is that it can only be heard, not seen. As hard as you try, you cannot see it with your eyes, nor can you grasp it by hand. Born of airy nothingness, it causes all sorts of things to float up, does it not? How, then, can you discuss another person based on what is formless and on what floats up from airy nothingness? Besides, aren't you yourselves sons of a widow? Is it right that you, as sons of a widow, should be saying things concerning a widow? Wait just a minute. I have something to show you." Producing a brass coin from her bosom, she asked:

"Can you see the rim of this brass coin?"

"No, ma'am."

"Do you see any inscription?"

"No, ma'am."

In tears, the mother said to them:

"This is the testament to your mother's struggle with death. The rim and inscriptions were worn away by my fingering it constantly for ten years. For most of us, life's vitality flows from the female–male principle of our life, which is concentrated in our passions and desires. Our thoughts, born of loneliness, lead to sorrow and heartaches. Because a widow is always lonely, she can never escape from her sorrows and heartaches. How could a vigorous and healthy woman be without feelings and desires, even if she is a widow?

"Some nights I would have nothing but the shadow of the dim, flickering light to commune with. On such nights I could hear only the sound of rain dripping from the eaves, or the leaves of the paulownia tree rustling to the ground, or the cry of a lone seagull as daybreak approached, for the crowing of the rooster would be too far away to hear. Unable to sleep, I would lie awake listening to the snoring of the young maidservant. To whom could I have confided my sorrow and sleeplessness then? It was at such times that I would spin this brass coin on the floor and then grope around for it. Sometimes I would find it resting against something that had blocked its path. After finding it I would spin it again and again, and by the time I had spun it five or six times the night would have passed and it would be daybreak. During the first ten years I came to spin the coin fewer and fewer times each year, and after those ten years had passed I needed to do it only once every five days, and then just once every ten days. Now my vitality has declined so much that I no longer have to spin it. Still, I have kept it in my bosom the last twenty years, wrapped in many folds of cloth. I kept it all these years so that I wouldn't forget what it did for me, but also because I wanted to look at it now and then as a reminder to myself."

When she had finished her story, the mother and her two sons embraced one another and wept.

On hearing this story men of virtue would say, "She should indeed be praised as a faithful wife." It is sad. Why wasn't this woman of fidelity and beautiful behavior discovered during her own times and why wasn't her name celebrated in later times? The answer is that the faithfulness of a widow, being a widespread observance now, is no longer considered exceptional unless she kills herself.

It was 1793, the year after I was posted as district magistrate of Anŭi. Just as the night was about to pass, half-awakened I heard several people whispering and sighing together sorrowfully in front of the main hall. It sounded like there was an emergency, but they were being careful not to disturb my sleep.

"Has the cock crowed?" I asked loudly.

"Yes, sir, three or four times already," replied an attendant who was close by.

"Is something the matter outside?"

"It's the niece of the clerk Pak Sang-hyo, sir. She married a fellow in Hamyang but soon was widowed. She just completed the second anniversary rites of mourning and then took poison. She's reported to be in critical condition. They want Sang-hyo to come quickly and help, sir, but he's on duty now and can't get away."

I gave the order for Sang-hyo to leave immediately.

Toward evening I asked, "Was that widow from Hamyang saved?"

"No, sir, she is dead," replied an attendant.

"Is that so," I sighed. "What faithfulness! She truly was faithful!" I called in a clerk of the district to enquire further.

"I hear Hamyang can now boast of a wife of exemplary faithfulness. I understand she is a woman originally from Anŭi. How old was she, who was she married to in Hamyang, and what was her conduct like since childhood? Is there anyone among you who happens to know?"

"She was one of the Paks, a family of county clerks for generations," several of the clerks reported sorrowfully. "Her father's name was Sang-il, and he passed away at an early age, leaving only the one daughter. Her mother also died early. She was totally devoted to the grandparents who raised her, and at age nineteen she became the wife of Im Sul-jŭng of Hamyang. Her in-laws were also a family of clerks in Hamyang. Sul-jŭng had always been rather sickly. Less than half a year after she began living with her husband's family, Sul-jŭng passed away. Not only did she strictly observe the first anniversary rites of her husband's death, she was perfectly filial in her devotion to her parents-in-law. Her relatives as well as the elders of Anŭi and Hamyang were therefore full of praise for her exemplary behavior, which has now been indeed confirmed."

An old clerk, who appeared deeply troubled, spoke up agitatedly at this point: "A few months before the wedding day, some people said, 'Since the bridegroom's illness has reached the very marrow of his bones, there is no prospect of his fulfilling his role as husband. Why not put off the day of the wedding?' Even her grandparents tried to talk her out of it quietly, but she was silent, making no response at all. As the wedding day approached, the Pak family had a man sent over to have a look at the bridegroom. Although he was handsome, he was so racked with illness and coughing fits that he was said to look like a mushroom standing and a mere shadow wandering about. Her family was greatly distressed and tried to call in another matchmaker, but the bride-to-be said to them, with a drawn look on her face, 'All the clothes I have sewn—who were they for and to whose measurements did I sew them? I'm going to keep the initial promise I made.' Her family, realizing her resolve, went ahead to receive the bridegroom as had been arranged. Although the wedding ceremony was performed, it was really no more than a matter of keeping faith with a suit of empty clothes."

Some time afterwards Yun Kwang-sŏk, the county magistrate of Hamyang, deeply affected by a wondrous dream he had, composed "The Life of a Faithful Wife." Yi Myŏn-je, the district magistrate of Sanch'ŏng, did the same. And Shin Ton-hang of Kŏch'ang, a scholar well versed in letters, has written a description of Mrs. Pak and her praiseworthy faithfulness.

From beginning to end Mrs. Pak was of one mind. She was widowed in her youth, and if she were to live alone in the world she would long have been an object of pity for the relatives and could not have escaped the malicious gossip of the neighbors. She must have thought a quick exit from life preferable to experiencing such things.

Alas! I believe she did not follow her husband in death at once because the immediate duty confronting her was to take care of her husband's funeral; she did not die after the funeral because she had the rites of the first anniversary of his death to take care of; she did not commit suicide after the first anniversary probably because she had to take care of the second anniversary rites. By following her husband in death at the same hour on the same day, after taking care of the second anniversary rites and completing the prescribed period of mourning, she finally accomplished what she had resolved to do from the very beginning. Isn't she indeed a faithful wife!

Notes

1. Ki-baik Lee, *A New History of Korea*, trans. Edward W. Wagner with Edward J. Shultz (Cambridge: Harvard University Press, 1984), 233.

2. Quoted by Ch'ŏn Kwan-u, *Hanguk sa ŭi chaebalgyŏn* (The Rediscovery of Korean History) (Seoul: Ilchogak, 1974), 191–92.

3. Quoted by Ch'ŏn Kwan-u in ibid., 192.

4. Ibid., 193. Pangye proposed many other significant reforms: reforms in education; the appointment of officials on the basis of merit only; an overhaul of the structure of local government; salaries for minor and local officials; and reform of the corvee and military draft systems.

5. Ki-baik Lee, *A New History of Korea*, 235.

6. In China, Korean scholars were also exposed to scientific and technological information from the West then trickling into China through the Catholic missions. Naturally, they were eager to gain firsthand knowledge of this information. A few became acquainted not only with this *sŏhak* (Western learning) but also with *sŏgyo* (Catholicism). See ibid., 239–42, and Ch'ŏn Kwan-u, *Hanguk sa ŭi chaebalgyŏn*, 175–78.

7. Ki-baik Lee, *A New History of Korea*, 236.

8. Kim Yun-shik and Kim Hyŏn, *Hanguk munhak sa* (A History of Korean Literature) (Seoul: Minŭm sa, 1973), 35.

9. Trans. Peter H. Lee in *Anthology of Korean Literature*, rev. ed., comp. and ed. Peter H. Lee (Honolulu: University of Hawaii Press, 1992), 222.

10. Ibid., 224–25.

11. Perhaps to deflect criticism, Yŏnam prefaces "Hojil" by claiming it is not his own work but an anonymous story he found written on the wall of a shop he chanced upon in North China.

12. My translation is based on the hangŭl version in *Yijo hanmun tanp'yŏnjip* (Yi Dynasty Short Fiction in Chinese) trans. and ed. Yi U-sŏng (Seoul: Ilchogak, 1978), 316–27, at 321.

13. Ibid., 272.

14. Ibid.

15. Ibid., 259. The name Yedŏk combines two Chinese characters that mean "filth" and "virtue." The author thus might be suggesting that one grows out of the other.

16. Quoted by Pak Ki-sŏk, *Pak Chi-wŏn munhak yŏngu* (The Literature of Pak Chi-wŏn) (Seoul: Samjiwŏn, 1984), 114.

17. My discussion of this work is based on the version in *Yijo hanmun tanp'yŏnjip*, trans. and ed. Yi U-sŏng, 288–92 and Kim Yŏng-dong, *Pak Chi-wŏn sosŏl yŏngu* (A Study of *Pak Chi-wŏn's Fiction*), exp. ed. (Seoul: T'aebak sa, 1993), 63–67.

18. Kim Myŏng-ho, *Yŏrha ilgi yŏngu* (A Study of *Jehol Diary*) (Seoul: Ch'angjak kwa pip'yŏng sa, 1990), 254–55.

19. Pak-Chi-wŏn, *Yŏrha ilgi*, trans. Yi Yi-hwa (Seoul: Minjok munhwa ch'ujinhoe, 1980), II:147–48.

20. In June 1995, in conversation with Kim Myŏng-ho, the brilliant young

scholar who has written probably the best book so far on *Yŏrha ilgi* (see note 18), I mentioned that I was puzzled by Mrs. Pak's behavior. His laconic reply was that his students were puzzled too! He then added that in Mrs. Pak's time an arranged marriage was based on morally binding commitments—*ŭiri kyŏrhon,* as he called it. Once betrothed, the young woman therefore believed she was morally obligated to marry, and she may have considered that obligation more important than her life. Besides, a canceled engagement would have stigmatized the woman for life, even if the cancellation had been agreed to by both sides. Finally, Professor Kim said, quoting Lu Hsun, morality can kill, too.

21. Quoted in Pak Ki-sŏk, *Pak Chi-wŏn munhak yŏngu,* 35.

22. This translation of "Yŏllyŏ Hamyang Paksshi chŏn pyŏngsŏ," the first complete translation of the work as far as I know, is based on the hangŭl version in *Yijo hanmun tanp'yŏnjip,* trans. and ed. Yi U-sŏng, 288–92, and the hanmun version in Kim Yŏng-dong, *Pak Chi-wŏn sosŏl yŏngu,* 63–67.

10

Notes on P'ansori

When we think of literature today we usually think of the written word in printed texts. But of course there is another, much older form of literature that has existed through much of human history. I mean oral literature. Some of the oldest literary works of the West originated in oral literature: *The Iliad, The Odyssey,* and *Beowulf,* the oldest English epic, just to name a few.

P'ansori is one of the most important forms of Korean oral literature. Indeed it is enjoying a surge of renewed popularity in Korea today. To better understand p'ansori, we should understand certain aspects of oral literature. First, in an oral culture—that is, a culture without a writing system—an event can be preserved only in memory. Descriptions of events therefore need to be put in memorable words—that is, in words and phrases that are highly rhythmic with "heavy patterning and communal fixed formulas," facilitating memorization. As Walter J. Ong has pointed out, "in an oral culture, experience is intellectualized mnemonically."[1]

Having its own form and economy, oral literature differs significantly from written literature. Its principal features are necessitated by the central role memory plays in its composition, transmission, and delivery or performance. A few of these key features are also central to p'ansori.

The first of these is redundancy—the repetition of key words and phrases to aid the memory of speaker and also audience, and to help maintain a sense of narrative continuity. Because spoken words vanish as soon as they are uttered, an oral narrative, whether prose or verse, tends to move more deliberately and

rhythmically. Redundancy is a central feature of oral literature precisely because it is a natural part of human thought and speech. In
contrast, "sparsely linear or analytic thought and speech is an artificial
creation," facilitated and promoted by "the technology of writing."[2]

Furthermore, when the speaker is addressing a large audience,
repetition is required by the very circumstance. Since not everyone
can catch the words the first time, it is to the advantage of the
speaker to repeat the same or equivalent words two or three times.
Such repetition is welcome to the audience for an oral narrative,
unlike to the silent reader of a written text. Besides, redundancy
gives the speaker more time to prepare what to say next.[3]

Another key feature of oral literature is formula. For ease of
memory, thoughts are expressed in rhythmic, balanced, and formulaic patterns, "in repetitions or antitheses, in alliterations and asso-
nances, in epithetic and other formulary expressions." For example,
it is easier to remember not just "the soldier but the brave soldier";
not just "the princess but the beautiful princess"; not just "the oak,
but the sturdy oak."[4]

In an oral culture there is neither need nor occasion for verbatim
repetition.[5] And even if there were, how could the accuracy of the
repetition be verified? Another important characteristic of the oral
narrative, therefore, is that the singer or narrator never gives exactly
the same performance of the same work twice. Each work varies
from performance to performance, "depending on audience reac-
tion, the mood of the poet or of the occasion, and other social and
psychological factors."[6]

In an oral narrative such as p'ansori that is both sung and spoken,
instead of a fixed text there is a tradition of performances that the
singer-narrator has inherited and against which his or her particular
performance is judged. The singer-narrator therefore has freedoms
as well as obligations. While not departing too far from the story
line, the singer-narrator must display his or her own talents to the
maximum and must improvise to satisfy the needs of a particular
occasion and audience. What the singer-narrator provides in each
performance, as Ong has observed, is the act of "remembering in a
curiously public way—remembering not a memorized text, for

there is no such thing, nor any verbatim succession of words, but the themes and formulas that he has heard other singers sing. He remembers these always differently, as rhapsodized or stitched together in his own way on this particular occasion."[7]

Every oral narrative performance therefore requires considerable improvisation, in contrast with a performance based on a fixed, written text. In Shakespeare's *Hamlet*, for instance, we can see how the needs of the playwright differ from those of the actor. Whereas the actor might feel an urge to improvise in order to better please the audience, the playwright wants the actor to adhere to the text. Thus, Shakespeare the playwright instructs his comic actors to speak "no more than is set down for them" (*Hamlet* 3.2.38). In a p'ansori performance, on the contrary, the singer-narrator *must* improvise, to better fit his or her material to the occasion and audience. In this sense, each performance of an oral narrative is a collaboration between the singer-narrator and the audience. A successful performance is a communal event, requiring a genuine rapport, even an intimacy, between performer and audience. Chŏng Pyŏng-uk, a noted scholar of p'ansori, goes so far as to say that a p'ansori performance without "enthusiastic audience participation" is as unthinkable as a p'ansori performance without a drummer.[8]

In Korea there was traditionally a drastic split between the culture of the literate upper classes and the culture of the unlettered lower classes. That of the upper classes was based on the written word (almost exclusively hanmun) and that of the unlettered common people was based on the spoken word—that is, spoken Korean. The situation was somewhat like the split in medieval and Renaissance Europe between the lettered and unlettered classes. In Korea this split between the text-based "high" culture and the speech-based "low" culture lasted almost to the end of the nineteenth century. It was out of the indigenous, "low," oral culture that p'ansori developed. Originally performed by and for the common people, it was transmitted orally until the first half of the nineteenth century, when several p'ansori works were first written down.[9]

The consensus among Korean scholars is that p'ansori originated in the early eighteenth century in Chŏlla Province in south-western Korea as an outgrowth of the narrative shaman song. Since the narrative shaman song included both sung and spoken parts, it did not require much modification to develop into a wholly secular performance art featuring protagonists who were ordinary men and women instead of heroes and spirits.[10] One of the stages in this transformation was the development of the performance "from a recitational chant to a dramatic song."[11]

P'ansori has just two performers: the singer-narrator, or *kwangdae,* who stands, and a seated drummer, or *kosu.* Probably because it originated in performances for common people by itinerant troupes of entertainers, p'ansori requires a minimal number of characters and virtually no props. All the kwangdae needs is a hand fan and a straw mat large enough to accommodate himself or herself and the drummer. Traditionally the performance took place practically any-where: in the village marketplace, in the town square, in the court-yard of a well-to-do merchant, or in the royal palace before the king. Thus all the world was its stage.

The performance usually begins with a *hŏduga,* a brief song usually unrelated to the work about to be performed. The hŏduga allows the kwangdae to loosen up the vocal cords, bring the voice into tune, and take a quick measure of the audience. In a place like the village square or marketplace it also probably helped draw a crowd and quiet them for the beginning of the performance. In this way, it worked a little like the attention-drawing opening scenes of Shakespeare's plays—for example, the appearance of the ghost in *Hamlet* or the street brawl in *Romeo and Juliet.*

The kwangdae's fan can represent anything, while the mat can stand for any location the audience's imagination can accommo-date. The kwangdae plays all the parts—male, female, young, old, even the nonhuman roles—and reproduces all the sounds, including those of nature. Because the performance of a complete p'ansori work would take five to eight hours, the kwangdae would usually perform only those parts of a work that he or she was known to excel in. Today, most complete p'ansori performances run from three to four hours with one brief intermission.

P'ansori includes sung passages in verse, called *ch'ang,* and spoken passages in prose, *aniri.* The ch'ang are "built around single themes" and can stand alone "as well-formed structures with their own internal integrity." The aniri introduce the ch'ang or serve as "bridges between songs, scenes, and juxtaposed events."[12] This mix of sung and spoken passages is essential to the dramatic narrative of p'ansori, but it also provides moments of rest. Singing for hours on end would be too exhausting for both the performer and the audience. On the other hand, the reputation of a kwangdae depended mainly on the quality of his or her singing. Those who incorporated too many spoken passages were scorned as *aniri kwangdae.*[13]

Another fascinating feature of p'ansori is the kwangdae's singing voice. It is not a beautiful voice in the Western sense, but more a gritty, husky voice. It has often been said that before kwangdae can master their voices, they must sing until their vocal cords have bled and healed.

There were originally twelve p'ansori works, or *madang,* but the number had declined to six by the late nineteenth century. Today only five works survive and are regularly performed: the *Ch'unhyang ka* (Song of Ch'unhyang), *Shim Ch'ŏng ka* (Song of Shim Ch'ŏng), *Hŭngbu ka* (Song of Hŭngbu), *Sugung ka* (Song of the Water Palace), and *Chŏkpyŏk ka* (Song of the Red Cliff).[14] A sixth work, *Pyŏn Kang-soe ka* (Song of Pyŏn Kang-soe), is also performed today in its traditional form as p'ansori.

Although p'ansori began as a performance art of and for the common people, it soon attracted a large middle-class audience as well as the patronage of the upper classes. In thus acquiring a varied audience it resembled Shakespeare's plays as they were originally performed. And just as Shakespeare had to cater to the varying tastes and demands of his broad-based audience, so did the kwangdae. If p'ansori was to thrive, kwangdae had to adapt their performances to the differing expectations of the various classes of people in their audience. P'ansori thus became more complex, accommodating multiple levels of diction and meaning and even developing a kind of doubleness in structure, language, and theme.

Since p'ansori was always closely linked to the other popular art forms of the common people, such as folktales and folk songs, it incorporated many folk elements. Each p'ansori work has "two aspects: core and accretion."[15] At the narrative core is a fairly simple version of a well-known folktale with an archetypical theme, such as the trials of a filial daughter of a poor parent, a devoted wife harassed by an evil official, or a good-hearted but feckless man ill-treated by his wealthy but cold-hearted brother. What makes the p'ansori narrative so complex and lengthy, as well as unique, is the accretion that has developed in the process of dramatizing this core story. This accretion, according to Marshall R. Pihl, includes materials as various as "legend, folktale, narrative shaman song, narrative folk song,"[16] and even bits of shijo and kasa.

While the core story of the surviving p'ansori works remained more or less unchanged, with each accretion the work became more complex. And it was in the accretion part of the p'ansori, which Pihl calls the *realization,* that each singer-narrator could showcase his or her special gifts of singing, narration, characterization, or dramatization. It was also in this part that much of a work's humor, satire, and secondary characters developed over time in response to the demands of different audiences. Thus, in the realization part, material that was little related to the core story—even "contradictions and inconsistencies"—sometimes entered the work.[17] As Pihl explains it:

> The kwangdae, as an entertainer more concerned with immediate performance than with the literary work as an entity, would draw upon his capacity for improvisation to suit the tastes of his listeners, with the result that he might alter an episode in the course of its performance in a way inconsistent with other episodes of the narrative. He would skip some detail here and add some detail there, interpolate snatches of Chinese verse or Korean folk songs, indulge in impressionistic flights of cataloguing (flowers, skills, clothing, place names, medicines, and so forth), and even change the sequence of the episodes themselves—practices to which surviving texts and modern performances bear witness.[18]

And because audience members, who were acquainted with the story line came to see how a singer-narrator handled certain dramatic episodes he or she was best known for, they would be not troubled by minor "factual inconsistencies or even contradictions between episodes."[19]

As Cho Tong-il has suggested, this double-layer narrative structure consisting of core and accretion is reflected in p'ansori's multifaceted language.[20] Along with the lyrical, formal, and formulaic, p'ansori incorporates language that is earthy, indecent, and above all humorous. Humor, of course, cuts both ways: it both affirms and subverts, exposing the light as well as dark sides of reality. In *Chŏkpyŏk ka* for instance, formal (and often formulaic) diction is used to tell the fantastic stories of the heroes and villains of *Sanquo zhi yanyi* (Romance of the Three Kingdoms). On the other hand, the grim reality of war is represented in the common soldiers' coarse, lewd, and humorous descriptions of their grievances, misfortunes, and suffering—including in some versions the sodomizing of a defeated soldier—all of which are interpolations composed by the kwangdae.

Thematically, too, there is a double vision at the heart of p'ansori. Tragedy and comedy exist side by side. Nearly all the extant p'ansori express the pain and suffering of the common people, but in the end everything comes out perfect.

We can see this thematic double vision, for example, in the difference between the outer and inner themes of *Hŭngbu ka*. On the surface *Hŭngbu ka* tells of two brothers who could not be more different in character, outlook, and values. Nolbu, the elder, is a selfish, cruel, unscrupulous, money-grubbing man who will let nothing block him from getting rich. He even forces his own brother and his family out on the street. Hŭngbu, the younger brother, on the other hand, is a kind, unselfish man who is unable to make a living for himself and his growing family because he is too good-hearted and gullible. In a world where Nolbu is a success, Hŭngbu is bound to be a failure. He is a fool who is utterly unfit to be a husband

and father, his lack of selfishness rendering him incapable of providing for his family.

Forced out by Nolbu from the house the brothers shared, Hŭngbu and his family are reduced to homelessness and starvation. When Hŭngbu returns to his brother to plead for help, he is chased away with a beating. Our pity for Hŭngbu and his family, however, is balanced by the comic depiction of the foolishness of Hŭngbu and his wife. Though unable to support themselves, they have produced twenty-five children. All is made well, however, by the miraculous intervention of two swallows: good-hearted Hŭngbu is showered with riches after he rescues an injured swallow, while Nŏlbu, trying to duplicate his brother's good fortune, is ruined for his deliberate cruelty to another swallow.

This story, as we can readily see, is little more than a fairy-tale version of life. But underneath it lurks the darker inner theme, the dark comedy of the work. The two brothers appear to represent two extreme types. While Nolbu stands for the worst tendencies of a commercial, materialistic, cash-nexus society, Hŭngbu seems a caricature of an exemplary gentleman in an ideal Confucian society. One is an object of scorn, the other an object of laughter. Nolbu has sold his soul to feed his greed, perhaps thus embodying the apprehension generally felt by people toward the money-worshiping society that was emerging in Korea during the eighteenth and nineteenth centuries. Hŭngbu, on the other hand, perhaps represents the shattered dream of an ideal society. Though kind and morally upright, he is a misfit in a world where someone like Nolbu can acquire riches and social prominence.[21]

Sugung ka, though in form an animal fable, differs little from *Hŭngbu ka* in its thematic pattern. Although the characters in the story are animals, such as the tortoise, fish, rabbit, and fox, their behavior and relationships are unmistakably human, and we have no difficulty recognizing in their actions those of people in contemporary Chosŏn society. The surface story is a humorous account of a rabbit's escape from a tortoise and the sea king, into whose clutches he had fallen through the folly of his own vanity. But again this lighter outer comedy is balanced by a darker inner comedy that satirizes the corruption and abuse of power by the king and his courtiers: the constant bickering between the civil and military officials, their shirking of difficult or risky tasks, official appointments based on family connections rather than merit or ability, and, worst of all, the readiness of the king and his court to sacrifice the lives of the common people for their own interests. Although the king and his followers come in for the harshest criticism, the story spares no one. For both the rabbit and the king are betrayed by their delusions of self-importance.[22]

This complexity of narrative structure, language, and theme is perhaps nowhere more powerfully illustrated than in the best-loved p'ansori, *Ch'unhyang ka*. *Ch'unhyang ka* is the story of two teenagers who fall in love across a huge class divide in the rigid social hierarchy of the Chosŏn period. Because she is the daughter of a retired kisaeng, Ch'unhyang too is considered a kisaeng and thus is consigned to the *ch'ŏnmin,* the lowest class in Chosŏn society. Her lover, Master Yi, son of the local magistrate, is near the very top of society. Despite their social disparity, they are joined together, though in an unofficial, almost clandestine marriage—the boy's parents know nothing about it. The consummation of their love, however, is gloriously celebrated in songs of passionate lyricism, always one of the high points of the performance. Here as in Shakespeare, what is most lyrical or romantic is also erotic, even lewd. As in *Romeo and Juliet,* for example, the most lyrical protestations of love contain earthy puns or jests that bring the characters from their romantic heaven down to earth. This mixture of the lyrical and the profane is, of course, part of the complexity of p'ansori, and it gives both p'ansori and Shakespearean plays their realism.

But joy turns quickly to sorrow when the boy's father is abruptly transferred to the capital. The lovers have to separate, and the huge class divide between them now becomes all too painfully real. Even though they pledge eternal devotion to each other, they do not really know if they will ever meet again. The new magistrate demands Ch'unhyang's services, to which he believes he is entitled, since to him Ch'unhyang is only a kisaeng. When she refuses, he has her beaten, jailed, and threatened with death. After Ch'unhyang has endured what seems to be a very long absence with no word from her lover, Master Yi suddenly returns in triumph as an undercover royal inspector, and the story ends happily for Ch'unhyang, her mother, and Master Yi.

But this ending is wildly improbable, as are other aspects of the story. For in real life a girl like Ch'unhyang would have been no more than a temporary plaything for someone like Master Yi, scion of an elite family. And even if he were to plight himself to her in a moment of youthful passion, he would soon have forgotten her in favor of other women in other places. Ch'unhyang, too, would have understood the situation perfectly. At most, a child might have been born of their relationship—Ch'unhyang herself is just such a child—and she and her more experienced mother might have sought monetary compensation. Thus, the mutual devotion of the young lovers, the triumphant return of Master Yi (who has also just placed first in the state examination!), and the resulting happy ending are all part of a timeless fairy-tale version of life.

This surface story has made *Ch'unhyang ka* the best-loved of all Korean stories, but the work also contains a darker underside. For Chosŏn society, as we saw in chapter 9, the highest virtue a woman could aspire to was lifelong fidelity to her husband, both during his life and after his death. But this was an honor denied to the kisaeng, who was strictly a source of amusement for any man who could command her price. The tragedy of Ch'unhyang is thus the tragedy of a young woman at the bottom of society who dares to fall in love, the one thing forbidden to her. As Cho Tong-il has pointed out, Ch'unhyang's problem is that she is a woman more than she is a kisaeng, a woman who struggles to break out of the bondage to which she is condemned by society. Though the daughter of a kisaeng, she is determined to exercise free choice over her body and mind. By remaining faithful to her lover-husband she attempts not only to rise above her social status but to claim her full humanity, the ultimate act of defiance against the ideology and mores of her society.[23] Such is the real tragedy and triumph of the Ch'unhyang story, and therein perhaps lies its enduring appeal.

To fully appreciate p'ansori, one must attend a live performance by a master kwangdae accompanied by an accomplished drummer. Merely to study a p'ansori text would be like merely studying the libretto of an opera. One would miss the extraordinary combination of singing and narrating, the vocal feats and the magical acting and dancing of the kwangdae, and the wonderful interplay among kwangdae, drummer, and audience. One would also miss the improvisation that is so much a part of every p'ansori performance, and which depends on the relationship among performers, audience, and setting.

This was brought home to me in the summer of 1995 when I attended a four-hour performance of *Shim Ch'ŏng ka* featuring Chŏng Sun-im, a singer-narrator I had never heard of. Originally, I had not wanted to see *Shim Ch'ŏng ka*. I thought I would find it depressing to sit through the pathetic scenes of the heroine's self-immolation for her foolish father, and I assumed the melodramatic happy ending would be totally unconvincing. How wrong I was. The experience turned out to be very different from what I had expected. Instead of being depressed I was exhilarated by the whirlwind of emotions generated by the performance, which was superb. Toward the end, having forgotten my misgivings about the improbable ending, I found myself joining in the audience's hand-clapping, foot-tapping celebration of the joyful reunion of the resurrected Shim Ch'ŏng and her father. When the performance was over we gave Ms. Chŏng and her two drummers a standing ovation. And as I left the theater, I was reminded once again that one attends a p'ansori performance not for the story but for the communal experience engendered by the tour de force performance of the kwangdae and drummer.

Notes

1. Both of these quotations are from Walter J. Ong, *Orality and Literacy* (London and New York: Routledge, 1982), 36.

2. Ibid., 40.

3. Ibid., 40–41.

4. Ibid., 34, 38.

5. Ibid., 58.

6. Ibid., 60.

7. Ibid., 145–46.

8. Chŏng Pyŏng-uk, *Hanguk ŭi p'ansori* (Korea's P'ansori) (Seoul: Chimmundang, 1981), 27.

9. Marshall R. Pihl, *The Korean Singer of Tales* (Cambridge: Harvard University Press, 1994), 66.

10. Cho Tong-il, *Hanguk munhak t'ongsa* (A Comprehensive History of Korean Literature), 2nd ed. (Seoul: Chishik sanŏp sa, 1989), 3:515.

11. Pihl, *The Korean Singer of Tales,* 61.

12. Ibid., 86.

13. Cho Tong-il and Kim Hŭng-gyu, eds. *P'ansori ŭi ihae* (Understanding P'ansori) (Seoul: Ch'angjak kwa pip'yŏng sa, 1978), 21.

14. Pihl, *The Korean Singer of Tales,* 63.

15. Cho Tong-il's words, quoted in ibid., 71.

16. Ibid.

17. Ibid.

18. Ibid., 84.

19. Ibid., 85.

20. Cho Tong-il and Kim Hŭng-gyu, eds. *P'ansori ŭi ihae,* 25.

21. In my reading of *Hŭngbu ka* I am indebted to the insightful discussion in ibid., 11–28.

22. See Im Kwŏn-hwan, ibid., 238–57. Im gives a thorough analysis of what each character and event in the story might stand for in Chosŏn society.

23. Ibid., 27.

11

Toward Modern Korean Literature

At the end of the nineteenth century, nearly four and a half centuries after hangŭl was promulgated, Korea still lacked a prose style capable of accurately representing spoken Korean. Hanmun was still the written language of educated and important men both in public and private life, and hangŭl—then called *ŏnmun*—was still the written language of women and men of the lower classes. It was not until domestic unrest and the looming menace of foreign intrusion jolted Korea out of its centuries of isolation that a movement toward the development of a hangŭl vernacular prose style began in earnest. This movement was part of a larger movement for nationwide reform and modernization whose impulse was at once nationalistic and populist. Driven by the growing specter of foreign domination, Koreans sought to reappraise their traditional values and institutions and reassert their national and cultural integrity. The National Language Movement was a means to this end. Its advocates began to forge a truly vernacular written language, which yielded a vernacular prose style that in turn led to the emergence of modern Korean literature during the first decade of the twentieth century.

By disseminating hangŭl throughout the nation, the proponents of the National Language Movement sought more than to merely Koreanize the written language. Their larger goal was to reinvigorate all that was indigenous in Korea's arts, history, language, and literature. They pushed for *ŏnmun ilch'i* (correspondence between the spoken and written languages) and sought to remove from the written language the foreign elements and influences that had so long dominated it. The use of hangŭl as the national written language, displacing hanmun, was for them both a practical and a symbolic act that expressed a number of deeply felt desires and beliefs: to create an enlightened and democratic society by making literacy universally attainable; to remove undue reverence for things Chinese; and to return to what was inherently and fundamentally Korean. How the movement came to embrace these important concerns is perhaps best illustrated by the efforts of Yu Kil-chun, Philip Jaisohn, and Christian missionaries to bring about the widespread use of hangŭl and a truly vernacular prose style.

As a young man of great promise and exceptional connections, Yu Kil-chun (1856–1914) studied for a year with Japan's foremost proponent of modernization, Fukuzawa Yukichi. Yu's exposure to modern ways was broadened in 1883, when he joined the first Korean delegation to the United States. He stayed in the United States for an additional year for the express purpose of absorbing Western knowledge. His first try at Koreanizing the written language had come in the spring of 1883 when, at the request of Pak Yŏng-hyo, then mayor of Seoul, Yu made plans to publish Korea's first newspaper. It is believed that he prepared the first issue in a hangŭl-hanmun mixed script. Although the newspaper was never published, it set a precedent for the *Hansŏng chubo,* a weekly newspaper inaugurated three years later that first experimented with a hangŭl-hanmun mixed script.[1]

In 1895 Yu published his *Sŏyu kyŏnmun* (Observations on a Journey to the West), an impressively comprehensive digest of his gleanings as well as reflections on what he believed to be the true meaning of modernization. Important as the contents of this work were, it was the prose style in which Yu wrote it that is of greater importance to our discussion here. For instead of writing the book entirely in hanmun, as was expected of a man of his learning and high position, Yu interspersed his text with Korean words and phrases in hangŭl. Warned in advance that his work was likely to be ridiculed for this breach of scholarly etiquette, Yu appended a preface in which he defended his use of a mixed script. The most important reason for adopting this style, he said, was to make his work accessible to as many Korean readers as possible, and for this he was willing to endure the ridicule of his fellow literati. "It is my regret that I could not write it altogether in Korean," he wrote, adding that he considered the nationwide adoption of hangŭl inseparable from his vision of a sorely needed program of reform and modernization for the nation.[2]

The hangŭl-hanmun mixed script of the 1890s, however, differed fundamentally from the one used today. The former was little more than the addition of a few Korean words and phrases in hangŭl to what was basically a hanmun text.[3] Nevertheless, this style signaled the beginning of the development of the mixed script used in South Korea today.

It was Philip Jaisohn (Sŏ Chae-p'il, 1866–1951) who accomplished the next, and most radical, step in promoting the use of hangŭl. Upon his return from exile in the U.S.—now Americanized in both education and citizenship—Jaisohn founded the Independence Club. Initially with the cooperation of the government, he also established the *Tongnip shinmun* (The Independent), a thrice-weekly newspaper that began publication on April 4, 1896. Single-minded in his dedication to the reform and modernization of Korea, Jaisohn—like Yu Kil-chun before him—considered the nationwide adoption of hangŭl an integral part of his program. He therefore put into practice the revolutionary step of publishing the paper entirely in hangŭl. In this he was helped by Chu Shi-gyŏng, who went on to become the most important of the early modern hangŭl scholars. In the opening section of the *Tongnip shinmun*'s first issue, Jaisohn informed his readers of the paper's policy of welcoming their letters for publication. He added, however, that the paper would not accept letters written in hanmun, and this reminder of the paper's strict, unprecedented policy of using hangŭl exclusively was repeated several times.[4]

Equally significant was the prose style used in the *Tongnip shinmun*. It differed markedly from all earlier hangŭl prose styles in that it approximated spoken Korean. The paper also introduced a number of other key reforms, such as spacing between words and phrases for easier comprehension. Even today one is struck by the simple, straightforward, natural Korean prose of the *Tongnip shinmun*. The only hanmun expressions permitted, though transcribed in hangŭl, were those unavoidable Sino-Korean words and phrases that had long since been adopted into the Korean language.

The contribution of the *Tongnip shinmun* to the promotion of literacy, enlightenment, and nationalism among Koreans during this time cannot be overestimated. The paper demonstrated for the first time that a simple hangŭl prose style that approximated spoken Korean could facilitate dissemination of information and knowledge and thereby greatly enhance literacy among the masses.

Although the *Tongnip shinmun* remained popular with its readers, the paper's uncompromising editorials and reports of official corruption and incompetence soon earned it the enmity of the government, which had provided part of the initial funding for the paper.[5] Consequently, in 1898—only two years after he founded the paper—Philip Jaisohn was once again driven from his native land.[6]

Many Korean scholars believe that the impact of the hangŭl translation of the Bible on the dissemination of hangŭl surpassed that of the newspapers. The hangŭl translation by Ross and MacIntyre of the Gospel of Luke appeared in 1882, thus preceding the *Tongnip shinmun* by nearly fifteen years.[7] By 1887 the entire New Testament had been translated into hangŭl by the same hands. The hangŭl New Testament found a receptive audience among Koreans, as indicated by the large number of copies distributed: 198,658 copies for the period 1883–1899; 38,006 copies in 1900; 16,814 copies in 1901; and 28,716 copies in 1902.[8]

Giving substance to these figures is the picture that has come down to us of the Christian missionaries' total dedication to their proselytizing. They appear to have gone everywhere in Korea, seeking out especially the women and the humbler people of the countryside. Like Philip Jaisohn, the missionaries believed they had to reach the masses and could best do so by promoting the use of hangŭl. It was this belief that drew them to their study of the

Korean language as well as their work of translating the Bible into hangŭl. In 1893, the Protestant Council of Missions in Korea established guidelines for the work of its members, including the following:

> All tracts should be written in hangŭl only.
>
> Proselytizing efforts should first be directed towards the people of the working classes, and only afterwards toward those of the upper classes.
>
> Special efforts should be made to convert women and educate young unmarried women. This is because the homemakers have the greatest influence on the raising of children.[9]

It was natural, then, that the missionaries should have chosen to cast their translation of the Bible in hangŭl, the hitherto despised written language of the women and humbler working people whom they sought to proselytize.

The efforts of the missionaries went beyond translation, however. They were also actively engaged in teaching the reading and writing of hangŭl to all they could reach, regardless of sex, age, or social status. The impact can easily be imagined, for within a short span of years practically every Korean convert to Christianity was literate in hangŭl. In the words of one scholar, the hangŭl Bible helped bring about a fundamental shift in attitude toward hangŭl:

> Just as students of the Confucian classics revered Chinese literature and Chinese characters, it was natural that the masses of people studying the Bible in hangŭl translation should come to hold hangŭl in reverence. As the hangŭl Bible, the carrier of the Divine word, came to be deemed precious, hangŭl itself in turn, as the medium of sacred thoughts, came to be deemed precious.[10]

But the hangŭl Bible also added an alien note by introducing to the Korean language new words, new expressions, and even new diction.[11] The Christian missionaries were determined to be faithful to their understanding of the scriptures as they translated them into hangŭl. And so whenever they had difficulty finding Korean words equivalent in feeling or meaning to those of the original text (Hebrew, Greek, or English), they coined new words and expressions either by drawing on Chinese characters or by combining two or more Korean words. The result was a prose style that has been called the "scriptural translation style," which has had a noticeable effect on the spoken language of Korean converts to Christianity.[12]

For a prose style that more closely approximated everyday speech, Koreans had to await developments occurring mainly in the new kinds of stories appearing in the newspapers. During the first decade of the twentieth century, the fiction serialized in the newspapers appeared mostly in two styles, hanmun with a sprinkling of hangŭl grammatical markers, and hangŭl only. Among those works written entirely in hangŭl were a handful that showed significant progress toward achieving verbal realism. We will look at two of them.

Both are brief, anonymous, satirical sketches with little plot or character development. They appeared in the *Taehan maeil shinbo* (Korean Daily News) in 1905 and 1906. What makes them significant is their supple style, capable of representing colloquial and idiomatic qualities previously absent in Korean prose. The first of these works, "A Dialogue Between a Blind Man and a Cripple," takes place between a fortuneteller and a maker of horsehair hatbands. The two men complain about the difficulty of earning a living in this period of so-called modernization. The blind fortuneteller grumbles that ever since modernization became fashionable, people have ceased hiring him to tell their fortunes. As for the crippled hatband maker, men no longer have any use for his product, since modernization has made short hair stylish for men. These complaints, however, form merely the comic surface of the dialogue; the sharpest barbs are reserved for unthinking followers of fashion, corruption in government, and blind reverence for newfangled things. One key passage goes as follows:

It looks to me like whether their heads are shaved off for "modernization" or "enlightenment," they are still filled with the same old antiquated ideas, even if on the surface they appear to be all caught up with "enlightenment" or "progress"; the fact is, they're still asleep—they're walking around town snoring. They're like a rotten old tree—fine-looking on the outside, worm-eaten on the inside.[13]

The second sketch, "The Misunderstanding of a Rickshaw Man," deals in one sense with the terrible, long-lived gap between the spoken and written languages in Korea. The sketch is based on a rickshaw man's comically absurd misapprehension of certain fashionable Sino-Korean phrases he has picked up from the important public men who ride in his rickshaw. Had he been educated, he could visualize the Chinese characters for these phrases, thereby grasping their correct meaning. But because he is uneducated, he doesn't even know that they are Sino-Korean. One such word he hears repeatedly is *chojik*, meaning "organizing" or "organization." Puzzled by the unfamiliar word, the unlettered fellow decides it is probably a mispronunciation of *chojip* (millet straw). Wondering what all these public men want with millet straw, he begins a series of hilarious misconstructions. Of course, the laugh is not on the rickshaw man but on an absurd situation that has been tolerated in Korea for too long. The anonymous writer then launches into savage criticism, though couched in comic language, of the blindness and incompetence of the country's leaders.[14] Works such as these marked an important advance toward a prose style capable of more accurately representing spoken Korean.

A further sharpening of the idiomatic and colloquial potential of hangŭl prose is evident in novels such as Yi In-jik's *Kwi ŭi sŏng* (The Voice of the Devil), serialized in *Mansebo* (Independence News) in 1907. These "new novels" may be seen as the penultimate step before the blooming of modern Korean literature in the second decade of the twentieth century. *Kwi ŭi sŏng* is generally considered Yi's best novel. Although it followed *Hyŏl ŭi nu* (Tears of Blood), Yi's first novel, by only a few months at most, it is altogether a different work, both in theme and in language. It has little to do with warring foreign powers, travel abroad, or popular education and enlightenment. In other words, it has little to do with the ideology of modernization, which played such a prominent part in *Hyŏl ŭi nu.* Instead, it deals exclusively with corruption and abuses of privilege in the last years of Chosŏn dynasty Korea: the unsavory aspects of the yangban-commoner relationship, domestic intrigues in a wealthy yangban household, and a tragedy resulting from a wife's jealous hatred of her husband's young concubine.

Although melodramatic—the plot is full of coincidences and ominous dreams—the novel shows considerable psychological depth and subtlety in characterization and narrative development. And above all, its language is remarkable. Despite a few vestiges of the hangŭl romances, such as formulaic phrases, prose passages of syllabic regularity, and verb endings more appropriate to oral literature, the language of *Kwi ŭi sŏng* is generally concise, vivid, and idiomatic, particularly in dialogue. From the beginning of the novel the characters are clearly differentiated, because each speaks in his or her own voice. For example, when we first meet the wife of Kim Sŭng-ji, a womanizing yangban official, her sharp and brutal words vividly delineate her character. Having just been told that her husband's young concubine has arrived from the countryside, she can hardly contain her rage. She vents her anger at the bondmaid standing beside her:

> You there, run over to the guest quarters and tell the master the Ch'unch'ŏn woman is here, the slut he's been waiting for day and night. Why, you, you, you. . . why don't you run along like I told you, instead of just standing there? Come here, you damned bitch, maybe I should do away with you first, you, you there![15]

In this brief passage, we can almost hear the snap and tang of the outraged wife's angry voice. What a passage like this suggests— and there are many like it in *Kwi ŭi sŏng*—is that hangŭl vernacular prose had finally come close to achieving the long-pursued goal of *ŏnmun ilch'i* and was now ready to become the principal vehicle of modern Korean literature. For in its idiomatic and colloquial suppleness and range, the prose of *Kwi ŭi sŏng* is not a bit inferior to that of Yi Kwang-su's *Mujŏng* (The Heartless, 1917), which ushered in the modern Korean novel.

Notes

1. Yi Kwang-nin, *Hanguk kaehwa sa yŏngu* (A History of the Enlightenment Period in Korea With Reference to the 1880s), rev. ed. (Seoul: Ilchogak, 1974), 64–65.

2. Yu Kil-chun, *Sŏyu kyŏnmun* (Observations on a Journey to the West), reprint (Seoul: Kyŏnmunhwa sa, 1965), 6.

3. Yi Ki-mun, *Kaehwagi ŭi kungmun yŏngu* (A Study of the Korean Language During the Enlightenment Period) (Seoul: Ilchogak, 1970), 17. The Kabo Reform of 1894 decreed the use of a similar mixed script in all official government documents. Yu was a member of the government committee that pushed this measure through.

4. *Tongnip shinmun* (The Independent), reduced ed., reprint (Seoul: Ilchogak, 1970), vol. 1.

5. In 1895, during Yu Kil-chun's brief tenure as minister of internal affairs, he promised Jaisohn financial assistance for his projected newspaper. The cabinet of which Yu was a member was ousted by a coup two months before the paper was to begin publication. Although the new cabinet reneged on all other promises made by its predecessor, it fulfilled the promise of financial assistance to Jaisohn, thus enabling him to begin publishing the *Tongnip shinmun* in April 1896. For a detailed account of these events, see Ch'oe Chun, *Hanguk shinmun sa* (A History of Korean Newspapers), rev. ed. (Seoul: Ilchogak, 1970), 51–53.

6. During his first exile from Korea (1884–1896) Jaisohn had studied medicine in the U.S. and become an American citizen. In 1898 he was forced to leave Korea when the Korean government complained about him to the U.S. legation.

7. There were several earlier translations of parts of the Bible into Korean—some consisting of only one or two of the gospels—dating back to 1790. See Kim Pyŏng-ch'ŏl, *Hanguk kŭndae pŏnyŏk munhak sa* (Literature in Modern Korean Translation: A History) (Seoul: Ŭryu munhwa sa, 1975), 23.

8. Ibid., 39.

9. Quoted in Kim Yŏng-dŏk, "Ŏnhae munch'e wa sŏngsŏ pyŏnyŏkch'e wa ŭi kwangye yŏngu" (Vernacular Style and the Translation of the Bible into Korean), *Ewha University Center for the Study of Korean Culture, Selected Essays* 6 (1966): 95–96.

10. Ch'oe Hyŏn-bae's words, quoted in Kim Pyŏng-ch'ŏl, *Hanguk kŭndae pŏnyŏk munhak sa,* 21.

11. Yu Ch'ang-gyun, "Kugyŏk sŏngsŏ ka kugŏ ŭi paltal e kich'in yŏnghyang" (The Effect of the Korean Bible on the Development of the Korean Language), *Tongsŏ munhwa* (Culture East and West) 1 (1967): 59–74.

12. This "scriptural translation style," as Kim Yŏng-dŏk calls it, remains to this day in the language of devout Korean Christians.

13. Song Min-ho, *Hanguk kaehwagi sosŏl ŭi sajŏk yŏngu* (A Historical Study of the Korean Novel During the Enlightenment Period) (Seoul: Ilchi sa, 1975), 182.

14. Ibid., 183–87.

15. Yi In-jik, *Kwi ŭi sŏng* (The Voice of the Devil) (Seoul: Chŏngŭm mungo, 1974), 25.

Works Cited

Chang Tŏk-sun. *Hanguk munhak sa* (A History of Korean Literature). Seoul: Tonghwa munhwa sa, 1987.

————. *Hanguk munhak ŭi yŏnwŏn kwa hyŏnjang* (Korean Literature from Early Times to the Present). Seoul: Chimmundang, 1986.

Cho Tong-il. *Hanguk munhak t'ongsa* (A Comprehensive History of Korean Literature). 2nd ed., 5 vols. Seoul: Chishik sanŏp sa, 1989. The most comprehensive history of Korean literature so far, especially for the premodern period. Indispensable for any serious student of classical Korean literature. Annotated bibliography after each section.

————. *Samguk shidae sŏlhwa ŭi ttŭtp'uri* (Explications of the Stories of the Three Kingdoms Period). Seoul: Chimmundang 1990.

Cho Tong-il and Kim Hŭng-gyu, eds. *P'ansori ŭi ihae* (Understanding P'ansori). Seoul: Ch'angjak kwa pip'yŏng sa, 1978.

Cho Yun-je. *Kungmunhak sa* (A History of Korean Literature). Seoul: Tongguk munhwa sa, 1949. One of the first histories of Korean literature. Professor Cho's strong views make it still worth reading.

Ch'oe Chun. *Hanguk shinmun sa* (A History of Korean Newspapers). Rev. ed. Seoul: Ilchogak, 1970.

Choe-Wall, Yang-hi, ed. and trans. *Memoirs of a Korean Queen.* London and New York: Kegan Paul International, 1985.

Ch'ŏn Kwan-u. *Hanguk sa ŭi chaebalgyŏn* (The Rediscovery of Korean History). Seoul: Ilchogak, 1974.

Chŏng Pyŏng-uk. *Hanguk ŭi p'ansori* (Korea's P'ansori). Seoul: Chimmundang, 1981.

Hanguk kojŏn munhak taejŏnjip (Collected Works of Classical Korean Literature). Seoul: Sejong ch'ulp'an konghoe, 5, 1970.

Hass, Robert. *Twentieth Century Pleasures.* New York: Ecco Press, 1984.

Hŏ Kyŏng-jin, *Hŏ Kyun.* Seoul: P'yongmin sa, 1984.

Hwang Chae-gun. *Hanguk kojŏn yŏryu shi yŏngu* (A Study of Classical Korean Poetry by Women). Seoul: Chimmundang, 1985.

Hwang P'ae-gang, Kim yong-jik, Cho Tong-il, and Yi Tong-hwan, eds. *Hanguk munhak yŏngu immun* (An Introduction to the Study of Korean Literature) Seoul: Chishik sanŏp sa, 1982.

Hyŏn Yong-jun. *Musok shinhwa wa munhŏn shinhwa* (Shaman Myths and Recorded Myths). Seoul: Chimmundang, 1991.

Im Ki-chung. *Chosŏnjo ŭi kasa* (The Kasa of the Chosŏn Dynasty). Seoul: Sŏngmungak, 1979.

Im Kwŏn-hwan. "T'okki chŏn ŭi sŏmin ŭishik kwa p'ungjasŏng" (Commoner Sensibility and Satire in "Tale of a Rabbit"). In *P'ansori ŭi ihae,* ed. Cho Tong-il and Kim Hŭng-gyu. Seoul: Ch'angjak kwa pip'yŏng sa, 1978.

Iryon. *Samguk yusa* (Memorabilia of the Three Kingdoms). Translated by Yi Pyŏng-do. Rev. ed. Seoul: Kwangjo ch'ulp'ansa, 1978.

Kang Han-yŏng, ed. *Kyech'uk ilgi* (Diary of the Year of the Black Ox, 1613). Seoul: Ŭryu munhwa sa, 1974.

Keene, Donald, ed. *Anthology of Japanese Literature.* New York: Grove Press, 1955.

Kim Hak-sŏng. *Kungmunhak ŭi t'amgu* (Explorations in Korean Literature). Seoul: Sŏnggyungwan taehakkyo ch'ulp'ansa, 1987.

Kim, Huran. "Shin Saimdang: Perfect Woman and Artist," *Koreana* 4, no. 2 (1990): 48.

Kim Mun-gi. *Sŏmin kasa yŏngu* (A Study of the Kasa of Common People). Seoul: Hyŏngsŏl ch'ulp'ansa, 1983.

Kim Myŏng-ho. *Yŏrha ilgi yŏngu* (A Study of *Jehol Diary*). Seoul: Ch'angjak Kwa pip'yŏng sa, 1990. The best study of *Yŏrha ilgi* to date.

Kim Pu-shik. *Samguk sagi* (History of the Three Kingdoms). Translated by Yi Pyŏng-do. Seoul: Ŭryu munhwa sa, 1977.

Kim Pyŏng-ch'ŏl. *Hanguk kŭndae pŏnyŏk munhak sa* (Literature in Modern Korean Translation: A History). Seoul: Ŭryu munhwa sa, 1975.

Kim Tal-chin, trans. and ed. *Hanguk hanshi* (Korean Poetry in Chinese). Vol. 3. Seoul: Minŭm sa, 1989.

Kim Tong-yŏng, *Kasa munhak nongo* (Essays on Kasa). Seoul: Hyŏngsŏl ch'ulp'ansa, 1977.

Kim Yŏl-gyu and Shin Tong-uk, eds. *Samguk yusa wa munyejŏk kach'i haemyŏng* (The *Samguk yusa* and Analyses of Its Literary Value). Seoul: Saemun sa, 1980.

Kim Yŏng-dŏk. "Ŏnhae munch'e wa sŏngsŏ pŏnyŏkch'e wa ŭi kwangye yŏngu" (Vernacular Style and the Translation of the Bible Into Korean). *Ewha University Center for the Study of Korean Culture, Selected Essays* 6 (1966).

Kim Yŏng-dong. *Pak Chi-wŏn sosŏl yŏngu* (The Fiction of Pak Chi-wŏn). Exp. ed. Seoul: T'aehak sa, 1993.

Kim Yong-suk. *Chosŏn yŏryu munhak ŭi yŏngu* (A Study of Chosŏn Dynasty Women's Literature). Seoul: Sungmyŏng yŏja taehakkyo ch'ulp'ansa, 1979. The best study of the writings of Chosŏn women, especially *Hanjung nok.*

———. *Hanguk yŏsok sa* (A History of the Customs and Manners of Korean Women). Seoul: Minŭm sa, 1989.

Kim, Yung-Chung, ed. and trans. *Women of Korea: A History From Ancient Times to 1945.* Seoul: Ewha University Press, 1979.

Kim Yun-sik and Kim Hyŏn. *Hanguk munhak sa* (A History of Korean Literature). Seoul: Minŭm sa, 1973. Though limited in scope (coverage begins with the mid-1700s), this is a provocative study.

Kwŏn Yŏng-ch'ŏl. *Kyubang kasa kangnon* (The Forms of Kyubang Kasa). Seoul: Hyŏngsŏl ch'ulp'ansa, 1986.

————. *Kyubang kasa yŏngu* (A Study of Kyubang Kasa). Seoul: Iu ch'ulp'ansa, 1980.

————, ed. *Kasa munhak taegye* (An Encyclopedia of Kasa). Vol. I, *Kyubang kasa*. Sŏngnam: Hanguk chŏngshin munhwa yŏnguwŏn, 1979.

Lee, Ki-baik. *A New History of Korea*. Trans. by Edward W. Wagner with Edward I. Shultz. Cambridge: Harvard University Press, 1984.

Lee, Peter H. *Korean Literature: Topics and Themes*. Tucson: University of Arizona Press, 1965.

————, comp. and ed. *Anthology of Korean Literature*. Rev. ed. Honolulu: University of Hawaii Press, 1992.

————. *Poems From Korea: A Historical Anthology*. Honolulu: University Press of Hawaii, 1974.

Lee, Sang-beck. *The Origin of Han'gŭl*. Translated by Dugald Malcolm. Seoul: Tongmunkwan, 1957.

McCann, David R. *Form and Freedom in Korean Poetry*. Leiden: E.J. Brill, 1988.

Ong, Walter J. *Orality and Literacy*. London and New York: Routledge, 1982.

Pak chi-wŏn. *Yŏrha ilgi* (Jehol Diary). Translated by Yi-Yi-hwa. 5 vols. Seoul: Minjok munhwa ch'ujinhoe, 1980.

Pak Ki-sŏk. *Pak Chi-wŏn munhak yŏngu* (The Literature of Pak Chi-wŏn). Seoul: Samjiwŏn, 1984.

Pak No-jun. *Koryŏ kayo ŭi yŏngu* (A Study of Koryŏ Songs). Seoul: Saemun sa, 1990.

Pak Pyŏng-ch'ae. *Koryŏ kayo ŭi ŏyŏk yŏngu* (A Study of Koryŏ Kayo: Words and Meaning). Seoul: Kukhak charyowŏn, 1994. The most thorough study of these poems.

————. *Koryŏ kayo ŭi ŏyŏk yŏngu*. Rev. ed. Seoul: Kughak charyowŏn, 1994. Published posthumously by Professor Pak's students.

Pihl, Marshall R. *The Korean Singer of Tales*. Cambridge: Harvard University Press, 1994. The best study in English of p'ansori.

Rutt, Richard. *The Bamboo Grove*. Berkeley: University of California Press, 1971. An indispensable introduction to shijo; Bishop Rutt's are among the finest of all shijo translations.

————. *A Biography of James Scarth Gale and a New Edition of His History of the Korean People*. Seoul: Royal Asiatic Society, Korea Branch, 1972.

————. "Flower Boys of Silla." *Transactions: Korea Branch of the Royal Asiatic Society* 38 (1961): 1–66.

———— and Kim Chong-un. *Virtuous Women: Three Classic Korean Novels*. Seoul: Korean National Commission for UNESCO, 1974.

Samguk yusa yŏngu nonsŏnjip (Selected Essays on the *Samguk yusa*). Vol. 1. Seoul: Paeksan charyowŏn, 1986.

Shim Ch'ang-sŏp. "Samguk sagi yŏlchŏn ŭi munhakchŏk koch'al" (A Literary Examination of the *Yŏlchŏn* Section of the *Samguk sagi*). *Munhak kwa chisŏng* (Literature and Intellect) 10, no. 1 (Spring 1979): 181–205.

Shin Hyŏng-shik. *Samguk sagi yŏngu* (A Study of the *Samguk sagi*). Seoul: Ilchogak, 1981.

So Chae-yŏng. *Ko sosŏl t'ongnon* (A Comprehensive Study of Early Classical Korean Fiction). Seoul: Iu ch'ulp'ansa, 1983.

Song Min-ho. *Hanguk kaehwagi sosŏl ŭi sajhŏk yŏngu* (A Historical Study of the Korean Novel During the Enlightenment Period). Seoul: Ilchi sa, 1975.

Tongnip shinmun (The Independent). Reduced ed., reprint, vol. 1. Seoul: Ilchogak, 1970.

Yi Im-su. *Yŏga yŏngu* (A Study of Koryŏ Songs). Seoul: Hyŏngsŏl ch'ulp'ansa, 1988.

Yi In-jik. *Kwi ŭi sŏng* (Voice of the Devil). Seoul: Chŏngŭm mungo, 1974.

Yi Ki-mun. *Kaehwagi ŭi kungmun yŏngu* (A Study of the Korean Language During the Enlightenment Period). Seoul: Ilchogak, 1970.

Yi Kwang-nin. *Hanguk kaehwa sa yŏngu* (A History of the Enlightenment Period in Korea With Reference to the 1880s). Rev. ed. Seoul: Ilchogak, 1974.

Yi U-sŏng, trans. and ed. *Yijo hanmun tanp'yŏnjip* (Yi Dynasty Short Fiction in Chinese). Seoul: Ilchogak, 1978.

Yi, Yi-hwa. *Hŏ Kyun ŭi saenggak* (Hŏ Kyun's Thoughts). Seoul: Yŏgang ch'ulp'ansa, 1991.

Yi Yong-bŏm. "Ch'ŏyong sŏlhwa ŭi il koch'al" (A Consideration of the Ch'ŏyong Story). *Kungmunhak nonmunsŏn* (Selected Essays on Korean Literature). Vol. 1. Seoul: Minjung sŏgwan, 1977.

Yu Ch'ang-gyun. "Kugyŏk sŏngsŏ ka kugŏ ŭi paltal e kich'in yŏnghyang" (The Effect of the Korean Bible on the Development of the Korean Language). *Tongsŏ munhwa* (Culture East and West) 1 (1967): 59–74.

Yu Kil-chun. *Sŏyu kyŏnmun* (Observations on a Journey to the West). Reprint. Seoul: Kyŏnmunhwa sa, 1965.

Index

A

Admonition kasa, 123–129
Admonitory Words to Women
   (*Naehun*), 124–125
Agricultural reform, in Shirhak
   movement, 172–174
Alphabet, Korean, 3, 4–5, 8, 10n.3
Aniri, 201
"Arirang," 33, 40–41, 42

B

Bamboo Grove, The (Rutt), 77
Basho, 81
Bear totem, 64
Bible, hangŭl translation of, 212–214
Book of Lesser Learning (Sohak),
   125
Buddhism
   of Hŏ Kyun, 154–155, 156
   hyangga and, 16, 17
   in *Kuun mong*, 159, 163
   in *Samguk yusa*, 51–52, 54, 66, 67,
      159
   withdrawal from world in, 162, 163

C

Ch'ae Cha, 72
Ch'ang, 201
Chang Hong-jae, 169
Chang Tŏk-sun, 8, 112

Chat'an ka (song of lament), 124,
   132–135
"Che mangmaeka" (Requiem), 21–22
China
   Shirhak movement and, 174
   written language (Hanmun), 3, 4–5,
      6–9
"Chindallae kkot" (Kim Sowŏl), 41, 42
Ch'oe Kyŏng-ch'ang, 120, 122
Chŏkpyŏk ka (Song of the Red Cliff),
   201, 203
"Ch'ŏngch'un kwabu ka" (Song of a
   Youthful Widow), 134–135
Chŏngjo, King, 103–104, 188
Chŏng Mongju, 78–79, 82
Chŏng Pyŏng-uk, 159, 199
"Ch'ŏngsan pyŏlgok" (Song of
   Green Mountain), 31–35
Chŏngsu, 69
Chŏng Sun-im, 207
Chŏng Yag-yong, 6
Ch'ŏn Kŭm, 83–84
"Choshin's Dream," 69–71
Chosŏn period, 6, 25–26
   Japanese invasions in, 143–144,
      169–170, 171
   prose fiction of, 159–164. *See also*
      Hong Kiltong chŏn
   status of women in, 111–112, 114,
      123, 126, 132–133, 164–165,
      170, 181–193, 206–207
   women' literature of, 96–136
   See also Shirhak (Practical
      Learning) movement

Kichung Kim is professor of English at San Jose State University, where he has taught since 1966. Educated in both Korea and the United States, Kim received a doctorate in English from the University of California, Berkeley. His work on modern and classical Korean literature has been extensively published.